WHEN BASEBALL ISN'T
WHITE, STRAIGHT
AND MALE

WHEN BASEBALL ISN'T WHITE, STRAIGHT AND MALE

The Media and Difference in the National Pastime

Lisa Doris Alexander

McFarland & Company, Inc., Publishers

Jefferson, North Carolina, and London

LIBRARY OF CONGRESS CATALOGUING-IN-PUBLICATION DATA

Alexander, Lisa Doris.
    When baseball isn't white, straight and male : the media and
difference in the national pastime / Lisa Doris Alexander.
        p.   cm.
    Includes bibliographical references and index.

    ISBN 978-0-7864-7113-3
    softcover : acid free paper ∞

    1. Baseball — Social aspects — United States.   2. Mass media
and sports — United States.   I. Title.
    GV867.64.A38 2013
    796.357 — dc23   2012044029

BRITISH LIBRARY CATALOGUING DATA ARE AVAILABLE

Cover photograph © 2013 Mike Liu

Manufactured in the United States of America

*McFarland & Company, Inc., Publishers
    Box 611, Jefferson, North Carolina 28640
    www.mcfarlandpub.com*

Table of Contents

Preface

"Given the small numbers of Black men who actually make it to professional sports, the visibility of Black male athletes within mass media speaks to something more than the exploits of actual athletes. Instead, the intense scrutiny paid to sports in general ... operates as a morality play about American masculinity and race relations."— Patricia Hill Collins[1]

"Baseball has made magnificent strides and set the tempo for other facets of our society to do the same. But baseball is still quite imperfect."— Jackie Robinson[2]

Baseball, in one form or another, has existed in the United States for well over one hundred years, and during that time it has become an important part of the nation's history and culture. Because of its longstanding presence, baseball has helped to create and maintain national sensibilities on a variety of topics, including race, class, gender, and sexual identity through the use of symbolism and imagery. Many baseball books discuss the sport's history or deal with the financial aspects of free agency and competitive balance. While those aspects of baseball are important and fascinating, given the sport's longevity and continued influence, it is particularly important to ask what Major League Baseball (MLB) conveys about power relations along the lines of race, class, gender, and sexuality.

From the very beginning, professional baseball was a raced space: a place where race and/or ethnicity play a predominant role. For example, unlike the National Basketball Association or the National Football League, professional baseball was briefly a racially integrated space at its inception. Black players like Moses Fleetwood Walker, his brother Welday Walker, and John W. (Bud) Fowler played professional baseball.[3] However, a "gentleman's agreement," which expelled U.S.–born black and dark-skinned Latin players from MLB from the late 1800s until 1947, solidified the league as a white space to such an extent that separate leagues were created to accommodate the banned players. The message was that U.S.-born and non–U.S.-born black players were not "good enough" to play MLB, and even if they were, these players were certainly not welcome. The reintegration of professional baseball, starting

1

with the 1947 signings of Jackie Robinson and Larry Doby, and the fact that MLB is one of the most racially/ethnically diverse of the U.S. professional sports leagues, illustrate the ways in which race has played, and continues to play, a dominant role in the league.

This book engages the principles set out in an essay, "Reading Sport Critically," by Susan Birrell and Mary McDonald, which involves "focusing on a particular incident or celebrity as the site for exploring the complex inter-related and fluid character of power relations as they are constituted along [various] axes."[4] Scholars have used this methodology to analyze how athletes such as Michael Jordan, Wayne Gretzky, and O.J. Simpson have been framed by popular media. To read sport critically, scholars choose the representations of particular sporting events or personalities and treat those representations as cultural texts in an effort to read sport texts in much the same way that literary scholars utilize textual analysis to interpret traditional literary texts.[5] Though reading sport critically can help illuminate the different ways power operates within specific sporting moments, Birrell and McDonald point out that "we cannot settle once and for all which relations of power are always and everywhere most important. What we can say as cultural critics is that at this historical moment, at this particular place, these discourses on race, gender, sexuality, and class were produced around this incident."[6] For the present work, each of the following chapters is an attempt to read media representations of an incident involving a baseball player and/or controversy to determine what messages are being conveyed.

This analysis focuses on a few salient and controversial moments from the 1995 season through the 2011 season to determine their cultural meanings which in turn illustrate the persistence of various "-isms" in MLB and American culture overall. The year 1995 makes an ideal starting point since this was the year MLB returned from its eighth work stoppage in twenty years, and the first that caused the cancellation of the World Series. For many this was a seminal moment in baseball history. What makes these particular incidents so interesting and controversial is the fact that they highlight the intersection of multiple discourses and reveal larger themes and issues that impact society at large. At the same time, these incidents and stories seemed to move beyond the sport pages. As Josh Suchon points out, "Dan Rather and Peter Jennings were talking about [these situations]; not just Dan Patrick and Peter Gammons."[7]

Chapter 1 looks at how the salience of race/ethnicity and nationality became visible through the controlling images, or stereotypes, that were created and/or exploited during the 1998 McGwire/Sosa home-run chase. Because the home-run race was taking place against the backdrop of President Clinton's sex scandal, Mark McGwire was revered as the nation's hero despite allegations of performance-enhancing drug use. Sammy Sosa's status as a non–U.S.-born black player subjected him to controlling images based both on race and nationality and assured that he would play second fiddle to McGwire regardless of the final homerun totals.

Chapter 2 analyzes how race and nationality influenced the different ways in which issues of sexual identity were discussed for Mike Piazza and Kazuhiro Tadano. These players' racial identities influenced the ways in which questions surrounding their sexual identity played out in the press. In addition this chapter looks at the evolution of attitudes regarding homosexuality within baseball culture.

Chapter 3 argues that issues of race, nationality, class, and objectification became salient when Alex Rodríguez signed a mega-contract worth approximately $25 million annually for ten years. When Rodríguez began his professional career, he was able to translate his U.S. citizenship into a larger starting salary than many non–U.S.-born players are able to earn. In 2001, because the Texas Rangers not only wanted the best player they could sign, but they also wanted to appeal to a Latino fan base, Rodríguez was able to use his ethnicity to sign one of the largest contracts in sports history. Lastly, A-Rod was able to use his physical attractiveness to attract a large female fan base; however, the focus on his attractiveness sometimes overshadowed his talent on the field.

Chapter 4 looks at how society's very definitions of race came into play when Effa Manley became the first woman inducted into baseball's Hall of Fame in 2005. During the mid–twentieth century, when many believed racial categories were fixed, Manley was able to navigate between racial categories, and this movement shows how fluid racial identities can sometimes be.

Race is described as a salient issue once again in Chapter 5, which analyzes Barry Bonds's record-breaking seasons starting in 2001. Bonds's complicated relationship with sportswriters, the specter of performance-enhancing drugs, and his age as well as race, combined to influence how Bonds's achievements are framed.

Chapter 6 discusses how issues of race, nationality, and reputation intersected during Major League Baseball's continuing efforts to purge performance-enhancing drugs from the sport.

Finally, Chapter 7 looks at the ways MLB honors Jackie Robinson, and brings up questions surrounding how we view history and how race influences the narratives we tell about baseball's past, present, and future. Though all of these incidents span over one decade and a multitude of people, places, situations, and identities, they are indicative of the ways in which media frame how the -isms operate in MLB specifically and American culture more broadly.

Introduction

"Fundamentally, baseball is what America is not, but has longed or imagined itself to be. It is the missing piece of the puzzle, the part that makes us whole [...] a fit for a fractured society. Baseball is about connecting: America is about breaking apart. America, independent and separate, is a lonely nation in which culture, class, ideology, and creed fail to unite us; baseball is the tie that binds. — John Thorn[1]

We believe baseball is more than a sport. It is a window into our nation's culture, diversity, heritage, and determination to succeed at every opportunity."— Bank of America[2]

Since the *New York Mercury* dubbed it "the national pastime" in 1856, the U.S. baseball establishment has evolved from a regional form of entertainment to a multibillion dollar global industry.[3] Since its humble beginnings, baseball has become an integral part of our history and culture and one of the few things that unites the nation. However, in 1995 when Major League Baseball (MLB) returned from its eighth work stoppage in twenty years, and the first that caused the cancellation of the World Series, something had changed. According to sports columnist Leonard Koppett, "What would not be resumed was the unquestioning sense of loyalty and personal need in those fans who felt betrayed, and the manufacture of such feelings in the fans to come."[4] Whether or not baseball has regained its position as our national pastime is debatable, but what has not changed is the fact that professional sport in general, and MLB more specifically, still captivates fans, generates billions of dollars in revenue per year, and helps create and maintain national sensibilities regarding race, class, gender, and sexuality through the use of symbolism and imagery.

Most people understand and relate to sports through media: we watch games on TV; stream games over the Internet; access highlights on ESPN or FOX Sports Net; post game updates on our Facebook page; tweet about the cool play we just saw; and call into radio talk shows to complain about our favorite team or player's latest misstep. Given that media is an embedded part of the sports landscape, it is safe to say that sports journalists are as much a part of the sports establishment as players, managers, and team owners. Every year the Institute for Diversity and Ethics in Sport releases a Racial and Gender Report Card for all of the team sports in the United States. Beginning in 2006 the Institute began investigating whether or not women and people of color were fairly represented within the newspaper sports hierarchy. Richard Lapchick, who has been publishing the Racial and Gender Report Cards for almost two decades, wanted to get at these essential questions: "Is the coverage of athletes and sports in the media fair and accurate when women and people of color are the subjects of the reporting and are women and people of color fairly represented on today's newspaper and dot com sports department staffs?"[5] The 2008 Report showed that 94 percent of sports editors were white and 94 percent were male; 88 percent of the columnists were white and 93 percent were male; and 87 percent of the sports reporters were white and 91 percent were male.[6] Unfortunately, the 2010 Report showed little to no change in the percentages.

As media continue to encroach into citizen's everyday lives via television, radio, internet, cell phones, and iPods, how an event is covered by media representatives becomes just as important, if not more important, than the event itself. Our interaction with sports is mediated through sportswriters and commentators and that makes their articles, blogs, and talk shows fair game for media and sports scholars. In a sports context, sportswriters and commentators have tremendous power to influence the ways in which fans and the general public view persons and events. Anyone who has read a *Spider-Man* comic book or seen the immensely popular films of the same name is familiar with the adage: with great power comes great responsibility. Unfortunately, sportswriters and commentators have not always framed athletes, sporting events, and controversies in a "fair and balanced" manner, particularly where various-isms (racism, classism, sexism, and heterosexism) are concerned.

Even if sportswriters' dramatically homogeneous background is set aside for a moment, race would still play a role in what sportswriters choose to write about and how they choose to write about it, because according to Critical Race Theory, we are "imprisoned by the history of racial subordination in America"[7] and exist in a society where "racism is an integral, permanent, and indestructible component."[8] This is not to say that all sportswriters are racists; however, there is a school of thought that suggests that everyone who is exposed to this "history of racial subordination" is informed by such racism. For the purpose of this discussion it is helpful to differentiate between *racist* behavior and policies that are designed to have a "differential or harmful effect on minority groups," and *racial* behavior and policies that are "neutral in intent but ... have a differential or harmful effect on minority groups."[9] For example, when NBA Commissioner David Stern imposed a dress code for the players to follow during press conferences, some labeled the move as racist, a charge that seemed a bit unfair. Because almost 80 percent of the NBA is comprised of players of color and because the dress code applied to *all* NBA players, but not the predominantly white team ownership, it would be more accurate to describe the code as racial.

Despite the role sport plays in U.S. popular culture, black feminist thinkers have not enthusiastically embraced sport as a site of analysis, though Jarvie and Reid argue that "a resurgence of black feminist writings on sport would help to challenge Eurocentric, masculinist and feminist thought which has at times pervaded the sociology of sport."[10] With the energy, finances, and time poured into sports annually, sports leagues in general and MLB in particular seem to be especially ideal institutions for black feminist thinkers to analyze. Black feminist scholar Patricia Hill Collins is correct: sport operates as a morality play about race relations.[11] It is particularly important to ask what MLB conveys about power relations along the lines of race, class, gender, and sexuality. Therefore, this book seeks to analyze Major League Baseball using black feminist thought and Critical Race Theory with the goal of exploring the meaning of specific events in order to illustrate the persistence of inequities with American society generally and MLB more specifically.

One of the core themes of black feminist thought, which will be discussed throughout this work, deals with controlling images. Collins argues that controlling images are "the gender-specific depiction of people of African descent within Western scholarship and popular culture."[12] Stereotypes become controlling when "elite groups, in exercising power, manipulate ideas [and use] these controlling images [...] to make racism, sexism, poverty, and other forms of social injustice to appear natural, normal, and inevitable parts of everyday life."[13] Traditionally, for black feminist thinkers, controlling images help define black women as objects and/or the other and reinforce the subjugation black women face in everyday life. For example, Collins discusses the image of the mammy which historically justified "black women's economic exploitation as house slaves and [was] sustained to explain black women's long-standing restriction to domestic service."[14] Controlling images are not limited to black women, and as such may vary due to gender, class, ethnicity, and so forth; despite those variations, the outcome, maintaining the status quo, remains the same.

Another aspect of black feminist thought that this book will rely on is the notion of intersectionality. Defined by Critical Race Theory (CRT) scholar Kimberlé Crenshaw, intersectionality argues that analyzing race and gender separately would not be equivalent to the analysis of their intersectional relationship because "the intersectional experience is greater than the sum of racism and sexism."[15] This means that analyzing race, class, gender, and sexuality separately is an inadequate method of analysis and that analyzing these factors together would provide a more complete analysis. For example, when discussing black women's oppression, it would be inadequate and quite difficult to differentiate between the racial oppression and gender oppression black women face. Intersectionality dictates that the racial oppression black women experience is related to their gender and their gender oppression is connected to their race.

Though not a core component of black feminist thought, white privilege is routinely addressed by black feminist scholars. The term white privilege has gained a lot of saliency in recent years and in her influential article, "Unpacking the Invisible Knapsack," Peggy McIntosh defined it as "an invisible package of unearned assets which I can count on cashing in each day, but about which I was 'meant' to remain oblivious."[16] McIntosh cites privileges that range from the mundane (i.e., finding flesh-colored bandages and blemish cover) to the more substantive (i.e., not having race work against her should she need medical or legal assistance). Collins later argues that white privilege allows "whites [to] routinely attribute their own success not to unfair advantage emanating from their group classification as whites in a racial formation that privileges whiteness, but to their *individual* attributes, such as ability, talent, motivation, self-discipline, and hard work. Within this logic of irresponsible individualism, they are not responsible for anyone but themselves."[17] Scholars of CRT take white privilege a step or two further. Stephanie M. Wildman and Adrienne D. Davis agree with McIntosh and Wise when they write, "When we look at privilege we see several things. First, the characteristics of the privileged group define the societal norm, often benefiting those in the privileged group. Second, privileged group members can rely on their privilege and avoid objecting to oppression and third, privilege is rarely seen by the holder of the privilege."[18] They argue that the law is complicit in creating and perpetuating white privilege, and arguably other systems such as sports and media are complicit as well. In the same vein as white privilege, George Lipsitz argues that there is a possessive investment in whiteness and that "white Americans are encouraged to invest in whiteness, to remain true to an identity that provides them with resources, power, and opportunity."[19] This possessive investment in whiteness can manifest itself in many ways in the sporting realm, and the most obvious would be if a sportswriter chooses to ignore racist and/or racial issues within sports. When reading a story or watching commentators discuss an incident on ESPN, fans have to ask themselves how a sportswriter's race, and the privileges associated with that race, influence how the story is being told.

Once fans and scholars know who is telling the story, the question becomes how would someone go about understanding and explaining the roles race, ethnicity, nationality, and sexual orientation play in the reading of these stories? For that, this book turns to Critical Race Theory, which is used primarily in legal circles and focuses on the social construction of race and how laws perpetuate oppression and privilege. It may seem odd to rely on a legal theory to discuss sports, but there is a connection. Though most people believe it is a recent phenomenon, historically sports and the justice system have a nasty habit of bumping into each other. Jack Johnson, Muhammad Ali, Curt Flood, and let's not forget O.J. Simpson, each dealt with the justice system long before Michael Vick, Barry Bonds, and Roger Clemens began their legal entanglements. In order to grasp how an athlete or sporting incident is framed, sports scholars not only have to scour newspaper articles and ESPN recordings but also grand jury testimony, congressional hearings, and federal indictments. Given the continued intersection between the sports establishment and the justice system, having a grasp of legal theory can only benefit sports researchers.

Richard Delgado and Jean Stefancic outline several common tenets within CRT. The first argues that "racism is normal, not aberrant, in American society. Because racism is an ingrained feature of our landscape, it looks ordinary and natural to a person in the culture."[20] Here, CRT scholars maintain that their goal is not to eliminate racism, because that is impossible. Instead, the ultimate goal is to lessen some of racism's debilitating effects. In this book, the goal is not to try to abolish racism in sport, because that would be impossible. The goal is to make visible some of the ways that race and other inequities operate in baseball and baseball journalism.

A second component of CRT has to do with interest convergence: the notion that "white elites will tolerate or encourage racial advances for blacks only when such advantages also promote white self-interest."[21] For example, the elimination of de jure segregation through the *Brown v. Board of Education* decision was not to move the nation in line with the principles of the constitution, but because the "separate but equal" ideology hampered the United States' reputation abroad during the Cold War. In that same vein, MLB did not begin to reintegrate because the team owners believed in equality; owners did so to win games and to make money by courting black fans.

Third, CRT scholars acknowledge that racism is a complex phenomenon and that works in a myriad of different ways. One of those ways is what CRT Scholar Charles R. Lawrence III terms unconscious racism. According to Lawrence,

> Americans share a common historical and cultural heritage in which racism has played and still plays a dominant role. Because of this shared experience, we also inevitably share many ideas, attitudes, and beliefs that attach significance to an individual's race and induce negative feelings and opinions about nonwhites. To the extent that this cultural belief system has influenced all of us, we are all racists. At the same time, most of us are unaware of our racism. We do not recognize the ways in which our cultural experience has influenced our beliefs about race or the occasions on which those beliefs affect our actions. In other words, a large part of the behavior that produces racial discrimination is influenced by unconscious racial motivation.[22]

Lawrence hypothesizes that in a society where overt racism is no longer tolerated, the negative attitudes created by the shared racist history will find an outlet. This book contains multiple examples where these negative attitudes have found an outlet within the baseball establishment.

Finally, CRT scholars argue that "the traditional claims of the legal system to neutrality, objectivity, color blindness, and meritocracy [act] as camouflages for the self-interest of dominant groups in American society."[23] Like the justice system, sport, and MLB particularly, often is framed as a neutral and objective site based on merit: the only subject that matters is a player's ability on the field. The ways in which issues of race and privilege operate in the legal realm are certainly connected to the ways in which race and privilege operate in the sport arena.

Unfortunately, neither sport nor the justice system has ever been based solely on merit, and there is ample evidence to suggest that neither are operating on a level playing field. According to Kevin Hylton, "Sport, just like the law, can be observed as a key tool in the subjugation of black people and the magnification of the place of 'race' as a major mediating factor within society. Sport, like the law, is supposed to be a 'level playing field,' however there is a body of knowledge to suggest otherwise."[24] While merit certainly counts, it has never been the sole arbiter of who is on the field and who is not, who makes the most money and who makes the league minimum, or, of equal importance today, who ends up in the front office and who does not, and who ends up in the press box and who does not.

If writer Gerald Early is correct when he hypothesizes that there are "only three things that America will be known for two thousand years from now when they study this civilization: the Constitution, jazz music, and baseball. They're the three most beautifully designed things this culture has ever produced,"[25] it behooves everyone to study what baseball says about our civilization. This book is an attempt to do just that.

1

Mark McGwire, Sammy Sosa and the Politics of Race and Nationality

"The home run is America—appealing to Americans' roots of rugged individualism and their fascination with grand scale. They gape at one of McGwire's blasts the same way they do at Mount Rushmore, Hoover Dam and the Empire State Building."—Tom Verducci[1]

"Babe Ruth was, along with George Washington and Abraham Lincoln, one of the greatest popular heroes in American popular culture, adulated, almost worshipped, never equaled. For that reason his record number of home runs per season was, and still is, the most famous record in American past, and hence in American psychology it has become nothing less than a symbol of heroic triumph, unequaled, powerful, solitary, upright, public."—Edward Said[2]

One of the most hallowed records in sports remains the single-season home-run record. In 1961, Yankees outfielder Roger Maris broke Babe Ruth's 34-year-old record, and for thirty-seven years, no player even came close to reaching Maris's controversial record: the year Maris broke Ruth's record Major League Baseball (MLB) moved from having a 154-game season to a 162-game season to accommodate the addition of two expansion teams. Because Maris was able to play in more games, there were some who questioned the record's validity. When the 1998 season began, only thirteen players had ever hit more than 50 home runs in a single season.[3] In 1998, former St. Louis Cardinals first baseman Mark McGwire, who is white, and Seattle Mariners center fielder Ken Griffey, Jr., who is black, inched toward breaking the single-season home-run record, and both were quickly joined by Chicago Cubs right fielder Sammy Sosa, who hails from the Dominican Republic. The home-run chase provided both a diversion from the Clinton administration's scandal involving intern Monica Lewinsky and placed baseball back in the nation's popular consciousness. In addition, the 1998 home-run race illustrates how race, ethnicity, and nation function in American society through the use of controlling images.

As discussed in the introduction, black feminist scholar Patricia Hill Collins defines controlling images as "the gender-specific depiction of people of African descent within Western scholarship and popular culture [that] are most closely tied to power relations of race, class, gender, and sexuality."[4] According to Collins, power, which involves the use of available resources to achieve desired outcomes, can be exercised through the creation and/or manipulation of controlling images or stereotypes which "are designed to make racism, sexism, poverty, and other forms of social injustice appear to be natural, normal, and inevitable parts of everyday life."[5]

Controlling images of blacks in the United States, and of black men in particular, is "that of a violent physical people, habitually involved in criminal activity, entertainment or sports."[6] and Collins argues that black men "were depicted primarily as bodies ruled by brute strength and natural instincts [and] relegating Black men to the work of the body was designed to keep them poor and powerless."[7] While work of the body has traditionally kept black men poor, the professional sport and the entertainment industry, both of which qualify as body work, are also framed as two of the few ways black men can gain money and status in American society. However, those financial and social status gains have a catch when popular culture merges "the athlete, the gangster rapper, and the criminal into a single black male persona."[8] There are few ways for black male athletes to challenge controlling images because their status as athletes reinforces existing stereotypes.

While baseball has certain advantages, including helping to increase the number of black millionaires and playing a significant role in nation's move toward racial integration, MLB is still a raced space and in the case of the home-run race, the different ways in which Sammy Sosa, who is a non–U.S. born black player, was relegated to the sidekick role illustrates Collins's notion of these controlling images and their effects. Sosa's Dominican heritage complicated a situation sometimes characterized as a black-white racial dichotomy. Analyzing the discussions surrounding McGwire, Griffey, and Sosa provides insight into the ways in which the controlling images mask the intersection between racism and bias based on national origin, and also sheds some light on how popular media frame the ways in which power operates in MLB.

Politics and Baseball

Despite the intense press coverage the home-run race garnered, it was not the year's lead story. During the 1998 season, American television and print media were riveted as special prosecutor Kenneth Starr revealed the details of President Bill Clinton's affair with White House intern Monica

Lewinsky. For *New York Post* columnist Mike Lupica, the home-run chase provided "a place every single day that we could go that had nothing to do with what did or didn't go on at the Oval Office."[9] For FOX baseball commentator Tim McCarver, whose book proclaims that 1998 was the best baseball season ever, "a baseball star was preferable to a prosecuting Starr."[10] Other baseball fans seemed to agree; according to *Sports Illustrated* Tom Verducci:

> The ball has healing power. About two weeks ago a fan left a voice-mail message for Cincinnati manager Jack McKeon, whose Reds had walked McGwire 11 times in six games before the weekend. "Please pitch to McGwire," the fan pleaded. "This is what we need. This is what the country needs to help with the healing process and all the trouble that's going on in Washington. This will help cure the ills of the country."[11]

While many people seemed to recognize and embrace the home-run chase as a diversion from more controversial matters, it is possible that the events on the field were more closely linked to the scandal in Washington than audiences realized. The importance of the timing of the home-run race cannot be underestimated, since it took place "at the same time as the other pinnacle of American symbolic life, the president, has been debased and devalued."[12] As such, "whenever [McGwire] hit the ball and scored still another home run he was, in effect, symbolically making up for Clinton's shortcomings and sins."[13] Given the revered place the home-run record holds in American popular culture, the perceived downfall of one icon, the president, had to be replaced by the ascendance of another icon, the single-season home-run record holder. When the president could no longer epitomize the elite white American male power structure, journalists exercised power by resurrecting the single-season home-run holder to epitomize the power structure. The home-run chase essentially became a national election, and thus received a similar level of media coverage.

The Changing Face of Baseball

As McGwire, Griffey, and Sosa moved toward Maris's record, *New York Times* columnist Harvey Araton noticed that "at the far end of the 20th century, in a country with still-painful racial wounds, we have a white man, a black man and a Hispanic man in this contest of Men Chasing Maris."[14] Those still-painful racial wounds Araton refer to may help account for the disparate ways the "Men Chasing Maris" were framed by sport journalists.

Araton's observation regarding the racial makeup of the "Men Chasing Maris" highlights baseball's changing demographics. In 1961 when Maris broke Ruth's home-run record, professional baseball had been a reintegrated space for just three years: the Red Sox were the last team to sign a U.S.–born black player in 1959. MLB reached a glass ceiling during the 1970s, when approximately 25 percent of major league players were black.[15] Since then, there has been a steady decline of U.S.–born black players while, at the same time, there has been a rapid increase in the number of players born outside the United States. In 1989, the year Griffey Jr. and Sosa entered the majors, 70 percent of the players were white, 17 percent were black, and 13 percent were Latin.[16] By the time the home-run chase began in 1998, the percentage of white players had declined to 59 percent, the percentage of black players had fallen to 15 percent, and the percentage of Latin players had jumped to 25 percent[17]—a phenomenon highlighted by a 2005 White Sox TV ad which stated, "To win you need speed, defense, and discipline, and the Department of Immigration."[18] The commercial emphasizes the importance of non–U.S.-born players and helped create a new image of what a major league player and team should look like. In addition, the commercial highlights the deficiencies inherent in a black-white paradigm view of race relations. If one quarter of the League's rosters are made up of non–U.S-born players, then framing baseball's racial issues within a black-white paradigm where "Latinas/os are rendered invisible"[19] is inadequate and unacceptable.

With Griffey, McGwire, and Sosa, the composition of the "Men Chasing Maris" accurately depicts not only baseball's changing demographics but changing demographics in the United States as a whole. In 1990, the cover of *Time* announced the "browning of America" and census information proclaimed that "1 American in 4 defines himself or herself as Hispanic or non-white. If current trends in immigration and birth rates persist, the Hispanic population will have further increased an estimated 21 percent, the Asian presence about 22 percent, blacks almost 12 percent and whites a little more than 2 percent when the 20th century ends."[20]

Bootstraps and Banana Republics

As the 1998 season progressed and sport journalists began to realize that Maris's record was within reach for at least one of the sluggers, the press coverage exploded, and the story moved from the sports page to the front page. In the beginning, Griffey and Sosa handled the increased media scrutiny better than McGwire. But at the same time, the media coverage was not equitable: in early August, *Sports Illustrated*'s Gary Smith visited all three players in a three-day period, and while there were thirty journalists waiting to talk to McGwire (down from fifty the previous day), there were only nine journalists for Griffey, and Smith was the lone writer talking to Sosa. At that time,

Smith notes that McGwire had 42 homers, Griffey had 39, and Sosa had 36.[21] This raises the question: if all three players had a legitimate chance to break Maris's record, what accounted for the disparate coverage? If the analysis by Edward Said quoted earlier in this chapter is accurate and the home-run record-holder functioned as a surrogate president, then, as perfunctory as it may seem, it follows that McGwire would receive more media attention as the president is legally required to be born in the U.S. and has historically been white.

Of the three players, Griffey Jr. seemed to have the advantage where media exposure was concerned. As *Time* magazine's Joel Stein pointed out, Griffey "has been in the spotlight since he was Little Kenny, when his father, outfielder Ken Griffey, Sr., used the Cincinnati Reds locker room as a day-care center."[22] Despite the fact that Griffey Jr. was considered one of the best all-around players in the game as well as being one of the most popular, sport journalists did not flock to him the same way they flocked to McGwire. It is possible that writers were blessed with extrasensory perception and foresaw Griffey's eventual slump, which caused him to finish the season with a highly respectable, AL-leading, yet not record-breaking, 56 home runs.

Though McGwire did not have the same extensive history with sport journalists that the young Griffey had, he was still an eleven-year veteran who was not unfamiliar with the media. Any familiarity McGwire had with the spotlight manifested itself as contempt. As Gary Smith observed, "You have this feeling that if you ask the wrong question, he might chomp your head off, and you would absolutely deserve it, so you wait for someone else to ask it."[23] Another reporter remarked that "McGwire often acts like he'd rather get hit in the head with a Randy Johnson fastball than answer one more question from the media."[24] Despite McGwire's sour attitude, sports journalists continued to stalk him at every stop. There were so many journalists from across the country clamoring for interviews that the Cardinals began holding pregame press conferences specifically designed for McGwire to field questions about the home-run race.

While sports journalists flocked toward McGwire and Griffey to a lesser extent, Sammy Sosa was unknown to most people outside Chicago despite playing in the third-largest media market in the United States. Because Sosa had never hit more than 40 home runs in one season, his name was nowhere near the list of players predicted to break Maris's record at the beginning of the season. But once baseballs started flying out of Wrigley Field, writers started paying attention. And as the *Arizona Republic* columnist Pedro Gomez pointed out, Sosa's new-found dominance may have had something to do with "the long-held belief within management circles that a foreign player rarely blossoms until he grasps a certain command of the English language.

It's hardly a coincidence that his career skyrocketed at about the same time his English skills flourished."[25] Gomez's statement highlights the lack of support non–U.S.-born players, particularly Latin players, receive when they enter the majors. Gomez points out that "when a club signs a player from the Far East, it typically hires a full-time employee to help the player get accustomed to life in the U.S. When a young Latin player is promoted to the majors, he typically must lean on the club's other Latin players for support."[26] While MLB has literally changed in complexion, the rules and bureaucracies governing baseball remain static, which puts some non–U.S.-born players at a disadvantage and privileges one language over another: by not providing interpreters for all non–U.S.-born players who are not fluent in English, MLB is exercising power by imposing language values. The onus is on the players to learn English instead of asking managers and coaches to learn Spanish, which sends the message that English is more important.

When Sosa's accomplishments brought him into the national spotlight, according to Douglas Looney from the *Christian Science Monitor,* "His story makes us tingle. Here's a guy who sold oranges and shined shoes in the Dominican Republic to help his desperate family survive."[27] The way Sosa's background was framed was reminiscent of the infamous "pull yourself up by your bootstraps" myth, which urges people, particularly underrepresented racial and ethnic groups, to believe in the possibility of economic independence without systemic help. Sosa's rise from a poverty-stricken shoeshine boy to baseball millionaire became a popular trope in media discussions, particularly because many Dominican players had similar backgrounds. Sosa's story served the dual function of presenting audiences with both an authentic success story as well as framing Latin players as "funny-sounding Latino[s] from a banana republic."[28]

Since sport has been framed as "a way out" of impoverished environments, focusing on Sosa's "rags to riches" story admonished blacks and poor whites — the message being that if a Latin player who comes from such an impoverished environment can pull himself up by his bootstraps, then so can anyone else. Though Sosa's story proved popular with the national press, that persona was drastically different from the reputation Sosa had in Chicago before 1998. As one *Time* magazine article pointed out:

> Until this year, Sammy Sosa was widely considered to be a Big Creep. The rap was that he was a selfish player, a braggart who couldn't deliver when it counted. Last year, up for a new contract and trying to impress his owners with gaudy numbers, he hit 36 homers but made a mess of it on the way, leading the league in strikeouts, having a worse on-base percentage than some pitchers and being so reckless on the bases that his normally mellow manager [Jim Riggleman] had to scream at him in the dugout on live television.[29]

Framing Sosa as a selfish player and a braggart evokes the controlling images used to frame Latin players throughout the 1950s and 1960s. According to Marcos Bretón, at the time sportswriters framed Latin players as "'moody,' 'hot-tempered,' and, worst of all, 'not a team player.' These labels were rooted in negative white perceptions of Latinos, labels that took hold and became a burden even the great players had to carry."[30] Though Sosa's popularity was beginning to increase, sportswriters were still able to frame Sosa with the stereotypes historically associated with Latin players.

As the season continued, the moniker "big creep" quickly faded. *Sports Illustrated*'s Steve Rushin wrote, "While McGwire can appear constipated in press conferences, Sosa has used them to hone his lounge act [...]. He likes to mix clichés as if they were paints, creating colorful new images [...]. Even when he says nothing at all, he seems to be sharing a confidence."[31] Tom Verducci added that Sosa's "coyness adds fun to what has been a remarkably uplifting Home Run Chase [...]. You would think it impossible to hit 54 home runs quietly. Yet here's Sosa, having tiptoed to the doorstep of history. He's the one with the wink and the smile. He looks just like a Little Leaguer."[32] Given McGwire's hostility toward the media, Sosa's new attitude proved to be a welcome change and provided a sharp contrast to McGuire's sour attitude. Sosa's new attitude plays into Collins's notion that professional athletes "who earn large salaries but who are deferential and appear to uphold American values are acceptable."[33] In order for Sosa to be included in the home-run race narrative, he had to hone his lounge act, to use Rushin's phrase, distance himself from the controlling images usually associated with Latin players, and not emulate McGwire's surly behavior.

McGwire was arguably able to get away with behaving like a churl in front of the cameras because of his white privilege: "an invisible package of unearned assets which I can count on cashing in each day, but about which I was 'meant' to remain oblivious."[34] One of the privileges Peggy McIntosh outlines in her seminal work on white privilege is the ability to "swear, dress in secondhand clothes, or not answer letters without having people attribute these choices to the bad morals, the poverty, or the illiteracy of my race."[35] McGwire could and did swear and refuse to answer questions — and sportswriters, the overwhelming majority of whom were also white, chalked up his behavior to shyness and not to the bad morals of his/their race.

Who's the Man?

As McGwire and Sosa neared and finally surpassed Maris's home-run record, fans and sportswriters alike noticed that the treatment and coverage was far from equitable or without bias. At one point, Sosa was quoted in newspapers and magazines across the country as saying that "baseball has been berry, berry good to me."[36] While Sosa does have a noticeable Spanish accent, it is difficult to believe that sportswriters could not differentiate between "very" and "berry." It is also possible that sportswriters, and maybe even Sosa himself, were referencing the classic *Saturday Night Live* skit with Garrett Morris portraying a Latin ballplayer named Chico Escuela who had difficulties with English. At the same time, this is not the first time that sportswriters have misquoted Latin baseball players. In an episode of ESPN's *Outside the Lines* titled "Language Barrier," Bob Ley recalls that Anglo reporters would quote Roberto Clemente "not only verbatim, but with phonetic emphasis on Clemente's difficulties with English."[37] For example, if Clemente said he "hit" the ball, journalists would quote him as saying he "heet" the ball. The trend continued into 2005 when *Sports Illustrated*'s Rick Reilly missed White Sox manager Ozzie Guillén's point by phonetically quoting the skipper as saying "Jew are racis son of a beech. If I was black, could jew be sayeeng these theengs? An beside, Spaneesh ees groweeng so fas een thees country. Why no writers lur Spaneesh?"[38] Though Reilly did not provide a translation for Guillén's quote, it would be safe to say that the quote should have read: "You're a racist son of a bitch. If I was black you wouldn't be saying these things. And besides, Spanish is growing so fast in the country, why don't writers learn Spanish?" In addition to phonetic quotations, journalists in the 1950s and 1960s sometimes went so far as to change Latin player's names: Roberto Clemente became Bob Clemente and Orestes Miñoso mysteriously became Minnie Minoso. Clemente described the position Latin players found themselves in as being a double minority: "singled out for being dark skinned and unable to speak the language."[39] The practice of phonetically quoting Latin players is a manifestation of that double jeopardy because the disempowered and silenced Clemente, and other Latin ballplayers, particularly dark-skinned ones, were made to appear to be ignorant or uneducated. This method of reporting, with the "berry good" misquote, helped frame Sosa as more of a sidekick character than a legitimate threat to Maris's record, as audiences were left with the impression that Sosa had the English-language skills of a child; after all, *Sports Illustrated*'s Tom Verducci had already compared Sosa to a little leaguer.

Sosa's behavior could also be read as playing down to a controlling image usually reserved for U.S.–born blacks: the role of the sidekick. The sidekick controlling image has a long and pervasive history in U.S. popular culture and is usually characterized as being "friendly and deferential; he was loyal both to dominant societal values [...] as well as to individuals who seemingly upheld them; he projected a safe, nonthreatening black identity; and he was defined neither by his sexual prowess nor by any hint of violence."[40] In terms of being friendly, deferential, and nonthreatening, despite accomplishing similar feats, Sosa deferred to McGwire in order to achieve acceptance and recognition, even going so far as to refer to McGwire as "the man" during a joint press conference.[41] At the end of the season, the *Sporting News*'s Michael Knisley seemed to congratulate Sosa for playing the sidekick when he wrote: "[Sosa] was everything baseball needed in its summer of joy: agreeable, tactful, even-tempered, and compassionate. His deferral to McGwire had just the right combination of respect and coyness."[42] Framing Sosa as a deferential sidekick further separated the two home-run hitters and made it easier for journalists to tout equality, since Sosa was being embraced by sportswriters specifically and America more generally, while reifying racial hierarchies. At the same time McGwire was still "the man" while Sosa was "the sidekick."

In addition to being framed as deferential and nonthreatening, sidekick characters, or the "black buddy" as they are sometimes called, are conceptualized as asexual. For the sidekick image to be successful, media representatives must "eliminate all aspects of the black buddy's life that would compete with the black buddy's loyalty to his partner. Many black buddies are depicted as not having families or any type of relationships, sexual or otherwise, that might distract them from their main purpose of being loyal to the White protagonist or to their jobs."[43] While journalists continuously referred to McGwire's son, despite the fact that he was divorced and did not have custody of his son, references to Sosa's wife and children were almost nonexistent. Sosa's entire persona was reduced to competing with McGwire for Maris's record and helping the Cubs reach the postseason for the first time in almost ten years. Sosa's situation presents an interesting conundrum. Sosa was depicted as embodying one set of stereotypes based on race in an effort to avoid stereotypes based on national origin. On the other hand, it is possible that media representatives molded Sosa's behavior and image to fit into the already existing symbol of the sidekick constructed to disempower U.S.–born blacks as well as Latinos/as living in the United States. Cultural critic bell hooks (who does not capitalize her name) condemns the practice of using black characters as sidekicks, which "includes us and subordinate[s] our representation to that of whites, thereby reinscribing white supremacy. While superficially appearing to present a portrait of racial social equality, mass media actually works to reinforce assumptions that [we] should always be cast in supporting roles in relations to white characters."[44] Though hooks speaks specifically about U.S.–born black characters, the practice functions in a similar manner for blacks throughout the diaspora.

By framing Sosa as a sidekick, the message was that the slugger should leave the offensive heroics and press conferences to the more articulate

McGwire. As mentioned earlier in this chapter, when dark-skinned Latinos integrated the majors in the 1950s, sportswriters would often describe Latin players as "hot dogs" or "showboats," using labels that had their roots "in negative white perceptions of Latinos."[45] While McGwire was framed as being shy, if Sosa had behaved in a similar manner, he would have to carry those negative labels usually associated with Latin players. At the same time, if Sosa did in fact use press conferences to "hone his lounge act" as Rushin claims, the behavior served as a way to increase his publicity without alienating media representatives and/or as an attempt to move past the controlling images often attached to Latin players.

The American vs. the Foreigner

Eventually the way the home-run chase was framed shifted from being strictly McGwire vs. Sosa to an "us" vs. "them" race between the "American" vs. "the foreigner." According to Bill Dedman from the *New York Times*, "In all precincts, nationality is up for grabs. McGwire is often referred to as 'the American,' and Sosa as 'the foreigner.'"[46] This framing of Sosa as a "foreigner" reinforces the notion that Latinos are

> not "real" Americans, notwithstanding their long established roots within the U.S. borders. Latinas/os [are viewed] as foreign others — those "little brown peons" who try to take advantage of, without being entitled to, "American" jobs and health, education, welfare, and social security benefits [and] this nativistic animus, based upon Latinas'/os' perceived alienness, is targeted indiscriminately at all Latinas/os, regardless of citizenship.[47]

McGwire allowed sportswriters to portray him as heir apparent to Maris's record by not contesting the image: he was the *American* hero whom everyone could rally behind, and everything that Sosa was not. CNN anchor Larry King summed up the comparison perfectly when he characterized McGwire and Sosa as "an odd couple all right: white and black. One was a middle-class guy from California; the other has been dirt poor in the Dominican Republic. One grew up speaking English, the other Spanish. Mark McGwire was shy, Sammy Sosa was extroverted."[48] This binary characterization allowed those in power to manipulate Sosa's image in an effort to keep McGwire at the forefront of the home-run chase. What is interesting about the positioning of McGwire as "the American" and Sosa as "the foreigner" is the fact that Sosa had been an American citizen for three years by the time the 1998 season began.[49] However, Latinas/os are framed as alien regardless of their actual citizenship status. Tying citizenship to race does not allow Sosa to be viewed as an American since McGwire has already claimed that mantle and the former did not readily fit into the mainstream definition of American (i.e., white, middle-class, native-born).

As the home-run chase continued, the American/foreigner (white/other) binary thinking that separated McGwire and Sosa went from the newspapers and news programs to the audience. Journalist Bill Dedman asked the question, "Who are you rooting for in the home run race? And why? The answers are not so simple. It does not take long for the vexing issues of race and national origin to creep onto the field [...] awkward pauses and disagreements renew the long, uncomfortable relationship between the national pastime and [race,] the national enigma."[50] Framing the home-run race as an either/or question perpetuates binary thinking and moved the uncomfortable relationships between baseball, race, and nationality to the forefront as journalists began analyzing the coverage McGwire and Sosa received. In interviewing residents of a predominantly Dominican neighborhood in New York, *New York Times* writer David Chen found that

> the Dominicans also wonder why McGwire has received so much more media coverage than Sosa, even though they both have been in hot pursuit of the home run record. After all, some contend, Sosa is carrying a team that is vying for the playoffs. "It's always McGwire, McGwire, McGwire; there's too much McGwire," complained Charles Rosario, who works at an electronics store in Washington Heights. "I think it's because McGwire is American, and white, and Sosa is a Dominican, and black. Americans want to see McGwire break the record."[51]

While journalists were slow to recognize that they were producing unequal and racialized coverage of McGwire and Sosa, fans, particularly fans of Dominican heritage, certainly noticed. When *USA Today* conducted a poll asking who people wanted to win the contest, seventy-nine percent chose McGwire and, according to Rick Reilly, "columnists all over the country started pulling their hair out. [Hall of Famer] Hank Aaron said he thought people favored McGwire over Sosa because Sosa is 'from the Dominican Republic and also happens to have black skin.' In an Internet interview last week one of my colleagues, Gary Smith, wondered if 'unconscious racism' was at work in the coverage."[52]

Smith brings up the concept of unconscious racism, which, according to Critical Race Theorist Charles Lawrence III, hypothesizes that in a society where overt racism is no longer tolerated, the negative attitudes created by the shared racist history will find an outlet.[53] If Lawrence is correct and everyone in the United States internalizes the same racist history, in the case of the home-run chase, this shared history could lead sportswriters and audiences to express the belief that Sosa was not good enough to be the home-run record holder. One of the ways sportswriters manifest this unconscious racism is through the seeming ease with which they framed Sosa as McGwire's sidekick, a controlling image that reaffirms the racial hierarchy within the United States, with the white male at the top and "the other" at the bottom.

62

The disparate coverage McGwire and Sosa received when they actually broke Maris's record demonstrates how both media representatives and MLB used the resources at their disposal to emphasize the fact that they wanted "the American" to break the record. In a scene that seemed scripted from a Hollywood movie, on September 7, 1998, when Sosa's Cubs met McGwire's Cardinals in Busch Stadium during the last week of the season, McGwire had 60 home runs and Sosa had 58. Maris's widow and children, MLB Commissioner Bud Selig, and several hundred journalists attended the game in anticipation of McGwire's historic homer. When McGwire broke Maris's record with a solo homer that barely stayed fair, newscasts across the country preempted their programming to cover the event. The scene was surreal: McGwire picked up and hugged his son as he crossed home plate and then he took time to briefly talk to and hug Maris's children. McGwire then embraced Sosa, who had rushed over from right field to congratulate him, and later in the game the Blue Angels soared overhead to mark the occasion.

While Ruth's record stood for thirty-four years and Maris's record stood for thirty-seven years, McGwire held the record for five days before he was forced to share it with Sosa. On September 13, 1998, Sosa hit a two-run shot in the fifth inning against the Brewers for his 61st home run, and then hit a solo shot in the seventh to surpass Maris. The scene surrounding Sosa's triumph was drastically different from McGwire's. *Sports Illustrated*'s Gary Smith, who had earlier introduced the notice of unconscious racism into the home-run chase discussion, points out the differences when he asked these questions

> Where was the commissioner? Where were the 600 media members? Where were the Blue Angels screaming over the stadium's rim? Where was America looking last weekend when Sammy Sosa of the Dominican Republic belted four baseballs over the ramparts and through the palace door to halt the coronation of Mark McGwire? Where were the zillion camera flashes? Where were the major-network cameras? Don't try to explain away the disparity between the national response to Mac's 62nd and Sammy's. Don't open America's chest and search for rotting racial reasons why the Caucasian is creaming the Hispanic in magazine covers and slo-mo replays.[54]

As Smith points out, the celebration for Sosa was much more subdued than the one for McGwire, and Smith blames racism, conscious and/or unconscious, for the disparity. Granted, McGwire did get to the record before Sosa.

However, there was no way of knowing when the celebration planning began which of the sluggers would get to the record first or, more importantly, who would have the most home runs at the end of the season. McGwire may have been the first to 62, but there was still no guarantee that Sosa would not pass him and be the official record holder before the season was finished — a situation which could have been berry, berry embarrassing for MLB.

Though many sportswriters were still basking in the glow of McGwire's triumph, a few journalists, in addition to the aforementioned Smith, questioned the motives behind Sosa's snub. As *Chicago Sun-Times* columnist Dave Van Dyck pointed out afterwards, "It was just short of a national disgrace. Let's just hope that the seeming snub of Sammy Sosa came only because he was the second to get to 62 home runs, not because he is considered a second-class citizen."[55] Here, Van Dyck acknowledges the racial hierarchy within the United States, which is problematic for Sosa because "[r]acial inequality in this country is assessed through the prism of the Black-White paradigm and Latinas/os are rendered invisible in this construct of race relations."[56] What makes Sosa's treatment even more egregious is the fact that at the time, the Cubs were owned by the Tribune Company which publishes both the *Chicago Tribune* and the *Los Angeles Times* and is one of the largest media companies in the United States. While McGwire's accomplishment was front-page news across the United States, Sosa's was relegated to the sports pages even by the team owners whose best interest would/should have been the promotion of their most popular player. Finally, Joel Stein and Julie Grace of *Time* magazine quote the Rev. Jesse Jackson's letter to Commissioner Bud Selig which read in part, "Sammy deserves the same infrastructure support [as McGwire], but he has not received it. While he will receive many honors in the coming days, it is a little after the fact. There was time to anticipate and to be there for him."[57] Stein and Grace conclude, "Baseball, for the moment, was very, very bad to him."[58] Referencing both Sosa's and the *Saturday Night Live* "berry, berry good to me" quote/misquote further admonishes journalists who not only snubbed the slugger's record-tying feat, but who also had essentially ignored Sosa's accomplishments throughout the season while subtly hinting at the racial and nationalistic undertones for the snub.

From a racial standpoint, it makes sense that MLB would choose McGwire as the heir apparent because:

> History suggests that Anglo baseball fans, especially men, would more likely identify with McGwire [...]. Likened variously to Paul Bunyan and John Wayne, McGwire is the prototypical all-American slugger [...]. A fitter version of Babe Ruth, he clearly was the fans' favorite to break a record set in 1961 by Roger Maris, who was a Yankee like Ruth and therefore an acceptable replacement for the legend. The sequence thus made sense in terms of race: Ruth, Maris, McGwire.[59]

This historical lineage highlights the likelihood that neither Sosa nor Griffey, whose chances of breaking the record had subsided by this point, had any chance of capturing the mantle reserved for legendary sluggers regardless of the number of home runs they would eventually hit — a situation that would prove fortuitous when Barry Bonds broke the single-season home-run record in 2001. The Ruth, Maris, McGwire sequence also assumes that Anglo baseball fans could not or would not identify with non-white or non–U.S.-born home-run hitters and, at the same time, erases the slugger who held the all-time home-run hitting record at the time: the non-white Henry Aaron. Given the options, McGwire was clearly the more acceptable choice to continue the white American home-run hitter lineage.

What Is Androstenedione and How Do You Pronounce It?

Clearly the praise heaped upon McGwire's offensive explosion was much greater than what Sosa received. While racism, conscious or unconscious, and what some dubbed as "simple" patriotism may help explain the differential treatment, the fact that McGwire's accomplishments may not have been *wholly* legitimate further heightens the discrepancy. Prior to McGwire's breaking the home-run record, before planning for the celebrations had even begun, Associated Press reporter Steve Wilsten spotted a bottle of androstenedione ("andro") in McGwire's locker. Andro is a hormone naturally produced by the body that may enable athletes to train harder and build muscles faster than they would otherwise.[60] At the time, MLB banned only illegal drugs, though there was no testing system in place to detect substances, legal or otherwise. Steroids and other performance-enhancing drugs were implicitly acceptable under baseball's rules and regulations. McGwire spoke openly about the fact that he had been using andro for over one year, though shortly after the story broke, he stated that he stopped ingesting the substance. It is curious that even in light of McGwire's admitted use of a performance-enhancing substance the nation would still continue to celebrate his accomplishments over Sosa's. In essence, McGwire's white privilege would shield him from any criticism concerning andro.

What is even more intriguing is the fact that sport journalists' attitude toward andro seemed just as cavalier as McGwire's. The *Sporting News*'s Steve Marantz and Michael Knisley wrote

> Not that [McGwire's] perfect. His use of the over-the-counter supplement, androstenedione, makes us wonder about his judgment. A substance incompletely researched, banned from the NFL, NCAA and Olympics, barred from the shelves of major dietary supplement chains, is dubious. We question that blind spot, yet

perversely, find him more appealing because of it, in the way Cindy Crawford's mole accents her beauty.[61]

Even with McGwire's legal yet potentially unethical use of performance-enhancing drugs, the slugger was revered by fans and journalists alike. Instead of condemning the use of performance-enhancing drugs, McGwire accused the AP reporter who originally wrote the andro story of "snooping," and Cardinals manager Tony La Russa wanted all AP reporters banned from the clubhouse.[62]

Clearly the support for McGwire on this issue took myriad forms. John Hoberman lamented that "public interest in sporting success outweighs public interest in drug-free sport [which] does reflect the historical record, and it is also compatible with the response to Mark McGwire in his role as a kind of Paul Bunyanesque distraction from the meltdown of the Clinton presidency."[63] This reverence in the face of character flaws once again harks back to the connection between the home-run chase and government scandal as President Clinton posted record approval ratings when news of the sex scandal broke.[64] It is almost as if despite his admission of using andro, McGwire was issued a free pass that meant that the controversy would not be allowed to stain his image. In both cases, the symbol of the white American male power structure was manipulated to allow for what was being framed as a momentary lapse in judgment. The controversy also effectively shows how entrenched the racial/nationality hierarchy within the home-run chase is: the white American remains on top despite questionable practices, while the "black foreigner" who refrained from using performance-enhancing drugs, as far as the public knew, was still relegated to the background. Few in MLB or the media at large questioned the validity of McGwire's record based on his use of andro or the consequences of his admission. Indicative of how the andro story was framed by media representatives, Daniel Okrent from *Time* remarked:

> Whatever else [andro] does, it can't help a player's timing, his hand-eye coordination, his ability to discern a slider from a splitter. But even if andro improved his power by an unlikely, oh, 5 percent, then instead of 70 home runs, McGwire this year would have hit ... maybe 67. Take 5 percent off a 450-ft. missile, and you've got a 427-ft. missile — long enough to clear any fence save center field in Detroit's Tiger Stadium.[65]

Sportswriters created a narrative that McGwire's andro use did not enhance his performance and they continued to frame him as the prototypical home-run slugger. In the end, the Blue Angels still flew over Busch Stadium, McGwire was still named *Time*'s Man of the Year as well as *Sport Illustrated*'s and the *Sporting News*'s Player of the Year, and, in what was probably an unintended consequence, the "sales [of andro] exploded by a factor of 10, to more than $50 million annually."[66]

The free pass McGwire was issued for using a performance-enhancing drug became even more important in light of later events. During a game versus the Devil Rays in 2003, umpires discovered cork in one of Sosa's shattered bats. Sosa was ejected from the game and suspended for seven games as players are not allowed to use altered bats during games. Though Sosa claimed it was an honest mistake — he used the corked bat during practice, which is allowed, but grabbed the wrong bat during the game — the backlash was swift and decisive. The difference in treatment was not lost on everyone, as *USA Today's* Christine Brennan noted: "Across the months and years, McGwire's big-boy-next-door image somehow never was seriously tarnished by his use of a substance that would have gotten an Olympic gold medalist immediately and unceremoniously kicked out of the Games, sans his or her medal. Sosa's image, on the other hand, is on the verge of cracking into a thousand pieces virtually overnight."[67] MLB quickly X-rayed all of Sosa's bats, including the ones he had used in 1998, which were in the Hall of Fame, and found no other corked bats. The revelation did not help remake his image, as *New York Amsterdam News* columnist Jamie Harris wrote: "Sosa has discovered that in some quarters, he is viewed as being as black as O.J. Simpson. Whatever the truth may be, he is no longer perceived as the happy-go-lucky slugger of the Chicago Cubs. He is certain to finish his career in a cloud of suspicion."[68] Harris's view on the controversy subjugated Sosa's Dominican heritage and reinscribed the black-white binary so prevalent in American culture by invoking the O.J. imagery. Though using a corked bat is in no way similar to being tried for murder, the illusion of transcending one's race or ethnicity applied to both athletes. Prior to his arrest, Simpson "was an exemplary figure to the white world [and] he was the kind of black man whom whites like and desire to promote, a depoliticized icon of racial amnesia."[69] In her discussion of Simpson's trial and the aftermath, Kimberlé Crenshaw argued that "Simpson's fall from grace is potentially meaningful because it suggested that even the few who won the celebrity lottery might still be divested of everything on the basis of the one thing they continued to share with the rest of African Americans — their race."[70] Though Sosa's and Simpson's situations are not analogous, the outcomes were similar: though Sosa never "transcended" his ethnicity in the way Simpson was framed as doing, any goodwill Sosa garnered during the 1998 home-run chase was quickly revoked. The free pass McGwire was issued allowed him to coast through the andro controversy unscathed; however, because of both his dark skin and his "foreign" heritage, Sosa never received a "get out of jail free" card and was forever tarnished for his mistake. Essentially, "we have different rules for different athletes"[71]: one set of rules for white American athletes and another set of more stringent rules for everyone else.

The Hits Keep on Coming

When McGwire retired after the 2001 season due to a knee injury, he was fifth on the all-time home run list but no longer retained the single-season home-run record. Though McGwire kept a low profile during his retirement, after Giants outfielder Barry Bonds broke the single-season home-run record, journalists began taking a more critical look at McGwire's heroics. It seemed as though journalists were finally revoking McGwire's get-out-of-jail-free card, though arguably only because a black player dared break the record so soon after the nation basked in McGwire's glory. The home-run record holder was framed as a hero, a symbol of Americana, and as a U.S.–born white player. With this controlling image statistically shattered and the president no longer in need of a symbolic replacement, McGwire's character flaws, which at one point made him more appealing to the public, were now subject to scrutiny.

The discussion surrounding steroid use in MLB intensified in 2004 when former NL MVP Ken Caminiti, an admitted steroid user, died of a drug overdose. One year later, former McGwire teammate José Canseco published the book *Juiced: Wild Times, Rampant 'Roids, Smash Hits and How Baseball Got Big*, in which he chronicled the rise of steroid abuse in MLB. Canseco was not unfamiliar with MLB: he spent sixteen years in the Majors playing with the Athletics, Rangers, Devil Rays, and both Sox franchises. His many professional accomplishments include winning the Rookie of the Year Award in 1986, the AL MVP Award in 1988, and four Silver Slugger Awards, plus playing in six All-Star Games and becoming the first player in history to hit 40 home runs and steal 40 bases in a single season.[72] An admitted steroid user like Caminiti, Canseco led a life outside of baseball that was less than stellar. *New York Times* columnist Michael Chabon described Canseco as "greedy, faithless, selfish, embittered, scornful, and everlastingly a showboat. He is a bad man."[73] Once again, the controlling images historically applied to Latin players resurface to describe a contemporary Latin player. In the book, Canseco alleges that he helped McGwire inject himself with illegal steroids in the 1980s. According to *Sports Illustrated*'s Verducci, Canseco alleges:

> McGwire used steroids as far back as 1988, when he first discussed them with Canseco [...]. The Cuban-born Canseco seethes at what he perceives as the preferential treatment afforded McGwire by baseball and the media, attributing it to the fact that McGwire is white. In short, Canseco does his best to smash McGwire's iconic stature. The McGwire that Canseco knows refers to reporters with a homophobic insult, is socially awkward and, above all, is a chemically made slugger.[74]

Because of Canseco's off-the-field exploits, including more than one arrest on assault charges, sportswriters initially balked at his claims, and McGwire remained relatively silent over the accusations. However, at least one group of people was paying attention: the U.S. House of Representatives. In March 2005, the House Government Reform Committee conducted hearings to determine the extent of steroid use in MLB. Though McGwire did not officially exercise his Fifth Amendment right against self-incrimination, his evasiveness, as well as his comment that he was "not here to talk about the past," caused many people to conclude that there may have been some truth to Canseco's statements. After the hearing, *Newsweek*'s Mark Starr and Eve Conant wrote

> Bill James, the noted baseball historian, told NEWSWEEK: "I certainly think that McGwire's Hall of Fame candidacy is damaged." So, too, may be his legacy in the town where he is most beloved. On Friday, Congressman William Lacy Clay urged the Missouri State Legislature to remove McGwire's name from a five-mile stretch of I-70 that now honors him.[75]

The recriminations continued in 2007, when only 23.5 percent of the Baseball Hall of Fame voters included McGwire's name on their ballots, well short of the necessary 75 percent.[76] None of the subsequent votes have been anywhere close to the needed percentage required for induction.

Once praised as one of baseball's saviors, McGwire had officially fallen from grace and, as the running joke went for several months, became the first person in history to invoke the 4½ Amendment during his Congressional testimony. St. Louis radio personality Kevin Slaten echoed the changed public sentiment when he stated, "I don't think that [McGwire's] welcome here anymore. They had a celebration for him a few years ago before all of this started but he hasn't been back since to anyone's knowledge and I don't think he will be again. If he did he wouldn't be welcome."[77] Though McGwire successfully deflected steroid allegations in 1998, without the backdrop of a government sex scandal or a sidekick, his legacy was forever tarnished. It seems ironic that after relegating Sosa to the background of the home-run chase, it was another Latin player who knocked McGwire off the national pedestal.

Though it seemed that McGwire's image would be forever tarnished, when the St. Louis Cardinals hired the slugger as a hitting coach in 2010 and he finally admitted to using performance-enhancing drugs, there seemed to be a modicum of forgiveness (this issue will be discussed in more detail in Chapter 6). Sosa's career experienced a minor renaissance as well. After sitting out the 2006 season, Sosa signed a one-year contract with the Texas Rangers and performed better than many expected with 104 hits, 21 homers, and 92 RBI in 412 at bats. At the end of the 2009 season, when he officially retired, Sosa was sixth on the career home-run list. Ironically, Griffey Jr. surpassed both McGwire and Sosa by moving up to number five on that same list. Sosa will never again be considered the happy-go-lucky sidekick he was in 1998, though that is not necessarily a bad thing.

Parting Shots

It has been argued that "the home run is America — appealing to Americans' roots of rugged individualism and their fascination with grand scale,"[78] and that the single-season home-run record is the most famous record in sports because "it has become nothing less than a symbol of heroic triumph, unequaled, powerful, solitary, upright, public."[79] The 1998 home-run race gave MLB an opportunity to create the home-run slugger controlling image which could replace a damaged president as the epitome of the white American male power structure at a time when the league was becoming less white and less American. Mark McGwire became the poster child of the new prototypical slugger controlling image: a white American working- or middle-class male, who was uncomfortable with the spotlight, spoke proper English, was abrasive at times, had a personality flaw or two that only made him more loveable, and had a loveable sidekick waiting in the wings. However, the publication of José Canseco's tell-all steroid biography forced many journalists to rethink the feats accomplished in 1998 as well as the controlling image McGwire embodied. Though he had been celebrated as the game's savior and a national hero, McGwire's image, once coated with Teflon, was irreparably damaged. Despite the fact that Sammy Sosa accomplished very similar feats to McGwire's, he never received the same acclaim and, at the first sign of trouble, the goodwill he gained evaporated.

The inequitable media coverage of Sosa's feats, as well as his positioning as McGwire's always-smiling sidekick, reinforced the idea that people of color must always be in a subordinate position to whites. The sidekick image, usually reserved for U.S.–born black characters in popular culture, became superimposed onto Latinos and blacks throughout the diaspora. McGwire and the mostly white sportswriters utilized their power by allowing white privilege to relegate Sosa to a sidekick role. At the same time, placing McGwire on a national pedestal created and reinforced the idea that the American public could not/would not embrace a non-white or non–U.S.-born players as a national hero at a time when the number of Latin players reached 25 percent and the nation's demographics showed a "browning" of America.

The power dynamic in Sosa's case was more complicated. While sportswriters used their resources to frame Sosa as McGwire's sidekick, it is unclear to what extent Sosa was complicit with the creation and maintenance of that stereotype. At the same time, Sosa did experience a huge boost in popularity, which probably brought increased income, because of his willingness to play that particular role. On the other hand, by characterizing Sosa as a sidekick, MLB maintained a racial hierarchy in its ranks with white players on top and black and Latin players vying for second place. The message was that if Latin players are willing to play the subservient role to whites, they can move to second place in the pecking order, but no higher.

2

"Out" on the Field: Homosexuality and Our National Pastime

"Of all the major team sports, baseball, because of the individual nature of the game, would give a gay player the BEST shot at success. The NFL would sooner accept a member of al-Qaeda than an openly gay player."— Gerry Callahan[1]

"In competitive team sports there are at least two givens: One is that players want to win. The other is that being or appearing homosexual will bring shame to the team and the sport."— Harriet L. Swartz[2]

Out magazine editor Brandan Lemon argued that "the greatest sports stories involve the breaking of barriers"[3] at those times when the political sphere intersects with the sporting world. John Carlos and Tommie Smith brought international attention to racism in the United States with their Black Power salute during the 1968 Olympics. Billie Jean King struck a blow for the feminist movement by beating Bobby Riggs in the "Battle of the Sexes" tennis match in 1973. Before *Brown v. Board of Education*, which rendered segregated public schools unconstitutional, or Executive Order 9981, which desegregated the armed forces, Jackie Robinson and Larry Doby helped prove that racial integration could work.

Throughout the 1990s and 2000s, while the political realm argued over issues involving sexual identity such as same-sex marriage, domestic partner benefits, and so forth, the sports world seemed largely uninvolved. As of the end of the 2011 baseball season, no U.S. professional male team-sport athlete had come out during his career. The most recent U.S. team-sport athlete to come out was former NBA player John Amaechi in 2007, four years after he retired. The most prominent U.S. professional female team-sport athlete to do so was three-time Olympic Gold medalist and WNBA MVP Sheryl Swoopes in 2005. Despite a lack of players who have come out during their careers, Major League Baseball (MLB) has not *completely* ignored the issue, and the league's response to several incidents revolving around sexual identity may provide clues as to how MLB, which includes players, managers, coaches, and sportswriters, would react to the presence of an out ballplayer who is still playing.

Harriet L. Schwartz's observation that homosexuality would bring shame to sports, quoted at the beginning of this chapter, helps explain the reaction to Brendan Lemon's 2001 admission that "for the past year and a half, I have been having an affair with a pro baseball player from a major-league East Coast franchise, not his team's biggest star but a very recognizable media figure all the same."[4] Sportswriters quickly grabbed the story and ran with it, and thus intensified discussions regarding homosexuality in professional baseball. At the forefront of this intensified discussion was Mike Piazza and questions surrounding his sexual identity. The New York Mets catcher seemed to fit Lemon's profile of a recognizable East-Coast baseball player; however, Piazza was arguably the team's biggest star at the time.

Two years after questions surrounding Mike Piazza's sexual identity surfaced, the discussion turned to Japanese pitcher Kazuhiro Tadano. In 2002, Tadano was passed over during the amateur draft in Japan and later had difficulty finding a U.S. club that would sign him. These difficulties occurred despite one scout's assertion that Tadano "should have been a top five pick over there. He gets it up to 93–94 [mph] and he throws four different pitches for strikes."[5] Neither pitch location nor shoulder strength kept Tadano from being signed; it was his participation, while in college, in a sexually explicit video that contained sex acts involving two men that gave scouts pause. Sports media glossed over Tadano's story despite the national debate on gay, lesbian, and bisexual (GLB) rights occurring at the time, which included a U.S. Supreme Court decision in 2003 overturning state sodomy laws and the Massachusetts Supreme Court ruling in 2004 that the state's ban on same-sex marriages was unconstitutional.

Piazza and Tadano's situations demonstrate how sexual identity operates in American culture, raising the question: Why did the matter of Piazza's sexual identity attract so much attention? If questions surrounding Piazza's sexual identity created a media explosion, what factors may have accounted for the different way journalists handled Tadano's story? Arguably, Piazza's status as an elite white male, combined with the homophobia present in society at large, and sports culture more specifically, allowed questions surrounding his sexual orientation to turn into media spectacle. At the same, time race- and gender-based stereotypes regarding Asian masculinity dampened discussions about Tadano. By using the Piazza and Tadano stories as a starting point, we can also see an evolution, if any, in how MLB frames sexual identity.

Coming Out

The panic concerning gay players in MLB began in earnest in 1999 when former major leaguer Billy Bean's sexual identity was revealed in a newspaper article. A former member of the Tigers, Dodgers, and Padres organizations from 1987 to 1995, Bean published a 1999 autobiography, *Going the Other Way*, that painted a picture of professional baseball that included gay jokes, slurs, and other symptoms of rampant homophobia. Bean made the argument that, during his playing years, "baseball wasn't ready for a guy like me, no matter how well I played. The game wasn't mature enough to deal with a gay ballplayer."[6] Bean became the fourth athlete in a major American team sport to openly discuss his sexual identity following former NFL running back Dave Kopay in 1975, former NFL offensive lineman Roy Simmons in 1982, and former Dodgers and A's outfielder Glenn Burke one year later[7]; as with the aforementioned players, Bean waited until after he retired to come out. Reaction to Bean's story was mixed. Some players seemed to shrug their shoulders at the thought of a gay teammate, much like Bean's former teammate Brad Ausmus, who was quoted as saying, "It wouldn't have made any difference to me when we played together and it doesn't matter to me now."[8] Others took the opportunity to express their discomfort with the idea, such as Yankees pitcher Andy Pettitte who said, "There would be the question of being comfortable."[9] Bean responded to the reactions within MLB by writing, "The bonds of teammates, I was learning, were far stronger than prejudice [...]. The silence from other quarters was deafening. The baseball powers-that-be could not be bothered to call or issue a statement. Bud Selig [...] didn't seem to give a damn about the questions my stories raised."[10] The silence from both the commissioner's office and the Major League Baseball Players Association (MLBPA) was hardly surprising: heterosexuality was so normalized within MLB that it went unquestioned, and heterosexual privilege allowed those in power to ignore Bean's statements. It is automatically assumed that all male athletes in general, and professional baseball players more specifically, are heterosexual, which, by consequence, obscures both the presence of gay and bisexual athletes and the underlying homophobic environment within sports/ MLB culture. By coming out and discussing the homophobic environment within MLB, Bean may have helped MLB take its first steps toward combating homophobia and heterosexism. At the same time, the onus cannot fall solely on gay and bisexual players, as journalist Dave Zirin argues: "Given the current context, we cannot make demands on gay athletes to come out and risk their necks unless we are willing to hit the streets and do the same. If we aren't willing to stand up right now for our gay brothers and sisters, then we shouldn't expect an athlete to do it for us."[11]

Fighting Words

The possibility of out gay ballplayers and anti-gay sentiments within the clubhouse are interconnected, and speculation regarding gay ballplayers did not end with Bean's admission. In the same year Bean began openly discussing his sexual identity, *Sports Illustrated* ran an interview with former Atlanta closer John Rocker in which he expressed his feelings about a wide variety of topics. When asked about New York City, Rocker stated, "It's the most hectic, nerve-wracking city. Imagine having to take the [Number] 7 train to the ballpark, looking like you're [riding through] Beirut next to some kid with purple hair next to some queer with AIDS right next to some dude who just got out of jail for the fourth time right next to some 20-year-old mom with four kids. It's depressing."[12] The pitcher went on to disparage anyone who was not an English-speaking, heterosexual, white male, in addition to calling a Latino teammate a "fat monkey."[13]

Rocker's comments could be characterized as fighting words, which Critical Race theory scholar Charles R. Lawrence III defines as "those [words] 'which by their very utterance inflict injury or tend to incite to an immediate breach of peace,' and which are commonly understood to convey direct and visceral hatred or contempt for human beings on the basis of their sex, race, color, handicap, religion, sexual orientation, or national and ethnic origin."[14]

In response to Rocker's fighting words, Commissioner Bud Selig suspended the closer for 73 days with pay, fined him $20,000, and ordered him to undergo psychological counseling. Rocker was later fined an additional $5,000 by Atlanta for confronting Jeff Pearlman, the journalist who wrote the original piece. Not long after, the team sent Rocker to the minor leagues; however, that was due more to the closer's lack of production than to his remarks and behavior.[15] There were some who found the punishment too lenient and others who thought it was too harsh. In either case, though Selig was remarkably silent about Bean's account of anti-gay sentiments in the clubhouse, the punishment handed down indicated that Selig would not tolerate fighting words outside the clubhouse. However, when an arbitrator later reduced the suspension to 14 days and the fine to $500, some believed that MLB was excusing Rocker's racist and homophobic remarks.[16] In responding to Rocker's outburst, Bean wrote that the closer "simply got caught saying what some people think but are afraid to say. It's easier for baseball to blame the outburst on the player than look in the mirror. They need to make it clear that harassment won't be allowed on the field or in the locker room."[17] Granted, Selig's original ruling could be interpreted as cracking down on fighting words and other forms of harassment. If that were the case, then Selig would hand out similar punishments to other players who made racist and/or homophobic remarks. Unfortunately, that has not happened.

Having learned absolutely nothing from John Rocker's public outburst and the resulting condemnation, during the 2001 season, pitcher Julian Tavárez, who was with the Chicago Cubs at the time, called San Francisco Giants fans "a bunch of faggots" after they booed him during a game.[18] Instead of making yet another example out of Tavárez, and living up to Bean's hope that MLB would not tolerate such behavior, the league went in a different direction. According to former *Chicago Sun-Times* columnist Jay Mariotti, Selig, "whose heavy-handed stance in the Rocker saga represented some of his finest work, went mushy on Tavárez. He didn't issue a suspension and deferred to the Cubs, who criticized Tavárez, slapped him with a fine and pointed him toward the mound, where he kept his place in the rotation."[19] What makes the punishment, or lack thereof, so ironic and disappointing is the fact that the Cubs have one of the longest track records for any MLB franchise of embracing their GLB fan base.[20] For black feminist thinker Patricia Hill Collins, the recurrence of fighting words is evidence that "such speech is less an anomaly than a visible, tangible manifestation of deep-seated ideas and practices that permeate and define the social structure itself."[21]

Rocker and Tavárez were not the only people within the baseball establishment to utter fighting words. In 2007 the ongoing feud between White Sox manager Ozzie Guillén and Jay Mariotti devolved in a very public fashion. While Mariotti had a habit of calling Frank Thomas "the big skirt" and referring to former Cubs pitcher LaTroy Hawkins as LaToya,[22] Guillén upped the ante by calling Mariotti a "f— king fag."[23] Guillén was quick to apologize to the GLB community, but not to Mariotti, and the manager was fined an undisclosed amount and ordered to attend sensitivity training.[24] While one tirade could be characterized as the ignorance of that individual, three outbursts — that the press reported — signal a larger problem. To be fair, homophobic statements receive more coverage than statements accepting GLB players and rights.[25] At the same time, Rocker's, Tavárez's, and Guillén's comments, as well as the accompanied minimal penalties, were not simply isolated and unconnected incidents, they reflect a more overarching heterosexist and homophobic environment present in MLB and are "manifestations of an ubiquitous and deeply ingrained cultural belief system."[26] The utterance, publication, and acceptance of fighting words sends the message that gay players are not wanted in MLB and if they are already present, they should stay in the closet.

In fact, it could be argued that the type of behavior displayed by Rocker, Tavárez, and Guillén "benefits powerful white-dominated institutions"[27] like MLB. According to Lawrence III, "This kind of behavior keeps [subordinate groups] on edge, a little off balance. We get these occasional reminders that we are different, and not really wanted. It prevents us from digging in too strongly, starting to think we could really belong here [...]. It assures that those of us of real spirit, real pride, just plain leave — all of which is a substantial benefit for the institution."[28] While Selig's punishment of Rocker initially sent the message that fighting words were not tolerated in MLB, the public remarks occurring in such quick succession also sends a signal to gay and bisexual players that it may not be safe for them to come out. In addition, Selig's acquiescence on Tavárez's and Guillén's behalf could reflect the homophobic environment within MLB specifically and professional sports more broadly. The truth is a bit more complicated.

Just three months before Ozzie Guillén's homophobic tirade, former NBA player John Amaechi announced he was gay. Like Billy Bean's announcement several years earlier, the reaction was mixed. Phoenix Suns forward Grant Hill was quoted as saying, "The fact that John has done this, maybe it will give others the comfort or confidence to come out as well, whether they are playing or retiring."[29] The bombshell occurred during the NBA All-Star Game, when former players were giving interviews in an effort to promote the game and the league. During a radio interview with Dan Le Batard, former player Tim Hardaway said, "You know, I hate gay people, so I let it be known I don't like gay people and I don't like to be around gay people. I am homophobic."[30] Though MLB Commissioner Bud Selig's handling of Rocker's, Tavárez's and Guillén's fighting words was uneven and somewhat unsatisfactory, NBA Commissioner David Stern did not waste any time: he immediately banned Hardaway from making any further public appearances on behalf of the League and issued a statement which read: "It is inappropriate for [Hardaway] to represent us given the disparity between his views and ours."[31] The fact that Hardaway was no longer an active player might help explain the swift punishment; however, Stern's actions left no doubt in anyone's mind that fighting words would not be tolerated in the NBA.

Comfort and Finances

Two years after the Bean and Rocker stories broke, Brendan Lemon's editorial regarding his relationship with a major league player intensified the discussion regarding sexual identity in baseball. Lemon concluded that his partner would "have to deal with the initial media avalanche and the verbal abuse from some bleacher bums, and there'd be a teammate or two who'd have an adolescent 'Oh, my God, he saw me naked in the showers' response. Not to mention a nervous front-office executive or two. But I'm pretty confident there'd be more support from the team than he imagines [...]. Their prime concern is winning, not who you're sleeping with."[32]

Sportswriters again seized the opportunity to discuss how an openly gay athlete would be received by teammates and fans alike. Sports talk radio host Jim Rome posed the question about teammate reaction to baseball veteran Eric Davis, who replied, "I think it would go real bad. I think people would jump to form an opinion because everybody already has an opinion about gays already. But I think it would be a very difficult situation because with us showering with each other ... being around each other as men. Now you're in the shower with a guy who's gay ... looking at you ... maybe making a pass. That's an uncomfortable situation."[33] Davis's remarks echoed comments made earlier by Andy Pettitte and others in response to Bean's book. Concerns expressed by players had little to do with on-field production or fan reaction and had more to do with the prospect of being hit on by a teammate.

Attempting to debunk the notion that baseball players are somehow irresistible to both males and females alike, Bean responded by writing, "It infuriates me to think that players would actually believe that a gay teammate would be any less serious about his job than they are. It takes a huge amount of work to reach the majors, and I wonder if they really believe a player would sacrifice his career for a cheap thrill. Being gay doesn't mean you lack self-control."[34] One month after Lemon's editorial was published, ESPN's *Outside the Lines* discussed "The Gay Dilemma" with Lemon, Bean, and former major league umpire Dave Pallone. Host Bob Ley began by focusing not on the issue of comfort that was raised by some of the players, but on the one factor players and management can agree on: making money.

Ley pointed out that the Minnesota Twins, "who for years have suffered with lackluster attendance, are scheduled to recognize a gay and lesbian group outing, organized by an alternative magazine."[35] Since 2001, almost half of the major league franchises have hosted events catering to GLB communities including Atlanta, the Blue Jays, Pirates, Dodgers, and Rangers.[36] When discussing the Twins' effort, Dave St. Peter, former senior vice president of business affairs, stated, "This isn't about gay and lesbian, it's about baseball fans. And we're in the business of promoting our game, and that means that we need to be proactive and progressive."[37] At the same time, while many teams may go out of their way to accept and cater to GLB fans, accepting and providing a safe environment for gay players is a different matter, since, as Danae Clark discusses in her essay "Commodity Lesbianism," advertisers and/or MLB promoters can embrace GLB consumers without embracing GLB politics.[38] Using the racial integration of MLB as an example, Bean is quick to point out that both outcomes are linked to financial considerations since "baseball didn't integrate solely out of a humanitarian concern for opportunity and equality. The change didn't occur because management had the best interests of black athletes at heart. It occurred, like most changes in pro sports, because of competitive pressures and business considerations."[39] So MLB has to ask itself whether or not catering to GLB fans can/will translate into the League accepting an out player because of humanitarian concerns, or as a way to bring in more GLB consumers?

15-Word Response

In the months following Lemon's editorial, the discussion surrounding the possibility of an out ballplayer remained fairly abstract, since no active player had come out in response to the editorial. The discussion moved from abstract to specific following a 2002 interview with then Mets manager Bobby Valentine in *Details* magazine. When asked whether or not baseball was ready for an openly gay player, Valentine replied, "The players are a diverse enough group now that I think they could handle it."[40] Shortly after Valentine's interview was published, *New York Post* gossip columnist Neal Travis framed Valentine's statement as a "pre-emptory strike" due to "a persistent rumor around town that one Mets star who spends a lot of time with pretty models in clubs is actually gay and has started to think about declaring his sexual orientation."[41] Though Travis's column did not name names, it was clear to many that Travis was referring to Mike Piazza. According to *Pittsburg Post-Gazette* sports columnist Ron Cook, Travis "didn't have to [mention Piazza]. He's the only Mets star who fits that description."[42] It was common knowledge that the catcher had a weakness for club-hopping with supermodels and Playboy Playmates. There was no question in sportswriters' or fans' minds that Travis' article was referring to Piazza.

It took less than twenty-four hours for Piazza to respond. The catcher held an impromptu press conference prior to a game in Philadelphia where he declared, "First off, I'm not gay. I'm heterosexual. That's pretty much it. That's pretty much all I can say. I don't see the need to address the issue further."[43] Piazza went on to state, "In this day and age, it would be irrelevant. If the guy is doing his job on the field [...] I don't think there would be any problem at all."[44] On some level Piazza's comments seem disingenuous. If a player's sexual identity is irrelevant, as he claims, why go to the trouble of holding a press conference to publicly proclaim his heterosexuality? Though the catcher did not feel the need to address the issue further following the press conference, other baseball players, managers, and journalists continued to ponder whether MLB was ready for an openly gay player. Former Phillies manager Larry Bowa remarked, "I'd probably wait until my career was over.

If he hits .340, it probably would be easier than if he hits .220."[45] This sentiment underscored the notion that production on the field is far more important than life off the field. When asked whether or not he would accept a gay teammate, Yankees pitcher Mike Mussina replied, "I'm going to make the assumption that I already have, that there already is a player like that out there. I don't have any problems with it. It's part of society."[46] Mussina's comments underscored an important point that was missing from the discussion thus far: there have always been gay athletes in professional baseball, even, possibly, on the venerated New York Yankees.

In the wake of Piazza's actions, sport journalists shifted the focus of their writing from hypothesizing about gay players' identities to asking whether or not a player's sexual identity was cause for a press conference. Most columnists agreed that the *Post* column, which could not be substantiated, did not deserve this much attention; however, the lack of evidence did not stop anyone from writing about it. Some, like *San Francisco Chronicle* columnist Bruce Jenkins questioned Piazza's tactics: "You'd think he would just shrug it off, and that the Mets would have no reaction whatsoever."[47] *New York Times* columnist Harvey Araton agreed with Jenkins' puzzlement:

> Irresponsible and unfair as the item in the *New York Post* was, I'm wondering what the Mets accomplished or were even thinking with their unfortunate overreaction. The better response, for the sake of discouraging such future musings, would have been: You don't have the right to ask unless I want you to know. Instead, we had Piazza, a gentleman, calmly stating, "I'm not gay," in addition to a variety of Mets voicing anger and disgust, including [catcher] Vance Wilson, who chimed in with the gem, "He lives his life morally right."[48]

While some journalists like Araton may have questioned their right to know, many sportswriters continued to comment on the story. Gerry Callahan of the *Boston Globe* discussed the ramifications faced by an out athlete, saying, "It would affect his relationship with his teammates, his fans, the media, the advertisers. To think otherwise is to be as naive or as disingenuous as those who ask, 'Who cares?'"[49] At the same time, some sportswriters expressed discomfort with players' homophobic remarks; Araton facetiously referred to Vance Wilson's comment as a gem. Despite the seeming disapproval of homophobic and heterosexist comments, it could be argued that one of the largest obstacles keeping gay ballplayers in the proverbial closet is not teammate reaction but the almost inevitable media frenzy.

I Always Feel Like...

Due to the public nature of their professions, celebrities (actors, athletes, politicians, etc.), are under constant surveillance by news organizations.

Because of this, some celebrities are inclined to regulate their behavior, especially if they believe that their career will be jeopardized if they are outed (whether or not they are actually gay). The constant surveillance allows the media to operate much like Jeremy Bentham's conception of the panopticon, a circular prison structure designed so that inmates' behavior can be observed at all times. Because of the fear, or reality, of constant surveillance, inmates regulate their behavior regardless of whether or not someone is actually observing them. Though the panopticon began as a concrete prison structure, the concept has expanded to describe any state of constant surveillance, whether real or imagined. John Thompson argues that "the development of communication media provides a means by which many people can gather information about a few, and, at the same time, a few can appear before many; thanks to the media, it is primarily those who exercise power, rather than those over whom power is exercised, who are subjected to a certain kind of visibility."[50] With that in mind, it can be argued that the media serve as a makeshift panopticon, with the dual purpose of reporting on and regulating celebrity behavior. The combination of heterosexism and media surveillance keeps some celebrities in the closet. Thompson's analysis focuses specifically on politicians who, due to the nature of their job as public servants, arguably should expect a higher level of surveillance and accountability. Despite the fact that most sports celebrities do not appear to endure the same level of media scrutiny as actors, musicians, or politicians, arguably the hypermasculinity of the professional sporting environment offsets the decreased media surveillance.

Michel Foucault referred to the Panopticon as "a marvelous machine which, whatever use one may wish to put it to, produces homogeneous effects of power."[51] A media panopticon helps to reproduce the notion that the default sexuality of professional athletes is heterosexual, forces athletes to regulate their behavior regardless of their sexual identity, and helps to keep gay and bisexual players in the closet during their careers. The media scrutiny might also help explain why players are more willing to come out after they have left professional sports: the media panopticon is not as great if they are no longer in the spotlight. Consequently, if an athlete is no longer in the spotlight the need to discipline/control his behavior diminishes.

...Somebody's Watching Me

Though the discussion surrounding openly gay players in MLB was tabled after Piazza's press conference, the issue would return less than one year later due to a controversy with Kazuhiro Tadano. According to *Baseball America*'s Chris Kline, Tadano "was one of the most talented amateur pitchers in Japan [in 2002]."[52] Despite his talent, the right-hander, whom scouts expected to be chosen in the first round of Japan's amateur draft, was not chosen at all. If Tadano was as talented as scouts observed, the pitcher should have been picked up by a major league team; however, despite his being close to securing a deal on more than one occasion, that did not happen. Quietly, word circulated that "Tadano (along with several of his college teammates at Rikkyo University) was paid to take part in a pornographic video that contained acts of homosexuality."[53] Coming so soon after the Piazza media circus, and in spite of Bobby Valentine's declaration that baseball players could handle an openly gay player, multiple clubs passed on signing Tadano, arguably because scouts assumed he was gay.

The discrimination Tadano faced because of his participation in a sexually explicit video is indicative of how scared MLB was of having an out gay player. In this case, the mere hint of homosexuality was enough to keep Tadano out of both the Japanese professional leagues and MLB. After some time, Cleveland signed Tadano to a minor league contract in 2004, and the team made it clear that "they would support Tadano when the video became public knowledge."[54] When word of the video finally reached the U.S. sports media, Tadano quickly stated through an interpreter, "I'm not gay. I'd like to clear that fact up right now,"[55] adding that he participated in the video as a way to support himself while in school.[56] The fact that several major league clubs initially passed on signing Tadano is not that surprising; neither is the fact that at least one team put winning above other concerns, though Tadano's stint in the majors lasted only two seasons. What is interesting is the relative lack of attention Tadano's situation garnered.

The question surrounding Mike Piazza's sexual identity made national headlines while Tadano's taped same-sex encounter did not elicit the same level of media response. It is possible that sportswriters learned from the Piazza debacle and decided that a player's personal life was off-limits, but there is no evidence to suggest that is the case. The feeding frenzy that ensued in 2007 when former NBA player John Amaechi came out highlights sportswriters' continued interest in player's sexual identity. The varied response may be related to the fact that Piazza occupies a higher place within the masculinity hierarchy. According to Collins, there is a three-tiered masculinity structure: the top tier consists of "predominantly wealthy white men."[57] Men in the second tier have "greater access to white male power, yet remain marginalized [and consist of] working-class White men and Latino, Asian, and White immigrant men," while the bottom tier consists of black and indigenous men.[58] Because of his racial and nationality status, Piazza occupied the top tier of the masculinity structure — not to mention the fact that he was an already established player in the nation's largest media market, which helps to explain the increased media attention. For Collins, an elite white man in the top tier of the masculinity structure "so dominates positions of power and authority [that] the view of masculinity patterns is well known and is often taken as normal, natural, and ideal."[59] If Piazza represented these elite white men throughout his career, then any questions surrounding Piazza's sexual orientation would be more damaging to the white, male power structure and therefore should be avoided. Piazza's "outing" also raises the question of whether or not Piazza could still epitomize the white, American male power structure if he were gay. However, as mentioned at the beginning of this chapter, Tadano's struggle paralleled existing controversies that were gaining national attention at the time. As mentioned earlier, three months after Cleveland signed Tadano, the U.S. Supreme Court ruled that sodomy laws were unconstitutional,[60] and later that same year the Massachusetts Supreme Court ruled that the state's ban on same-sex marriages was unconstitutional.[61] Both decisions were interpreted as steps forward for GLB rights in the United States. Though Tadano quickly affirmed his heterosexuality, the difficulties he faced making it to the majors based on the mere perception of homosexuality coincided with discussions surrounding GLB rights in much the same way the integration of MLB coincided with the civil rights movements during the 1950s and therefore could have been framed as a much larger and more influential story than it was.

Another reason why Tadano's story was downplayed by sport journalists may have to do with unconscious stereotypes regarding Asian masculinity. As mentioned in Chapter 2, Charles R. Lawrence III's notion of unconscious racism hypothesizes that, since racism played a large part in America's shared past, all Americans unconsciously harbor negative opinions about nonwhites. Because society no longer tolerates overt racism the way it once did, the negative attitudes created by the shared racist history will find another outlet.[62] Some of those lingering attitudes concern sexuality and the construction of different masculinities. As Chong-Suk Han points out, "For decades, the mainstream media have usually portrayed Asian men as meek, asexual houseboy types or as sexual deviants of some kind."[63] In the article "Representing and Reconstructing Asian Masculinities," Allen Luke goes further when he writes, "We have all the characteristics of something Other, something more feminine in the normative eye of Western sexuality: slender and relatively hairless bodies, differently textured and coloured skin and straight hair. In Western public representations of masculinity we are defined in terms of absence, lack or silence."[64]

As Luke points out, Asian men broadly, and, by extension, Tadano more specifically, are the opposite of the masculine ideal. At one point, *Details*, the same magazine that asked Bobby Valentine whether MLB was ready for an out player, "featured an item entitled 'Gay or Asian,' and challenged its readers to ascertain whether a given man was, in fact, gay or Asian."[65] This quiz that highlights how popular media frames Asian masculinity as congruent with homosexuality. These lingering stereotypes meant that not only did it seem as though Tadano's heterosexuality was *not* assumed, but questions surrounding the pitcher's sexual orientation were also framed as un-newsworthy.

It's a Man's World

Another reason sportswriters were drawn to Piazza's story is that players like him represent the physical embodiment of hegemonic masculinity. According to Robert Hanke, hegemonic masculinity "refers to the social ascendancy of a particular version or model of masculinity that, operating on the terrain of 'common sense' and conventional morality, defines 'what it means to be a man.'"[66] Contemporary models can be real persons such as Piazza or actor George Clooney, or fictional characters such as James Bond or Bruce Wayne from the *Batman* franchise; however, the exemplars are always "elite white men."[67] Furthermore, "because this group so dominates positions of power and authority, the view of masculinity patterns on [these elite white men] is well known and is often taken as normal, natural, and ideal. It becomes hegemonic in that the vast majority of the population accepts ideas about gender complementarity that privilege the masculinity of propertied, heterosexual, White men as natural, normal, and beyond reproach."[68]

Nick Trujillo's analysis of Hall of Fame pitcher Nolan Ryan, another exemplar of hegemonic masculinity, outlines five features of hegemonic masculinity in U.S. culture: physical force and control, occupational achievement, familial patriarchy, frontiersmanship, and heterosexuality.[69] Trujillo's features are helpful in understanding how media personalities generally, and Mike Piazza more specifically, embody these five characteristics and thereby represent what it means to be a man.

Not a physically imposing player like Jim Thome or CC Sabathia, as a catcher Piazza is required to withstand physical force far more than he is required to exhibit it. The squatting position catchers must sustain throughout the game takes a physical toll on players' knees, and in addition, the ability to hold on to the baseball after colliding with a charging baserunner is a necessity. Though Piazza has not exhibited much physical force throughout his career, the catcher did make headlines because of his control. During a regular-season interleague game with the Yankees in 2000, pitcher and notorious headhunter Roger Clemens drilled Piazza in the head with a fastball. Because Piazza had an unheard-of .578 batting average against Clemens, some speculated that the Yankee pitcher hit Piazza on purpose.[70] After the incident, Piazza did not charge the mound, a move which almost qualifies as standard operating procedure in that situation. Three months later, when the two met during the World Series, Piazza hit a pitch that caused his bat to explode into several pieces. The barrel of the bat rolled toward Clemens and he tossed the pieces toward Piazza, who was running toward first base.[71]

The scene of Clemens throwing the barrel of the bat toward Piazza was replayed endlessly for the duration of the Series, and sportswriters praised Piazza for maintaining his control during the confrontation. In this case, Piazza conforms to an element of hegemonic masculinity outlined by Collins but not by Trujillo—the fact that "'real' men exercise control not just over women but also over their own emotions."[72] By staying in control of his emotions, Piazza was framed as the "better" man in these situations. Clemens, the physical aggressor in both events, was admonished by journalists covering the series. Framing the event in this manner led audiences to believe that, at least in this baseball context, control is more representative of hegemonic masculinity than physical force, as Clemens's actions were framed as unacceptable.

The second component of hegemonic masculinity, occupational achievement, is not a problem for Piazza. Despite the fact that he was drafted in the 62nd round of the draft,[73] after thirteen years in the majors, twelve All-Star appearances, ten Silver Slugger awards, and one Rookie of the Year award, Piazza clearly had surpassed everyone's expectations. When he retired after the 2007 season, Piazza had more career home runs (427), a higher slugging percentage (.545), and a higher on-base plus slugging percentage (.922) than any other catcher in history, numbers that will almost guarantee Piazza induction into the Hall of Fame in 2013.[74] Since Piazza was also one of the highest paid players in the game during his career, the only professional achievement missing from Piazza's résumé is a World Series win, which has less to do with Piazza's abilities and more to do with the lackluster teams he played for.

Another aspect of hegemonic masculinity is frontiermanship or a "present-outdoorsman" persona.[75] While this aspect of hegemonic masculinity could be personified by the likes of John Wayne or Nolan Ryan, who spent most of his career playing in Texas and his off-seasons on a ranch, the image of the outdoorsman seems outdated. For Jay Clarkson, "the frontiersman [has been] replaced with a dapper, dashing man about town who sings to his wife, knows how to handle himself at high-class urban events, and takes time to enjoy a day at the spa."[76] The evolving nature of hegemonic masculinity illustrates how fluid the concept is because, as Robert Hanke acknowledges, "Hegemonic masculinity *changes* in order to remain hegemonic."[77] While Piazza could not be described as a frontiersman, the man-about-town classification seems more appropriate, especially for a New York baseball player. In 2001 Piazza shared the Toast-of-the-Town Award with Yankees shortstop Derek Jeter,[78] and as *New York Post* columnist Neal Travis pointed out in his "outing" article, Piazza seemed comfortable with the New York nightlife. Piazza's embodiment of hegemonic masculinity follows the Bruce Wayne model more than the John Wayne model.

Familial patriarchy posed a conundrum for Piazza and his embodiment of hegemonic masculinity. While Trujillo concluded in his study that "the media have reproduced Nolan Ryan as the archetypal husband and father and, in so doing, they have reaffirmed the hegemony of patriarchy,"[79] the same could not be done for Piazza since he was not married and did not have children. That being said, being framed as a husband and father are not the only ways to embody hegemonic masculinity and reaffirm patriarchy. In fact, dealing with Piazza's status as a bachelor and serial dater, sportswriters can relegate women to the background and render them disposable. In 2004 *Sports Illustrated*'s Rick Reilly proclaimed Yankees third baseman Alex Rodríguez "the man," but became frustrated by the player's unwillingness to embody the playboy image associated with being "the man." Reilly explained, "Some people just don't get their roles. A-Rod refuses to show up in *Star Magazine* with some blonde wearing too much lipstick and not enough dress. He does hit the bars for an hour after every game, but they're the bars with weights on the ends of them. Sigh. On second thought, maybe Mike Piazza is The Man."[80] Piazza's persona as a swinging bachelor helps explain why, when Neal Travis's article described a baseball player who "spends a lot of time with pretty models in clubs,"[81] sportswriters and fans immediately looked to Piazza despite the fact the article did not mention his name. Until his marriage to former Playboy model Alicia Rickter in 2005, Piazza personified the role Reilly thought "the man" should play, which helped reaffirm patriarchy, and expanded the dimensions of hegemonic masculinity from focusing solely on husbands and fathers to embracing the active bachelor lifestyle.

The fact that Piazza would often be accompanied by a woman wearing more makeup than clothing coincides with the final feature of hegemonic masculinity: heterosexuality. For Mike Donaldson, "heterosexuality and homophobia are the bedrock of hegemonic masculinity."[82] Collins agrees, as she contends that hegemonic masculinity mandates that "'real' men are also *not* gay or homosexual."[83] Arguably because heterosexuality is the most important aspect of hegemonic masculinity, the question concerning gay baseball players attracted a great deal of attention. Until the *New York Post* article was published, there had not been any questions surrounding Piazza's sexual identity, which was assumed to be heterosexual. Since Piazza had embodied the other features of hegemonic masculinity for such a long period of time, if the rumors surrounding his sexual identity were true, society would have to ask itself whether that was enough to remove Piazza from the hegemonic masculinity mantle.

Queer Eye for the Red Sox

One year after Cleveland signed Tadano to a minor league contract, in 2004, the Boston Red Sox won their first World Series in over eighty years. Framing themselves as "idiots," the Red Sox often resembled an unkempt little league team instead of the world champions. Partly because of the team's increased notoriety following the win and partially due to their scruffy-looking image, several members of the Red Sox agreed to appear on the television series *Queer Eye for the Straight Guy* to raise money for charity. Airing on Bravo beginning in 2003, *Queer Eye*

> is predicated on the basic assumption that straight men are unrefined, ungroomed, and simply need a gay man's help to attain a higher fluency of culture, charm, and sophistication. In each episode, the "fab five"—Carson (fashion), Kyan (grooming), Jai (culture), Thom (interior design), and Ted (food and wine)—inflict their areas of expertise on a hapless straight man, who, more often than not, is depicted as a clueless slob with a good heart and a woman who loves him the way he is but would like to see him improved.[84]

To that end, *Queer Eye* opened its third season by making over five Red Sox players: center fielder Johnny Damon, first baseman Kevin Millar, catchers Doug Mirabelli and Jason Varitek, and pitcher Tim Wakefield. The five were treated to manicures, pedicures, hair treatments, waxing, and fashion makeovers at the team's spring training facility. It is interesting to note that all of the players chosen to participate in the *Queer Eye* episode were framed as white and married; in addition, all but one of the wives were in attendance during the makeovers. Though Mirabelli, enjoying a rose-petal pedicure, began the episode by saying "Who said it was bad to be gay? I am now gay,"[85] *San Francisco Chronicle* reporter Gwen Knapp noticed that "in a few scenes, a couple of the Red Sox seem uncomfortable, and they're all incredulous that gay celebrities have visited their clubhouse. But the entertainment value of the show hinges on the culture clash between grungy jocks and style gurus."[86] The discomfort Knapp noticed was more amplified in the deleted scenes included on the DVD, which showed Wakefield visibly uncomfortable and agitated at having Carson in his personal space during a fitting[87] and just prior to the episode being aired, Mirabelli admitted, "We had a lot of fun. But if I had thought about it some more, I'm not sure I would have done it."[88] In interviews after the episode aired, Mirabelli and Millar quickly reminded reporters that the primary rationale behind taping the episode was to raise money to repair a little league field which was devastated by Hurricane Charley the year before.

Outfielder Johnny Damon, who seemed the least fazed and the most comfortable throughout the episode, discussed the matter with journalists and said, "If there's a gay guy in baseball, we have to help him out, I'd smack him on the butt, just like I do everybody else."[89] Damon's comments appeared less than two months after *Sports Illustrated* released a poll which gauged fan attitudes about homosexuality in sport. According to Jon Werthem, "Of 979 people interviewed, 86 percent agreed that it is O.K. for male athletes to participate in sports, even if they are openly gay, yet nearly a quarter of the respondents agreed that having an openly gay player hurts the entire team. 'It was like, I'm O.K. with this, but if you press me, I have some doubts,' says Doug Schoen, whose firm, Penn, Schoen & Berland Associates, conducted the poll."[90]

Though the *Sports Illustrated* poll did not ask players how they felt about openly gay athletes, and readers have no way of knowing how representative the sample was, the overwhelming number of respondents who agreed that openly gay male athletes could participate in sports is encouraging. When asked whether he would accept a gay teammate, the one baseball player Wertheim quoted in the piece, Ken Griffey, "laughed and said, 'Wouldn't bother me at all. If you can play, you can play.'"[91] This response prompted Wertheim to conclude, "Who knows? With attitudes like Griffey's, there will come a day when locker rooms and clubhouses cease to double as walk-in closets."[92]

It Gets Better

After the fighting-words incidents, Piazza's press conference, and *Queer Eye* guest spots, MLB, and U.S. team sports in general, moved out of the GLB spotlight. The same could not be said for the nation as a whole. In 2011, President Obama certified the repeal of the military's "Don't Ask, Don't Tell," a move that allows GLB service members to serve openly. The president also instructed the Justice Department not to defend the Defense of Marriage Act (DOMA), which defines marriage as a union between a man and a woman. DOMA is being challenged in several different court cases. Attorney General Eric Holder released the letter he sent to Congress, which read in part:

After careful consideration, including a review of my recommendation, the President has concluded that given a number of factors, including a documented history of discrimination, classifications based on sexual orientation should be subject to a more heightened standard of scrutiny. The President has also concluded that Section 3 of DOMA, as applied to legally married same-sex couples, fails to meet that standard and is therefore unconstitutional.[93]

In that same year, New York State became the sixth and largest state to allow same-sex marriage, joining Connecticut, Iowa, Massachusetts, New Hampshire, and Vermont. Unfortunately, against the backdrop of GLB communities' move toward legal and legislative equality were several high-profile suicides by GLB teenagers and young adults. As a response, syndicated columnist Dan Savage and his partner Terry uploaded a YouTube video with the simple message: it gets better. The It Gets Better Project, whose goal is to "show young LGBT people the levels of happiness, potential, and positivity their lives will reach — if they can just get through their teen years,"[94] became a phenomenon. Celebrities, politicians, community groups, corporations, and supportive individuals created and uploaded their own It Gets Better videos.

On June 1, 2011, the San Francisco Giants, hot off their World Series victory, became the first professional sports team to record an It Gets Better video. "Giants players Barry Zito, Sergio Romo, Matt Cain, Andres Torres and hitting coach Hensley Meulens"[95] participated in the video, which stated, "We speak for the entire Giants organization when we say that there is no place in society for hatred and bullying against anyone."[96] Less than one month later, the Chicago Cubs released their own video, which featured manager Mike Quade, Ryan Dempster, Marlon Byrd, Darwin Barney, and team owner Laura Rickets — who is openly gay. Shortly thereafter, the Red Sox released a video which featured manager Terry Francona, Kevin Youkilis, and Jason Varitek, who also participated in the *Queer Eye* episode. As of November 2011, the Orioles, Phillies, and Rays had released their videos, and three additional teams had announced their intention to record videos: the Twins, Mariners, and Nationals.[97] Given MLB's history of homophobic remarks, the fact that so many teams are signing on to the project is encouraging. Equally encouraging is the fact that not only has there been little to no mainstream backlash against the teams that have participated, but fans have also started online petitions to get their favorite teams to make a video. In the same way that multiple homophobic remarks may signal a larger homophobic environment, it is possible that multiple gestures against homophobia may signal a change toward inclusivity.

While it is certainly a good sign that teams are speaking out against anti-gay bullying, the news is not all positive. Just two months before the Giants released their It Gets Better video, Roger McDowell, a hitting coach with Atlanta, made a homophobic remark and made lewd gestures toward Giants fans. McDowell clearly was not paying attention when just two weeks prior, NBA star Kobe Bryant was fined $100,000 for using a homophobic slur during a game, though he was not suspended. McDowell quickly issued the obligatory "I'm sorry *if* I offended anyone" apology, was fined an undisclosed amount, and was suspended for two weeks without pay.[98] Commissioner Bud Selig issued a statement in conjunction with the discipline that read, "Major League Baseball is a social institution that brings people together and welcomes all individuals of different races, religions, genders, national origins and sexual orientations into its ballparks. Conduct by people associated with MLB that shows insensitivity to others simply cannot and will not be tolerated."[99]

Parting Shots

Though Gerry Callahan suggests that MLB would offer an openly gay athlete the best chance of success due to the individual nature of the game, the fact remains that no gay MLB player has come out during his career.[100] It is encouraging that eight teams have joined the It Gets Better Project, though it also disappointing that no NBA, NFL, or NHL team has signed on, which lends credence to Callahan's theory. When WNBA star and Olympic Gold Medalist Sheryl Swoopes came out in 2005, *Pardon The Interruption*'s Tony Kornheiser remarked that gay male athletes "are scared to death to come out and say if they are homosexual that they are, scared to death. [...] In fact, Mike Piazza went out of his way to run to a press conference to say I am not gay."[101] The brouhaha surrounding Brendan Lemon's editorial and Mike Piazza's alleged "outing" illustrate how media representatives regulate celebrity behavior which, in turn, effectively keeps gay athletes from coming out during their careers and sends heterosexual athletes running to press conferences to reaffirm their sexual orientation. Though the California Supreme Court struck down the state's ban on same-sex marriage and New York State legalized same-sex marriage, MLB has yet to find ways to discourage homophobic tirades from its members.[102] Is baseball out of touch with the changing political realities, or is baseball signaling the fact that the nation is not quite as ready as it seems to embrace equality based on sexual identity? At this point, there is no way to know for sure. When all is said and done, as Jim Buzinski, creator of outsports.com, points out, "Everybody will say, 'We aren't ready.' Society was not ready for Jackie Robinson. If you are going to wait for everybody to be ready, nobody will do it."[103]

3

The $25 Million Man: Alex Rodríguez, Objectification and Money

"There are three tiers of players in baseball. The first consists of Alex Rodríguez and Barry Bonds. The second is [St. Louis Cardinal first baseman] Albert Pujols. The third is everybody else."—Matt Crossman[1]

"Now this is what you're gonna do for me. You listening? It's a very personal, very important thing. Hell, it's a family motto. Now are you ready? Just checking to make sure you're ready, here it is: show me the money."—Jerry Maguire[2]

He was called sport's poster boy for greed.[3] It would not be too much of an exaggeration to say that Alex Rodríguez, his agent Scott Boras, Texas Rangers owner Tom Hicks, and baseball Commissioner Bud Selig were likened to four horsemen of the baseball apocalypse. In 2000, Rodríguez signed a ten-year contract with the Texas Rangers worth approximately $25 million per year. His total salary would be more than the assessed value of eighteen of the thirty major league teams and two million dollars more than Hicks paid for the Rangers in 1998.[4]

The largest professional sports contract in history was lambasted from almost every direction; as *Sports Illustrated*'s Tom Verducci noted, A-Rod's "contract is the smoking gun for disillusioned fans in their case against overpaid ballplayers."[5] Since, as the quotation opening this chapter points out, most agreed that A-Rod was one of the best players in the game, the collective animosity toward both the player and the contract was puzzling. Both the media and fans seemed to turn against A-Rod despite his continued exceptional level of production, which unfortunately did not help move the Rangers out of last place.

Despite the accolades, the contract was viewed as one of the final nails in baseball's coffin: the Collective Bargaining Agreement was set to expire in less than two years and everyone was bracing for the possibility of another work stoppage. However, in the September 9, 2002, edition of *Sports Illustrated*, Tom Verducci wrote, "The official announcement is about to be made in New York: Alex Rodríguez and his $252 million contract did not kill major league baseball as we know it."[6] This acknowledgment came after the Players Association (MLBPA) and team owners inked a labor agreement without a work stoppage for the first time in over thirty years.

The controversy surrounding A-Rod's contract highlights the intersection of race, nationality, and objectification, and presents workers "as constrained but empowered figures."[7] Work is "shaped by intersecting oppressions of race, gender, and class,"[8] and in the case of professional baseball, players' salaries in general and Rodríguez's salary more specifically can be discussed not only in terms of ability as one might expect, but also in terms of race and nationality.

Race enters the picture because Major League Baseball (MLB)'s power structure is organized with white owners (with one exception: Angels owner Arte Moreno), controlling a labor force comprised largely of black and Latin labor. Of course, this work is shaped by gender oppression, as women are barred from MLB, which denies them access to the sizeable income professional baseball players make. At the same time, while it almost seems absurd to describe contemporary professional baseball players as oppressed, it may be more accurate to think of them as exploited or constrained.

The A-Rod controversy also exemplified the fact that MLB resides in a bizarre parallel financial universe which is quite different from the reality most people are familiar with. In 2010, blacks and Latinos occupied the bottom rungs of the male socioeconomic ladder, with black males making 74 percent and Latinos making 65 percent of what white males earned.[9] During that same year the median income for white males was approximately $51,450 per year, while the media income for Latinos was $31,393 and the median income for black males was $37,496.[10] On the other hand, in professional baseball, players of color occupy the financial upper echelon: twelve of the twenty-five highest paid players during the 2011 season were men of color.[11]

In addition to exemplifying baseball's unusual economic situation, Rodríguez's contract also highlights objectification. Because of his attractiveness, Rodríguez was able to market himself in ways that few other baseball players were able to. His status as a matinee idol brought in a new legion of fans, primarily women, a segment of the population MLB was eager to attract. On the other hand, it could be argued that by objectifying Rodríguez, sportswriters shifted the focus away from his professional accomplishments, a shift that raises the question of how much control Rodríguez had over the ways his image was framed. In essence, foregrounding A-Rod's physicality allowed racism, classism, and nationalist bias to go uncontested.

The Boatload Mentality and Its Exception

According to ESPN baseball analyst Tim Kurkjian, in 1994 one American League scouting director observed that A-Rod was "the best amateur prospect I've ever seen. He might be the best player ever in the draft."[12] The Seattle Mariners, who had the first pick in the draft that year, signed Rodríguez to a three-year, $1.3 million contract. Signing such a lucrative deal as a rookie is not unheard of in MLB — for American players. According to Marcos Bretón and José Luis Villegas, as a general rule, Latin players, who are often not U.S. citizens when they begin their careers, are "attractive to major league scouts because they [can] be signed for less than American players, providing cheap labor like so many other Latin immigrants in other walks of life."[13] For example, in 1997, All-Star shortstop Miguel Tejada from the Dominican Republic would begin his career with the Oakland A's for only a two thousand dollar signing bonus, primarily because, like many other Latin players, Tejada "didn't have college offers to use as leverage against his meager bonus, or agents who could protect his interests, or parents who could help him maneuver through the land mines of modern-day major league sports. He was just a kid with precious few English skills and no other compelling options in his life but to play baseball."[14]

Because Latin players can be signed for less money, teams are subscribing to what is being called the boatload mentality: teams can "sign a 'boatload' of Latinos for little money and if only a couple make it to the big leagues, [the teams] still come out ahead. Instead of signing four [Americans] at $25,000 each, [teams can] sign 20 [Dominicans] for $5,000 each."[15] Almost every team has set up baseball academies in the Dominican Republic for expressly this purpose. Latin players like Tejada who do not have U.S. citizenship and the resources that citizenship provides must wait to take advantage of the financial benefits U.S. players gain: players such as Sammy Sosa signed with Texas for $3,500 and pitcher Pedro Martínez signed with the Dodgers for $8,000 three years later.[16] Ironically, the $3,500 Texas signed Sosa for is the exact amount the Dodgers signed Jackie Robinson for in 1946.[17] Perhaps coincidentally, and perhaps not, Tejada, Sosa, and Martínez are all dark-skinned, and would have been (and in some ways still are) classified as "black," and therefore banned from playing in the majors under the Gentlemen's Agreement in the early 20th century. Rodríguez, who is light-skinned, may have been able to "pass" and play professional ball at a time when U.S.–born blacks and dark-skinned Latin players were banned from MLB.

Since Alex Rodríguez was born in the United States, his nationality worked to his advantage in the negotiations. Scott Boras, his advisor, was able to parlay A-Rod's admission to the University of Miami into a negotiating advantage since the Mariners knew, as A-Rod remembered, "that if I walk[ed] into that classroom, then I [could not] go pro for three years,"[18] and the team would have lost out on a first-round draft pick. If A-Rod had grown up in the Dominican Republic, where his parents were from, it is likely that he would not have had someone like Scott Boras fighting for him. He likely would not have been able to use potential college entrance as leverage, and the initial contract probably would have more closely resembled Tejada's, Sosa's, or Martínez's. In this case, while it is tempting to discuss baseball's salary structure in racial terms (i.e., white players vs. black players vs. Latin players) the intersectional nature of A-Rod's situation reveals a more complex structure. Not only is it possible that race and ethnicity play a role in salary discussions, but a player's nationality also plays a role in determining his position in baseball's power structure.

Lower starting salaries are not the only disadvantage facing Latin baseball players. One of the most notable problems facing non–U.S. born players is the language barrier. Since English is not always the primary language of the growing number of Latin and Asian players, they encounter difficulties involved in communicating with managers, owners, and sportswriters. As noted in the discussion of the 1998 home-run chase, the language issue became prevalent again with Sammy Sosa when he was phonetically quoted as saying "baseball is berry, berry good to me,"[19] and again in 2003 when an Associated Press article discussing Sosa's corked-bat incident quoted the slugger as stating, "You got to stood up and be there for it."[20] ESPN's Bob Ley also pointed out that "while Asian players are customarily provided interpreters to assist with interviews, Latin players are not."[21] Given the smaller number of Asian players in the majors, it is possible and not at all cost prohibitive to provide each player with an interpreter. However, given the eagerness with which MLB teams have been courting "boatloads" of Latin players and Latina/o audiences, it seems counterintuitive not to provide at least one interpreter per team to help promote Latin players and sell the league to Latin and Anglo audiences. This reliance on English, despite the growing number of players for whom English is not their first language, "can only serve to entrench Latinas'/os' outsiderness, foreignness, and nonmembership in 'America.'"[22] As it stands, players must either rely on bilingual teammates or managers to translate, or avoid talking to the media altogether. Because of his dual citizenship and fluency with English, A-Rod bypassed the oppressions faced by many of his countrymen. Those Latin players who speak English well are singled out by sportswriters as "special" because of their fluency. In one MLB.com piece on Pedro Martínez, Marty Noble mentions:

> What makes Martínez unusual is that he speaks English almost flawlessly. That puts him among a small percentage of players in the game, regardless of heritage.

And it speaks well for the pitcher who is the most visible pitch man on the roster. Martínez' Spanish accent is evident when he speaks English, but his good grammar and syntax are equally apparent. He'll never be the one to use any of the phrases that ring through baseball clubhouses and cause the most tolerant grammarians to blanch.[23]

In this instance, Martínez, in addition to being a phenomenal pitcher, is recognized for his English language skills. Martínez was determined to speak English well, due mostly to the struggles his brother Ramon faced in the majors because he could not speak English. While praising Martínez's language skills, Noble's comment also contained an admonishment directed not only at non–U.S. born players but also at select U.S.–born players as well. Noble remarks that Martínez's flawless English places him within a small group of players "regardless of heritage," and separates Martínez from both non–U.S. born players and U.S.–born players with "poor" language skills as well. Noble privileges a particular way of speaking English, which has racial and economic implications.

The accolades Martínez received are in direct contrast to the treatment other Latin players receive. In his book *The New Face of Baseball*, Tim Wendel writes, "Talk to any Anglo beat writer about Manny Ramirez and he'll probably tell you that the Red Sox superstar is moody, not a good quote."[24] Wendel discussed the stereotype with bilingual *Miami Herald* writer Dan Le Batard, who observed that "far from being moody, Ramirez is simply shy in English."[25] In his own defense, Ramírez has been quoted as saying, "Perhaps the American press treats [Latin players] a little differently, since sometimes we don't feel so comfortable speaking English. And sometimes if a reporter comes along and they want to talk with us, someone might say no. It's not because we're being hateful but because we don't feel comfortable enough speaking the language."[26] Often, sportswriters label players with what they consider poor English-language skills as moody or unfriendly, which can limit the amount of press coverage those players receive. By labeling non–U.S. born players in this manner, sportswriters are able to "simultaneously grant power to the powerful and subjugate the subordinated."[27] By refusing to interview non–U.S. born players who do not speak "flawless" English, sportswriters effectively silence the players on an individual and cultural level and at the same time reinforce notions of linguistic superiority.

In contrast, A-Rod, who grew up primarily in the United States, would not be labeled as moody because of his language skills; he speaks "proper" English and has a barely noticeable Spanish accent, which is "a veritable boarding pass to many mundos."[28] In fact, English became so dominant in Rodríguez's life that when he was traded to Texas "he had to brush up on his Spanish [because he] was losing it."[29] The ease with which Rodríguez communicates with both the English-speaking and Spanish-speaking media helps increase his marketability. At the same time, his mannerisms and language skills proved to be a double-edged sword: "Some sportswriters [...] loved Rodríguez because he almost always said the right thing and was a natural spokesman. But some sportswriters [...] grew tired of A-Rod because he almost always said the right thing and was a natural spokesman."[30] In this instance non–U.S. born players are damned if they do and damned if they don't: players who do not speak "flawless" English are shunned, but players like Rodríguez who speak the way sportswriters want them to are viewed as being fake. It was almost as if sportswriters were not used to and did not know how to deal with an articulate Latino ballplayer.

The decreased publicity as well as the controlling image applied to Latin players because of their English-language skills places Latin players at a disadvantage that not only manifests itself during their playing career, but also has ramifications later. Collins argues, "Black women and men alike are more vulnerable than Whites to being excluded from professional and managerial occupations."[31] This exclusion plays itself out within MLB's power structure: on Opening Day of the 2011 season, there were four Latin managers (Manny Acta, Ozzie Guillén, Fredi Gonzalez, and Edwin Rodríguez, who resigned in the middle of the season) and only one Latin general manager (Omar Minaya). Having Latinos occupy these managerial positions could, in theory, help new Latin players with their transition to the majors as well as help effect change, particularly within MLB's disciplinary and hegemonic domains of power.

Regardless of the difficulties sportswriters faced in interviewing some Latin players, the number of Latin players continues to increase. As mentioned in the McGwire/Sosa discussion, in 2005 Latin players made up 25 percent of Major League rosters, and this number does not include U.S.–born Latinos like Rodríguez.[32] Even though A-Rod is not included in MLB's count of Latin players, the league continued using Rodríguez to market the sport to the Latina/o population. *Newsweek*'s Allison Samuels and Mark Starr argued, "A-Rod is the linchpin of Major League Baseball's increasingly aggressive marketing to Hispanics which explains why baseball's 2001 season opener Sunday showcased A-Rod's Rangers vs. the Toronto Blue Jays — and was played in San Juan, Puerto Rico."[33] During the 2003 and 2004 seasons, the Montreal Expos used the San Juan facility to play a portion of their home games before officially becoming the Washington Nationals.

Nor is MLB the only sports industry going to great lengths to court Latin players and fans. One year prior to the aforementioned MLB opening day game in Puerto Rico, ESPN launched a Spanish-language feed to cater to stateside Latina/o sports fans, and ESPN Deportes became a full-fledged cable network station in 2004.[34] While other sports leagues relied on holding

contests in international locales to draw Latina/o fans, MLB relied on Rodríguez and other Latin players as its key attractions. But at the same time, MLB
had plenty of talented Latin baseball players available to actively promote the
league. So what did Alex Rodríguez have that others did not?

Bringing Sexy Back

In addition to the accolades he received for his feats on the field, A-Rod's
physicality was attracting attention as well. Rodríguez made *People*'s 50 Most
Beautiful People list in 1998, and the magazine writers remarked, "It's [A-
Rod's] buff body underneath that caused a *Seattle Times* reporter to lose linguistic control. His physique, she opined, is 'as lovely as the glow of Mount
Rainier during a summer sunset.'"[35] *Sports Illustrated*'s Gerry Callahan mentioned that Rodríguez "appears to be as flawless as a hot fudge sundae,"[36] *Newsweek*'s Samuels and Star point out that Rodríguez "can also compete with
Hollywood's finest for position on the ladies' bedroom walls. He's a tall, buff,
soft-spoken charmer with caramel skin, shimmering hazel eyes and a boyish
smile."[37] When Rodríguez was listed as one of the sexiest athletes by FOX
Sports' *The Sports List*, one guest commentator remarked, "If I was Alex Rodríguez for a day I think I would probably see how many women *don't* want me,
that's what I'd do. I'd probably see how many women don't want to touch me.
You know he makes dudes go 'man, he looks fine, I hate him, he's pretty.'"[38]
Clearly Rodríguez made headlines not only because of his talent on the basepa-
ths, but also because of his physical attractiveness.

As Toby Miller points out in his book *Sportsex*, "Commercial sports today
are a site for activating the female gaze and even empowering it, part of a
momentum that is putting the public presentation of men under scrutiny in
the same way as women. Men, too, are becoming dependent on the gaze
directed at them."[39] In other words, almost everybody and everything can be
reduced to sexual objectification, and male public figures, at least in Rodríguez's case, do not balk at sexual objectification. Miller's analysis is suggestive
of Laura Mulvey's groundbreaking essay "Visual Pleasure and Narrative Cinema," first published in 1975. For Mulvey, "In a world ordered by sexual imbalance, pleasure in looking has been split between active/male and passive/
female."[40] This brings the question of whether or not pleasure in looking can
ever be passive/male or active/female as long as the sexual power imbalance
within society is maintained. Unfortunately Mulvey's viewpoint seems to dismiss the possibility of women actively seeking or deriving pleasure from view-
ing, a situation that is happening with Rodríguez. Later in her essay, Mulvey
writes, "According to the principles of the ruling ideology and the physical

structures that back it up, the male figure cannot bear the burden of sexual objectification."[41] As A-Rod's situation shows, not only can men bear the burden of sexual objectification, but they can use it to their advantage.

The objectification of athletes is usually mentioned in the context of female athletes and tends to manifest itself it two ways. In one instance, "news media, local communities, and in some cases [the athletes] themselves [...] emphasize the femininity of female athletes."[42] This form is evident when sports media highlight "women's difference or fragile youth" or provide more coverage of traditionally feminine sports such as gymnastics or figure skating as opposed to traditionally masculine sports such as basketball or soccer.[43] Objectification can also manifest itself when more emphasis is placed on an athlete's sexuality or physical attractiveness than on her athletic ability. One only has to browse any website devoted to tennis player Maria Sharapova or peruse *Sports Illustrated*'s swimsuit issue to see this form of objectification in action.

This objectification serves to disempower the increasing number of women and girls participating in sports. Even if that is the case, the objectification does not explain the purpose behind objectification of male athletes. In recent years sport media and publicity managers have realized that sexy male athletes are just as likely as sexy female athletes to attract viewers. This shift can be seen in the fact that "in the decades [prior] to 1993, women were three times more likely to be portrayed in a sexualized manner, but explicit and suggestively alluring representations of men had become much more common — up from 11 percent to 18 percent of images."[44] On the other hand, the increased objectification of male athletes could have less to do with appealing to the female gaze and more to do with alleviating criticism for objectifying female athletes as objectifying both female and male athletes would serve to "level the playing field." By increasing the ways in which male athletes are objectified, media makers create the impression that the objectification of female athletes is decreasing, when in actuality the objectification of male athletes is simply catching up.

The concept of intersectionality dictates that male athletes would experience objectification differently from female athletes because of the gender difference. In fact, the notion of differential experiences based on identity is one of the primary rationales behind black feminists' branching off and conceptualizing their own type of feminism, since black women experienced gender oppression differently from white women. It stands to reason that if black women and white women experience sexism differently due to their racial identity, then male and female athletes would experience objectification differently due to their gender identity. A-Rod's newfound attention was ideal from a marketing perspective: female fans enamored with Rodríguez would flock to games, often with marriage proposal posters in hand. However, was this a case of MLB objectifying and exploiting Rodríguez, or is A-Rod marketing himself in this manner? It was actually a combination of the two. Since both MLB and Rodríguez utilized physical attractiveness as a means to gain power in the form of increased visibility and an increased fan base, the result was more money for the player, the team, and the League. At the same time, the ways in which Rodríguez was objectified sometimes overshadowed his on-field achievements. Framing A-Rod through an objectified lens moved both his ethnicity and nationality, and the privileges and constraints associated with them, to the background. Instead of discussing the privileges Rodríguez received because of his nationality or the ways in which MLB exploits and marginalizes non–U.S. born players, the discussion centered around A-Rod's good looks.

It's All About the Benjamins

In 1998 Rodríguez became the third player in history to join the 40–40 club and, on defense, he had a .975 fielding percentage to go along with the homers and stolen bases. Though A-Rod missed part of the 1999 season due to an injury, during the 2000 season he had a .318 batting average (BA), a .399 on-base percentage (OBP), and a .622 slugging percentage (SLG). In that same year he hit 52 homers and drove in 135 runs.[45] The Sporting News's Jon Hayman wrote, before the contract figure was announced, that "many believe Rodríguez will establish himself as the greatest shortstop ever. Considering age and talent, he [...] could command a contract of $200 million-plus for eight or 10 years."[46] In the annual poll conducted by the Sporting News, which ranks the top thirty players in the game, A-Rod came in second behind Pedro Martínez.[47] Forgetting the actual sum for a moment, if that is possible, was anyone really surprised that A-Rod left Seattle and signed such a large contract?

Though some blame free agency for the increased number of large contracts, when Curt Flood, Andy Messersmith, and Dave McNally fought for free agency in the 1970s, money was not the primary rationale; free agency liberated players from the indentured servitude they endured under the reserve clause. The ensuing skyrocketing salaries could be characterized as an unintended consequence having to do with the artificially low salaries imposed by team owners before free agency. The increase in salaries is also directly proportional to the increase in television revenue, since "from 1971 to 1990 player salaries have risen 1,741 percent, while national TV money had gone up 1,742 percent."[48] In addition to being criticized as the cause for the ever-increasing player salaries, free agency is also criticized for the increased player movement, as individuals are free to sign contracts with the highest bidder. The Mariners lost pitcher Randy Johnson to free agency after the 1997 season and lost Ken Griffey in 1999, so player movement was something Mariners fans were intimately familiar with at the time. However, there was player movement before free agency, as ESPN's Jim Caple points out: "Whether a player was a superstar or a utility infielder, movement has been as unfortunate a part of baseball as organ music. Even though he retired eight years before free agency, Roger Maris played for twice as many teams as Mark McGwire has."[49] As Caple explains, player movement was just as, if not more, prevalent before free agency was instituted. The difference now is that in-demand players have a choice as to whether or not they spend their entire careers with a single team.

Rodríguez was *the* free agent during the 2000 off-season, but unfortunately, because of baseball's ever-increasing competitive imbalance, or the fact that there are some teams that are less likely to win games for reasons that have more to do with finances and less to do with talent, most teams understood that A-Rod would be out of their price range. MLB's Blue Ribbon Panel Report, created in 2000 to examine the League's financial status and future, noted that there was a "revenue difference of $125 million in 1999 between" the richest and the poorest teams.[50] It is no coincidence that from 1995 to 2011 the teams who maintained payrolls in the top ten won ten championships.[51] The exceptions were the Angels, whose payroll ranked fifteenth in 2002; the 2003 Marlins, whose payroll was twenty-fifth when they won the Series; the White Sox, whose payroll ranked thirteenth in 2005; the Cardinals whose payroll ranked eleventh in 2006 and 2011; and the Phillies, who were just barely outside the top ten at number twelve when they won in 2008.[52] Clearly, large payrolls do not automatically translate into World Series titles, as Rangers owner Tom Hicks would soon learn, but money certainly helps. In the end it was Hicks who won the bidding war and signed Rodríguez to the largest contract in sports history, one worth approximately $25 million per year for ten years.

In addition to his salary, Rodríguez received a $10 million signing bonus paid semi-annually over five years. Finally, as is customary in many baseball contracts, the Rangers included, performance-based bonuses that allowed Rodríguez to earn $50,000 for finishing sixth in MVP voting, $100,000 for making the All-Star Team, $100,000 for winning the Silver Slugger Award, and $200,000 for making both Baseball America's and the *Sporting News's* All-Star Team, for a grand total of $25.45 million in earnings in 2001.

Not all of the performance bonuses listed in A-Rod's contract were necessarily tied to performance. For example, MVP and newspaper awards are decided by the very journalists who often shun Latin players whose English proficiency is deemed insufficient. At the same time, All-Star team selections are based on fan voting via punch-ballots available at ballparks and, in recent years, over the Internet. The former method may exclude many working-class and lower-income fans from voting because they simply cannot afford to attend games. Latin players in smaller markets with limited English-language skills may not get the media exposure their on-field performance deserves, and therefore may not be able to capitalize on such bonuses. While it is true that many players in smaller markets suffer from a disadvantage due to the decreased amount of coverage, players with limited English-language skills have an extra hurdle to overcome. Since, as the *Outside the Lines* exposé on the language barrier pointed out, sports journalists are less likely to interview players with what they deem as poor language skills or label them as moody, listings in magazine and newspaper polls may also be limited, and that lack of exposure can deprive Latin players of income.[53]

Though Rodríguez's on-field numbers were clearly worthy of praise and media attention, he played in a smaller market, which should have limited his exposure. However, in today's pop culture environment, "Men can no longer get by on their achievements, as has long been the case, their appearance less important than their activities. Goodbye to all that. Boys just gotta be hot."[54] In A-Rod's case, the attention he received because of his physical attractiveness offset any negative impact playing in Seattle would have had. At the same time, the privileges Rodríguez has because of his citizenship empowered him to accumulate even more income based on performance bonuses, as did the extra media exposure he received because of his looks. This combination produced endorsements not readily available to non–U.S. born players with limited English-language skills or players deemed less attractive than Rodríguez.

Don't Hate the Playa, Hate the Game

The ink on the contract had not had a chance to dry before the outrage began. Rangers owner Tom Hicks was called "a fool and the harbinger of baseball's apocalypse."[55] Rodríguez's agent Scott Boras was called everything from "the most hated man in baseball" to the "Darth Vader of baseball," and was described by one team official as a man who "sees all the devious ways you can rip people off and make a bundle on 'em."[56] Rodríguez did not fare any better, as Blaine Newnham of the *Seattle Times* relayed a conversation he had with a Mariners fan who asked, "Do you know that $25 million would pay for 625 teachers a year?"[57] An article in the *Christian Science Monitor* calculated that Rodríguez would make about $49,000 per at-bat and that his "yearly salary is enough to pay for all of the Boston Ballet's expenses this year (with about $9 million left over),"[58] an analogy that privileges "high art" over popular entertainment and has both racial and class bias. When *People* magazine named Rodríguez one of the most intriguing people of 2000, the writers noted, "At least one official raised the possibility that Rodríguez might soon be remembered not as the superb athlete he is but as the catalyst for a bitter player-management showdown triggered by the game's financial inequalities."[59] Finally, Ross Atkins pointed out, arguably with tongue planted firmly in cheek: "Rodríguez could take some comfort in knowing that Oscar-winning actress Julia Roberts will make more this year, an estimated $51 million, according to *Parade* magazine's annual salary comparison of a cross section of Americans. On the other hand, there's little comfort in the fact that President Bush, the Rangers' former part owner, will make only $400,000 as the leader of the free world."[60] Some may argue that historically the president is underpaid, given the demands of the office, and this is not the first time a baseball player's salary has been compared to the president's. In 1930, when Babe Ruth was asked whether it was unusual for him to be making more than President Herbert Hoover during the Great Depression, Ruth replied, "Why not? I had a better year than he did."[61] Going back to Atkins's comparison between Rodríguez and Julia Roberts, the latter grossed income proportional to the revenue she generated. The $51 million Roberts made in 2001 relates to the $343.8 million her films grossed that year.[62] If Roberts's salary is related to the income she generates, then as the argument goes, an athlete's salary should reflect both his or her talent and the revenue she/he generates. When asked about the criticism his contract caused, Rodríguez replied, "Listen, the contract is what it is, and I'm proud of it. To me, it's symbolic for what I've worked for my whole life. It has been a huge point of criticism for a lot of people, but I can't control that. All I can control is how I go out and play on the field, try to back up what I earn."[63] Since Rodríguez was considered the best player in the game and he could arguably bring in a substantial amount of revenue for his team, it stands to reason that he would be one of the highest paid players in the game.

At the same time, Atkins brings up an interesting fact. Other entertainers such as Roberts make large sums of money as well. But unlike professional athletes, entertainers such as actors or singers typically do not receive the same criticism in regard to their salaries. Granted, the fact that other entertainers are not criticized in the same way athletes are does not negate the criticism athletes receive; however, it does point out a double standard with possible racial implications. One study by Martha Hill Zimmer and Michael Zimmer compared the salaries of professional athletes, singers, actors/directors, and musicians, as well as other entertainers, and found that "athletes are among the lowest paid entertainers, based on simple averages and after controlling for measured sociodemographic traits."[64] If we think of professional athletes as entertainers, it would seem that they are, in fact, underpaid compared to other entertainers. So if everyone agreed that Rodríguez was one of the best players in the game, if sportswriters predicted he would sign an unprecedented contract, and if entertainers in other fields make larger sums of money, where does the animosity come from?

Many sportswriters argued that A-Rod was not "worth" $25 million. That type of argument seemed predictable, given the amount of money involved. Rodríguez supporters were quick to point out that attendance rose by more than 28,000 in A-Rod's first year in Texas and by over 30,000 in 2001.[65] In addition, group sales rose 41 percent from 1999, merchandising revenue increased 25 percent, and the 1.6 million advance ticket sales sold before the season began were the most since 1994, when The Ballpark at Arlington opened.[66] Shortly after Hicks signed A-Rod, Forbes "listed the Rangers as the sixth most valuable franchise in baseball, worth $342 million. [Hicks states] 'We were never that high without A-Rod.'"[67] Going back to the Julia Roberts comparison, if an actor's salary is related to the income produced and Alex Rodríguez's presence with the Rangers generated new revenue, then it stands to reason that his salary should reflect not only his talent but also the profits he helped produce for the Rangers in general and Tom Hicks more specifically. Clearly, regardless of whether or not A-Rod is worth $25 million, his presence brought in a nice chunk of revenue for the Rangers. The animosity directed toward Rodríguez despite the increased revenue his presence brought to the team and its owner is puzzling.

Though A-Rod received the brunt of the criticism for the contract, what about the animosity toward Tom Hicks, who had the honor of signing A-Rod's paychecks? Most of the criticism directed toward Hicks was not because he *could* pay A-Rod $25 million per year, but because he actually *did* pay A-Rod that sum. In 2000, Hicks made Forbes's list of wealthiest Americans with a net worth of $750 million, which put him at only 382 on the list.[68] Journalists never ask if the owners, who are predominantly white, are "worth" all that money. It is doubtful that Hicks questioned A-Rod's worth on a monetary basis since Hicks saw his net worth and his standing on Forbes's wealthiest list increase after signing the shortstop.[69] James Richard Hill asserts, "Average fans consider their own salary and the meager increases doled out in the last few years in our competitive economic environment and often feel disgust for millionaire players protesting owners' attempts to constrict future pay raises."[70] If that is the case, then where is the outrage surrounding the Steinbrenner family, which owns and operates the Yankees, or White Sox owner Jerry Reinsdorf? Notice that Hill points out the disgust fans have toward the millionaire players but does not mention any animosity aimed at the billionaire owners. The discrepancy cannot solely be linked to visibility since the Steinbrenners are often in the spotlight more than their players — and are probably disliked by more people. Reinsdorf has the dubious distinction of being hated by both baseball and basketball fans in Chicago, though the disgust is not tied to his personal finances: in addition to owning the White Sox, Reinsdorf also owns the Chicago Bulls, and is considered by many to be at least partially responsible for breaking up the six-time championship team after Michael Jordan's second retirement in 1999. There are unfortunately very few who agree with Joel Shuman, who laments, "A part of me will always believe that if a player from a middle or working-class background — especially one as good as Rodríguez — can get twenty-five million a year from a group of rich owners who probably got their money on the backs of workers, so much the better."[71] Dave Zirin also noted fans' indifference to owners' wealth when he wrote, "The real obscenity of riches is not on the field but in the owner's box. As the inimitably prickly Barry Bonds once said, 'Nobody is complaining about the owners' salaries. So don't complain about us.'"[72]

One would think that sympathy would lie with the workers, as Shuman's and Zirin's sympathy seems to, instead of management, many of whom have never hit, thrown, or fielded a baseball. However, in baseball's alternate reality, the acrimony is aimed toward the players while the owners' wealth, which is considerably more sizable than the players' wealth, is ignored. Is it possible that the invisibility of Steinbrenner's and Reinsdorf's finances is the by-product of white privilege? Until 2003, when Arturo Moreno purchased the Angels, all of the major league teams were white-owned, and as Tim Wise points out in his essay on white privilege, "The virtual invisibility that whiteness affords those of us who have it is like psychological money in the bank, the proceeds of which we cash in every day while others are in a state of perpetual overdraft."[73] At the same time, as Peggy McIntosh writes, "Whiteness protected me from many kinds of hostility, distress, and violence which I was being subtly trained to visit in turn on people of color."[74] In essence, the team owners' whiteness may have protected them from the hostility leveled at the players' increasing income by rendering their income virtually invisible. At the same time, as Critical Race Theory scholar Derrick Bell points out, "To give continued meaning to their whiteness, whites must identify with the whites at the top of the economic heap, not with blacks, with whom most whites hold so much in common save their skin color."[75] Bell's acknowledgement of racial solidarity fits well with George Lipsitz's notion of a possessive investment in whiteness, which he argues "is about assets as well as attitudes; it is about property as well as pigment."[76] Since many of the sportswriters ignoring the team owner's finances are white, like the majority of the owners, leveling hostility toward Rodríguez's contract helps to maintain not only the team owner's white privilege but the sportswriter's privilege as well.

In addition to asking whether or not Rodríguez was "worth" the money, another way sportswriters displayed their displeasure with the contract was to focus on the entire sum of A-Rod's contract instead of breaking it down into its annual sum. Though $25 million is still a considerable sum of money, in sport salary terms, it sounds more reasonable than $252 million. In fact, Rodríguez's annual salary was comparable to those of several NBA players. In 2001, then Minnesota Timberwolves forward Kevin Garnett earned $22.4 million per year, and then Los Angeles Lakers center Shaquille O'Neal earned $21.43 million annually.[77] In 2004 Indianapolis Colts quarterback Peyton Manning, who is white, quietly dwarfed them all by earning slightly over $35 million for that season, and Pittsburgh Steelers quarterback Ben Rothlisberger earned almost $28 million for the 2008 season.[78] Since Garnett and O'Neal are black, touting Rodríguez as the $252 million man as opposed to the $25 million man cannot solely be attributed to race. However, it raises the question: is it possible that the sight of a *Latino* with $25 million in hand helps explain some of the hostility? Professional sports have been producing black millionaires for the past few decades; however, in the sports world, Latino millionaires are a more recent phenomenon. It is also possible that white journalists are more protective of MLB than the NBA since the overwhelming majority of NBA players are black, while MLB is still a predominantly white institution, at least for the time being.[79] That being said, sportswriters rarely asked if then New York Yankees designated hitter and purported steroid user Jason Giambi was worth the $23 million he received in 2008, though, admittedly, some did think former Houston Astros pitcher Roger Clemens was out of line when he asked for and received $25 million in salary arbitration during the 2004 off-season. In the same way that white privilege protected white team owners from the hostility white sportswriters leveled against Rodríguez's contract, Giambi's and Clemens's earnings were similarly shielded from criticism due to their white privilege. The criticism potentially sends message to other players that if the best player in the game does not deserve this much money then neither does anyone else. Though $25 million is still a sizable amount of money for a professional athlete, the controversy surrounding A-Rod's contract essentially creates a glass ceiling and subjects anyone attempting to break through that ceiling with a barrage of criticism. As Curt Flood remarked when criticized for challenging the reserve clause decades earlier, "A well-paid slave is nonetheless a slave."[80]

While Rodríguez continued to be constrained by the backlash the contract produced, he was still empowered by the fact that his abilities could command such a large sum of cash. At the same time, it was almost as if A-Rod's contract dwarfed his previous and continued professional accomplishments. *Sports Illustrated*'s Tom Verducci wrote, "Alex Rodríguez, the man who signed the richest contact in professional sports history, is synonymous with a number. That figure is bigger in every way than the one on the back of his Texas Rangers uniform. *Now batting, number 252....* He wears it wherever he goes."[81] The framing of Rodríguez's performance in terms of his contract harks back to the notion that workers can be empowered and constrained at the same time because, as Verducci's quotation indicates regardless of how Rodríguez performs on the field, the commentary is immediately brought back to the contract. While Rodríguez is empowered by the fact that he is still considered one of the best players in the game, he is, at the same time, constrained by the fact that his performance is couched in terms of the contract.

All Good Things...

Despite A-Rod's offensive and defensive production, the Rangers continued to languish in last place. During his 2003 MVP season, Rodríguez began to express his desire to win a championship, an outcome that clearly could not happen in Texas. The Rangers rewarded Rodríguez's MVP win by approaching him with the possibility of being traded. The speculation intensified before the engraving on A-Rod's MVP trophy was completed. In December 2003, the *Dallas Morning News* published reports that "the Rangers are willing to part with A-Rod in exchange for [Red Sox outfielder] Manny Ramírez and a financial package that liberates them from Rodríguez's expensive contract."[82] The deal would have involved the Red Sox paying an estimated $180 million over the next seven years remaining on A-Rod's contract in addition to a portion of Ramírez' $20 million annual salary. The deal would also compel Boston to trade their shortstop Nomar Garciaparra. The complexity of A-Rod's contract posed severe economic and legal hurdles to any team involved in trade negotiations. When it seemed as though the Rangers and Red Sox had worked out an amicable deal, the MLBPA, in an unprecedented move, rejected the proposal because, in their mind, the deal was less about restructuring the contract and more about reducing the amount of money Rodríguez would receive.[83] While Rodríguez himself was willing to take a reduction in salary to move to a winning team, the MLBPA did not want to set that precedent. It seemed as though Rodríguez would continue his tenure with the Rangers since there were few teams who could afford to restructure the contact to the MLBPA's satisfaction.

Fortunately or unfortunately, depending on the point of view, the one team that did have the financial resources to restructure A-Rod's contract in a way that would satisfy the MLBPA was interested. Though George Stein-brenner initially balked at paying such a high price for one player, the fact that the Yankees had not won a championship since 2000 caused him to reconsider. Since the Yankees consistently generate the largest revenue stream in MLB, it makes sense that that team would also have the largest payroll. Before signing Rodríguez, the Yankees maintained a $152.7 million payroll, which was by far the largest payroll in professional sports — though, to be fair, the other sports leagues in the United States have salary caps.[84] Since the ultimate goal of any team is to win championships, which can in turn bring in more revenue, it seemed that to Steinbrenner, money was no object. In March 2004, right before the start of spring training, the Rangers traded Alex Rodríguez to the Yankees for Alfonso Soriano and the ubiquitous "player to be named later," in a trade which forced Rodríguez to move from shortstop to third base.

The trade increased the Yankee payroll to $184.3 million: their infield alone, which included Jason Giambi, Miguel Cairo, Derek Jeter, and Rodrí-guez, earned $53.9 million, which was higher than the total payroll of eleven other teams at the time.[85] Despite the bloated overall payroll, few realized that the Yankees only paid Rodríguez approximately $16 million that season, which was less than what Jeter and Giambi were being paid at the time. Since Rodríguez changed positions and ultimately gave up the chance to go down in history as the greatest shortstop ever, it seemed only natural that the ani-mosity toward A-Rod and his contract would subside. Unfortunately for him, that did not happen.

When the Yankees played in Seattle for the first time during the 2004 season, MLB.com writer Mike Bauman asked the question, "Who wins the A-Rod boo-a-thon? Without a reliable, standardized measurement [...] this task is necessarily subjective. But the only thing you can say with certainty is that the competition is fierce."[86] When the Yankees played in Texas that season, the *Fort Worth Star-Telegram* distributed signs that read "A-Rat" for fans to display throughout the park.[87] Rodríguez was booed in Seattle and Texas for leaving, booed in Boston for not signing with the Red Sox, and booed every-where else both because of his monster contract and because he signed with the hated Yankees.

Same Stuff, Different City

To say that Alex Rodríguez's relationship with the Yankees, their fans, and the New York media has been acrimonious would be putting it kindly. During the 2005 season Rodríguez produced a .321 BA, .610 SLG, a place on the Latino Legends Team, and a second AL MVP award. The following season he was not nearly as productive. Rodríguez committed 24 errors, the most since 1997. During the American League Division Series against the Tigers, A-Rod went 1 for 14, and in one instance was demoted to batting eighth in the order. Fans booed him mercilessly, and teammates refused to come to his defense, but his lackluster performance did not seem to be at the heart of the matter. According to Tom Verducci, "I asked Rodríguez why criticism of him from inside and outside the game is so amplified. 'We know why,' he said. The contract? That 10-year, $252 million deal that no one has come close to matching for six years? He nodded."[88] Though there was clearly no excuse for Rodríguez's performance, the contract helped magnify an already volatile situation.

After an abysmal year, the 2007 season seemed to bring out the old Alex Rodríguez. Though the Yankees began the season with a thud, A-Rod exploded. "In 23 games, A-Rod hit .355 and led the league with 14 home runs and 34 RBIs," capturing the Player of the Month Award for April.[89] The praise continued as he crept toward the 500 career home-run mark. Clearly something was different this season and everyone knew it: the historic contract that everyone reviled contained a clause that allowed A-Rod to opt out of his contract and become a free agent at the end of the season. After wrapping up his third MVP award, Rodríguez did opt out of his contract during the final game of the 2007 World Series; but, two months later, after much fanfare, A-Rod re-signed with the Yankees for another record-breaking $27.5 million over ten years.[90]

The Earth Is Round, and It's A-Rod's Fault

As of the 2011 season, Alex Rodríguez remained the highest paid player in baseball, commanding $27 million per season.[91] To be fair, most of the animosity surrounding A-Rod's contract eventually subsided: the animosity toward Rodríguez now concerns performance-enhancing drugs and his personal life. While the NFL and NBA both experienced lockouts during the 2011 season, MLB is still in its era of economic tranquility. Given baseball's relative stability, one wonders what the commentary would be if another player, particularly a Latin player, dared to ask for more money. As the quote at the beginning of this chapter opined, there are three tiers of players, and in that second tier are Alex Rodríguez and Albert Pujols. It just so happens that Albert Pujols became a free agent at the end of the 2011 season, and the discussions surrounding his potential contract had begun well in advance. Much like Rodríguez, Pujols is considered one of the best, if not *the* best player in the game today, but despite that moniker, Pujols earns $14.5 million per season, which does not even put him in the top 25 of the highest paid players.[92] Prior to the 2011 season, Pujols and the Cardinals were unable to reach an agreement, and while there was very little discussion regarding whether Pujols was "worth" or deserved more money, sportswriters agreed on one thing: the breakdown in talks was entirely Alex Rodríguez's fault.

During spring training, rumors swirled that Pujols was asking for a ten-year contract worth approximately $30 million per year, which is slightly more than the deal Rodríguez signed with the Yankees in 2007. Harvey Araton of the *New York Times* argued, "It was the Yankees who indirectly put the Cardinals in this uncomfortable and potentially ruinous position when they handed Rodríguez the richest contract in baseball history."[93] Writing for SI.com, Jon Heyman speculated that "the main goal for Pujols was always to top A-Rod."[94] Once again it never seemed to occur to many sportswriters that the three-time NL MVP, two-time Gold Glove winner, and nine-time All-Star *should* be one of the highest paid players in the game. No one noticed that because Pujols was born in the Dominican Republic, his starting salary in 2001 was half of what Alex Rodríguez earned in his rookie season[95] and despite the fact that his talent became obvious fairly quickly, it has taken almost a decade for his salary to match his skill level. Again, sportswriters seem to blame Rodríguez for signing the contract, but a small few blame the Yankees for actually offering the contract.

When the Pujols sweepstakes finally ended and the slugger signed a contract with the Angels worth approximately $25 million for ten years, the discussion over whether he was "worth" that much money was decidedly muted, though still present: one blogger noted that "from a pure baseball standpoint, this is probably an overpay."[96] Though the "worth it" discussion was not as popular as it was in 2001, Alex Rodríguez's legacy was still felt. As Jayson Stark pointed out, "Pujols' contract will go down in history as the biggest to a man who was not named Alex Rodriguez. Amazingly, his deal got done in the same hotel where the Texas Rangers once signed A-Rod for 10 years and 252 million of Tom Hicks' well-intentioned dollars."[97] Most of the discussions surrounding Pujols's move to the west coast were put in the context of Rodríguez's deals. The reality of the situation seems to be that Alex Rodríguez's contract is still seen as such a problem that it's affecting the media framing of a player's contract negotiations even after ten years.

Parting Shots

For Alex Rodríguez, the intersection of nationality, race, and objectification framed discussions of his historic contract. In essence, examinations of Rodríguez's career would be incomplete without these intersecting positions, oppressions, and privileges. A-Rod's entrance into the majors underscored the privileges U.S.–born ballplayers receive in terms of compensation. The combination of Rodríguez's athletic ability, physical attractiveness, and language skills helped elevate A-Rod past the rest of the increasing number of Latin players in the league. A-Rod's position in terms of ability, physical attractiveness, and language skills also helped create the conditions under which he could sign the largest contract in sports history. Despite his being considered one of the best players in the game, many sportswriters were surprised and outraged that any one player would be "worth" $25 million annually, though no one thought to ask whether Ranger owner Tom Hicks was worth his estimated $750 million. Unfortunately, "The problems arise when players realize their value, their significance to the game, and try to capitalize on their accomplishments. Then they are often held in the highest contempt."[98] In essence, Rodríguez was "safe" so long as he played the role of the objectified, nonthreatening, English-speaking athlete; however, when he demanded and gained compensation that was comparable with both his talent and the revenue he generates, A-Rod was framed as unworthy. Focusing attention on A-Rod's contract deflected attention away from the owner's finances, and that diversion allows the latter group's white privilege to remain intact and invisible.

By objectifying A-Rod, both MLB and Rodríguez can utilize physical attractiveness as a means to gain power in the form of visibility and an increased fan base, the latter of which leads to more money for everyone. It is also possible that the ways in which Rodríguez was objectified at times overshadowed his on-field achievements and allowed systems of oppression to go unrecognized. Objectifying A-Rod moves attention away from both his ethnicity and nationality, or the ways in which non–U.S. born players are exploited by MLB; the discussion centers around A-Rod's good looks. Whether Alex Rodríguez remains famous for his sex appeal or infamous because of his contract, one thing is certain: A-Rod still has the power and ability to remain one of the best players, if not the best player, in baseball.

4

Effa Manley and the Politics of Passing

"Passing is well-known among Black people in the United States and is a feature of race subordination in all societies structured on white supremacy. Notwithstanding the purported benefits of black heritage in an era of affirmative action, passing is not an obsolete phenomenon that has slipped into history."— Cheryl I. Harris[1]

"Narratives of passing, whether written by African American or by white authors, presume the African American internalization of the "one-drop" and the related "hypo-descent" rules. According to the one-drop rule, individuals are classified as black if they possess one black ancestor; the "hypo-descent" rule [...] assigned people of mixed racial origin to the status of the subordinated racial group. Originally deployed as a means of supporting the slavocracy and the Jim Crow system of racial segregation, then, these "rules" were internalized by African Americans who converted them from mere signifiers of shame to markers of pride."— Valerie Smith[2]

Though the previous chapters have focused primarily on players, baseball's power structure encompasses not only players but managers, general managers, owners, and sportswriters. One item that ties all of these people together is the National Baseball Hall of Fame in Cooperstown, New York. The Baseball Writers Association of America makes the final decision while everyone else waits to see if they will be inducted. In 2000, Major League Baseball (MLB) gave Cooperstown $250,000 to fund a study on the history of black baseball from 1860 to 1960. Researchers spent five years compiling an 800-page study with biographical and statistical information and put forward a list of 39 individuals for possible induction. Included on that list was Newark Eagles co-owner Effa Manley.

Even people who know absolutely nothing about baseball can name some of its heroes: Jackie Robinson, Larry Doby, Hank Greenberg, or Roberto Clemente. At the same time, when asked who Effa Manley is, even the most die-hard baseball fan would reply: "Who?" Manley's history and Hall of Fame selection presents an interesting case study, first because she was the first woman ever inducted into Cooperstown, and second, her racial background has been the source of some controversy. By all measures, Manley was a woman who was successful in an all-male business enterprise; in addition, it seems as though Manley was able to maneuver back and forth across the color line at a time when the demarcation between black and white appeared to be quite rigid. Manley's history, and the way that history was framed during her induction, highlights how the intersection of race and gender functioned during the World War II period and how fluid racial categories can be in the twenty-first century.

Prior to the Civil War, being able to define oneself as white meant the difference between owning property and potentially being regarded by law as a piece of property. After the Civil War, and following the 1896 *Plessy v. Ferguson* decision, which codified separate but equal, a person's racial classification became only slightly less dire, but still had everyday consequences in terms of access to property, education, legal standing, and basic human rights. Given the rights and privileges that whiteness conferred, states had a vested interest in defining who could benefit from white privilege and who could not. This possessive investment in whiteness was "about assets as well as attitudes; it is about property as well as pigment. It does not stem primarily from personal acts of prejudice by individuals, but from shared social structures that skew access to resources, opportunities, and life chances along racial lines."[3] Because of the benefits that whiteness conferred on citizens at that time, it should come as no surprise that people who were legally defined as black, but who did not necessarily look the part, decided to pass for white, primarily for economic reasons. Despite the use of the color line to separate people from different racial categories, there was still a great deal of fluidity, particularly as light-skinned black citizens moved from one side of the color line to the other.

Assumptions regarding Manley's racial background have swirled since the 1930s with some assuming she was black, some assuming she was white, and Manley never giving a direct and consistent answer to the question. According to Connie Brooks, Manley's niece, Effa was of "African-American, Native American, and German descent."[4] If Brooks's genealogy account was correct, in contemporary times, Manley's background could be classified as multiracial; however, in the 1930s and 1940s, when Manley was active in professional baseball, the pioneer would have been considered as black or colored. The question becomes: Was Manley a black woman who passed for white, as her decedents argue and black sportswriters at the time assumed; or was Manley a white woman who made a conscious decision to live as a black woman, as the Hall of Fame and contemporary baseball scholars claim? What were some of the historical implications of passing for one race or the other? How does Manley's perceived passing impact the way scholars deal with race and baseball broadly and Manley's achievements more specifically?

Effa Manley was born in Philadelphia in 1897 and moved to New York after graduating from high school. In 1933 she wed Abe Manley, a real estate mogul and numbers runner. The Manleys both enjoyed baseball, and in an effort to further legitimize his earnings, Mr. Manley purchased the Brooklyn Eagles in 1936. Quickly realizing that they could not compete with the Dodgers, who were still in Brooklyn at the time, the Manleys moved their franchise to Newark, New Jersey. Effa Manley served as co-owner and business manager for the team and focused on the day-to-day operations of the club. She functioned in much the same way as a general manager would today. Manley worked hard to make sure that the players projected an air of respectability, and she also tried to integrate the team into the community by securing jobs for players during their down times and working for community causes. She was treasurer of the Newark NAACP and often used games to raise awareness and funds for important causes. In one instance she had her "usherettes [wear] sashes that read 'Stop Lynching' and went throughout the stadium collecting funds" for various anti-lynching efforts.[5] During World War II, she invited all-black regiments to attend games for free, and in one instance she invited the black members of the Free French forces stationed at Fort Dix to a game. In her invitation written to the post commander, Manley slyly highlighted the issue of segregation in the armed forces by writing that "white members were also welcome [to attend the game], if there was room."[6]

Only the Ball Was White?

Professional baseball in the United States moved along a similar path in terms of creating and maintaining the color line. Contrary to the popular myth surrounding baseball's integration, Jackie Robinson was not the first black professional baseball player in the United States. For a brief period in the 1800s, professional baseball was a racially integrated space. In the days immediately after the Civil War, professional baseball teams were integrated, including U.S.–born black players such as Moses Fleetwood Walker, his brother Welday Walker, and John W. (Bud) Fowler. It was not until the late 1800s, possibly around the same time that *Plessy* was decided, that these players were pushed out of racially integrated professional teams.[7] Within baseball's color line, dark-skinned U.S.–born black and Latin players were unacceptable. Light-skinned Latin and Native American players were allowed. Just like the societal color line, baseball's color line could be fluid: light-skinned U.S.–born black men could play only if they could pass. The message was the black and dark-skinned Latin players were not "good enough" to play MLB, and even if they were, these players were certainly not welcome.

Once professional baseball began reintegrating their rosters in 1947, team owners naturally looked to Negro League teams for talent. Unfortunately, MLB owners had little respect for the contracts Negro League players had with their teams. In fact, one of the architects of MLB's reintegration, Brooklyn Dodgers owner Branch Rickey, referred to the Negro Leagues as a "racket,"[8] and he passed on signing future Hall of Famer Monte Irvin because he knew Manley would demand reparations. Rickey also "argued that there did not exist 'in a true sense such a thing as organized Negro baseball,'"[9] a sentiment that was not shared by Negro League team owners, players, and fans. Since Negro League team owners did not want to be portrayed as standing in the way of reintegration, most sat idly by while their best players were snatched from their rosters without any compensation. Not Manley. Manley threatened to sue any major league team owner who did not honor Negro League contracts. MLB team owners knew she was serious because in 1940 she sued and won a breach of contract dispute against Hall of Fame pitcher Satchel Paige. According to reports, Pittsburgh Crawfords owner Gus Greenlee traded Paige to the Eagles for a then unprecedented $5,000. After Paige promised but failed to report to the Eagles three times, the Manleys threatened to leave the Negro National League and eventually successfully sued Paige.[10] In 1947 Manley negotiated with Cleveland owner Bill Veeck to receive compensation for Eagles second baseman and future Hall of Famer Larry Doby, who went on to become the first black player in the American League. With that precedent in place, in addition to the real threat of lawsuits, major league team owners were forced to buy out Negro League players' contracts.

In addition to her stance on contracts, Manley is also best known for a very public spat with Jackie Robinson, who in a July 1948 issue of *Ebony* chastised the Negro Leagues for low player salaries, second-rate hotel accommodations, and uncomfortable travel arrangements.[11] Now Robinson was smart enough to know that it was the Jim Crow laws, not the Negro League owners, who were responsible for these problems. Manley's rebuttal was swift and uncompromising. She called Robinson "ungrateful and more likely stupid,"[12] and asked: "How could a child nurtured by its mother turn on her within a year after he leaves her modest home for glamour, success and good fortune? Jackie Robinson is where he is today because of organized Negro baseball."[13] In short, whether it was Jackie Robinson, Branch Rickey, or Satchel Paige, Manley wouldn't let anyone push her around.

If all there was to Manley was a shrewd business sense, even fewer people would recognize her name. Baseball was and still is a business, but her teams had to win and win they did. In 1946 the Eagles won the Negro League World

Series by beating the Kansas City Monarchs in seven games. Her rosters boasted several future Hall of Famers, including the aforementioned Larry Doby; Ray Dandridge, who is considered one of the best defensive third basemen in any league; Leon Day, who, on his first game back from serving in World War II, threw a no-hitter[14]; and Monte Irvin, who helped the New York Giants win two pennants and batted .458 in the 1951 World Series.[15] Manley also signed Don Newcombe, who is the only player in baseball history to win the Rookie of the Year, Most Valuable Player, and the Cy Young award, and was the first black pitcher to win 20 games in the major leagues.[16] Other Hall of Famers who played with the Eagles include first baseman George "Mules" Suttles, shortstop Willie Wells, catcher James Raleigh "Biz" Mackey, and pitcher Satchel Paige. Clearly Manley had an eye for talent.

After the Manleys sold the Eagles in 1948, Effa Manley continued to be a spokeswoman for the Negro Leagues by co-authoring the book *Negro Baseball ... Before Integration*, which championed black baseball pioneers. In addition, she continuously lobbied the baseball Hall of Fame in Cooperstown to induct Negro League players.[17] Because of her dedication to baseball, Cooperstown not only inducted several Negro League players but rewarded Manley by making her the first woman ever inducted into the Hall of Fame in 2006.

Lies, Damn Lies, and Statistics

Manley's induction process wasn't without its bureaucratic rigmarole. Between 1972 and 2005 the Veterans' Committee inducted only 18 Negro League players or owners into Cooperstown. The explanation for the paltry numbers was that valid statistical information was difficult to obtain and corroborate. The only reason statistical information was difficult to obtain was that, for the most part, white mainstream newspapers seldom covered Negro League games. While black newspapers did cover Negro League games, the data are not always complete, and corroborating that information requires painstaking effort. Essentially Negro League players were penalized twice: first they were penalized by MLB, which refused to sign black players; then they were being penalized again by white newspaper owners and sportswriters who didn't think the Negro Leagues were worthy of coverage. Clearly, this was a problem. MLB, more than the National Football League or the National Basketball Association, is cognizant of and finds great value in its history. As was mentioned earlier in this chapter, MLB funded an extensive study in an effort to obtain accurate statistical information, and as a possible unintended consequence, placated Hall of Fame voters. Not content to leave the consideration of these candidates to the Hall's Veterans' Committee, which had done very little for Negro Leaguers to that point, the Hall authorized a special committee of experts on black baseball. That committee chose 17 inductees, including Manley.[18]

To be clear, Cooperstown did not begin inducting Negro League players because the Society for American Baseball Resarch (SABR) members presented evidence or because the Manley family lobbied. They got on the ball, so to speak, because of a phenomenon known as interest convergence, or the notion that "white elites will tolerate or encourage racial advances for blacks only when such advantages also promote white self-interest."[19] The classic legal example of interest convergence has to do with the *Brown v. Board of Education* decision that struck down the "separate but equal" doctrine. In this case, the elimination of de jure segregation was not done in order to move the nation in line with the Constitution and the ideal of equality, but because the "separate but equal" doctrine hampered the United States's reputation abroad during the Cold War.[20] In that same vein, MLB did not begin to reintegrate their rosters because the commissioner and the team owners believed in equality or because they suddenly thought that segregation was wrong. MLB reintegrated first and foremost because baseball is a business. If a team wins games, it will have more revenue; in order to win games, it helps to have the best players. Both players and owners knew for quite some time that some of the best baseball players were in the Negro Leagues.

Another reason for baseball's reintegration has to do with MLB's first commissioner, Kenesaw Mountain Landis, who served from 1920 until his death in 1944. Research has teased out that it was Landis was one of the people responsible for keeping the ban on black players in place for so long. Landis was brought in after the 1919 White Sox scandal in an effort to bring respectability back to professional baseball. Prior to becoming commissioner, Landis was best known for stripping boxer Jack Johnson of his boxing title and throwing him in jail for mailing his white wife a train ticket; it has been argued that the thought of white female fans mixing with black players helped MLB remain segregated for so long.[21] Major league players and owners had known for quite some time that there was a lot of talent in the Negro Leagues. In addition, the Negro Leagues showed that black fans cared about baseball, and that the best way to tap into that revenue stream would be to sign black players. In essence, it was in the team owners' best interest to desegregate.

In that same vein, baseball's Hall of Fame began inducting pre-integration black players because, during his 1966 induction speech Ted Williams said:

> Baseball gives every American boy a chance to excel. Not just to be as good as anybody else, but to be better than someone else. This is the nature of man and the name of the game. I've always been a lucky guy to have worn a baseball uniform;

to have struck out or hit a tape-measure home run. And I hope that someday the names of Satchel Paige and Josh Gibson in some way can be added as a symbol of the great Negro players that are not here only because they were not given the chance.[22]

Here was one of baseball's best players speaking during the Hall's finest and most public moments, and Williams basically embarrassed the Veteran's Committee into action. Almost thirty-five years before Derrick Bell called for it, Ted Williams took the mantle and demonstrated "to other whites the economic harms, social disadvantages, and lost opportunities that white people have suffered and continue to suffer as a result of the pervasive and corrosive effects of social neglect which are linked directly to institutional racial inequality."[23] Williams understood that segregation in professional baseball not only deprived black players of the chance to showcase their talents but also prevented white fans from seeing some of the best players the game had to offer. By not inducting those same black players into the Hall, white sportswriters attempted, whether consciously or unconsciously, to "e-race" (Kimberlé Crenshaw's term for the color-blind ideal that dismisses the "dynamics of racial power"[24]) those players from baseball's history, depriving future fans of any knowledge of what black baseball had to offer. Prior to 1966, many sportswriters either did not notice or did not care whether Negro League players were in the Hall. After that five-minute speech, people began asking questions. For over thirty years, the Veterans' Committee managed to do just enough to remove the spotlight from their actions. If MLB had not intervened in 2000, which again brought media attention to the issue, and the not-so-subtle bypass of the Veterans' Committee, it is doubtful that the Negro Leagues would have the representation they do.

Who's Black, Who's White?

Though Manley's contributions to professional baseball are well documented, there has been some controversy regarding Manley's racial background. While Cooperstown understandably touted Manley's induction, many of the press releases described the team owner as a white woman who chose to live as a black woman, a characterization that her family vehemently refutes.[25] As mentioned earlier, Manley's niece Connie Brooks argues that Manley was African American, Native American, and German. Brooks went on to state, "Effa Manley was not white.... I don't understand reporters saying that she just liked black people. What kind of ignorance is that?"[26] And it is here that racial classification and the issue of passing enters the picture.

Manley herself is cause of much of the controversy: her description of her racial background seemed to change depending on her mood and who was asking the questions. Manley told the story: "My mother was a white woman. Her first husband was a Negro by whom she had four children. In the course of her sewing she met my father, who was a wealthy white man, and I was born as a result."[27] In other interviews, Manley freely admitted to passing for white in order to gain access to segregated spaces and opportunities.[28] Within baseball circles it was taken for granted that she was a black woman who sometimes passed for white. In one instance, Art Carter of the *Baltimore Afro-American* reported on a disagreement between Manley and other Negro League team owners over the practice of paying white booking agents to schedule games in major league ballparks. Carter wrote, "Mrs. Manley asserts that she wanted the profits of the league to stay within the racial group. I doubt it. I am skeptical of Mrs. Manley's sincerity in the matter, because at the same time she says she desires to see more of the dough reach the coffers of *her racial brethren* she hires a $50-a-week white publicity agent."[29] In another instance, in press coverage on the aforementioned rift between Manley and Satchel Paige, Manley was described as Abe Manley's "energetic wife" with no mention of her race, while in that same article Ed Gottlieb, booking agent for the Philadelphia Stars, and J.L. Wilkinson, owner of the Kansas City Monarchs, were both described as "white."[30] Lastly, Manley's obituary in the *New Pittsburgh Courier* described her as the "first black female executive."[31]

Assuming that Manley's descendants are correct, and Manley was a light-skinned black woman who sometimes passed for white, popular culture is littered with examples of light-skinned black characters passing for white, many of whom meet a tragic end. Some of the more popular examples are included in Walter Mosley's novel *Devil in a Blue Dress*, Philip Roth's *The Human Stain*, and Fannie Hurst's *Imitation of Life*. Interestingly enough, "women are more likely to be punished for passing than are men,"[32] a fate which Manley avoided. Critical Race Theorist Cheryl Harris argues, "Becoming white meant gaining access to a whole set of public and private privileges that materially and permanently guaranteed basic subsistence needs and, therefore, survival. Becoming white increased the possibility of controlling critical aspects of one's life rather than being the object of others' domination."[33] Gunnar Myrdal even discussed the phenomenon in his 1944 landmark study "An American Dilemma: The Negro Problem and Modern Democracy" when he wrote:

> Passing means that a Negro becomes a white man, that is, moves from the lower to the higher caste. In the American caste order, this can be accomplished only by the deception of the white people with whom the passer comes to associate and by a conspiracy of silence on the part of other Negroes who might know about it.... In the Northern and Border states it seems to be relatively common for light-skinned Negroes to "pass professionally" but preserve a Negro social life.... In view

of the advantages to be had by passing, it is not difficult to explain why Negroes pass, professionally or completely. It is more difficult, however, to explain why Negroes do not pass over to the white race more often than they actually do.[34]

As Mydral's quote points out, whiteness held tangible benefits in terms of jobs, housing, education, and general quality of life, particularly in a segregated society. These tangible benefits would help explain why some light-skinned black citizens would choose to pass. In Manley's case, the benefits included a job in the millinery business, which, she admits, would not have hired her if they believed she was black. Passing also allowed Manley to stay in first-class hotels where blacks could work in menial jobs but were not allowed to stay as guests.[35] Lastly, passing for white may have also widened her options as far as marriage was concerned: during the 1920s and 1930s marriage was the end-game for most women. Moving back and forth across the color line could allow Manley to draw from at least two racial pools without the societal ramifications. In fact, Manley stated that it was only when she drew the romantic intentions of a white gentleman that Manley's mother told her she was white.[36]

If Manley was a light-skinned black woman who was passing for white, she was hardly the only person in baseball who utilized the practice. As long as segregation in baseball existed, passing took place. As mentioned earlier, black players such as Bud Fowler, George Stovey, Moses Fleetwood Walker, and his brother Welday Walker played on integrated professional teams during the 1880s and 1890s. Professional baseball reached a peak of about a dozen black players, but slowly the numbers dwindled until there were none left. Once the handful of black players were escorted or pushed off professional teams, organized baseball entered the "Gentleman's Agreement" era. Once black baseball players were banned from playing integrated ball, whether it was official or unofficial, attempts to pass began to appear. In 1901 the manager of the Baltimore Orioles, John McGraw, became impressed with a black second baseman named Charlie Grant. As the story goes, McGraw "tried to pass Grant off as Charlie Tokohama, a Cherokee Indian."[37] When Grant's black friends congratulated him after a game, his cover was blown and he was summarily exiled.[38] In the end, it is virtually impossible for researchers to know with any certainty who was passing and who wasn't (unless, of course, as in the case of Grant, the effort failed miserably), since people who were passing typically did not advertise their actions.

If Cooperstown is correct and Manley was a white woman who made a conscious decision to live as a black woman, then Manley would have been participating in what Luther Wright, Jr., terms soulmaning: "passing for black in order to gain employment, education, and political opportunities."[39] As mentioned earlier, popular culture is filled with examples of blacks passing for white; however, there are far fewer examples of whites passing for black. Probably the best known example is John Howard Griffin, who wrote *Black Like Me*. Griffin darkened his skin and spent approximately one month in 1959 traveling throughout the South to get a firsthand look at how racism operated. Other passing narratives of this variety within popular culture are usually played for comic value. In a scene in the 1976 film *Silver Streak*, Richard Pryor convinces Gene Wilder to darken his skin with shoe polish and "act black" to avoid being captured by the authorities. The most egregious example is the 1986 film *Soul Man*, in which C. Thomas Howell plays a wealthy UCLA graduate who purposely overdoses on tanning pills and pretends to be black in order to gain a full scholarship to Harvard Law School. The most recent example comes from the 2008 film *Tropic Thunder*, in which Robert Downey, Jr., portrays a white actor who dons blackface for a film role. Griffin is the only one among these examples who takes the issue seriously, but even so, the passing is temporary.

As with passing, there are examples of soulmaning not only in popular culture but in the real world as well. In 1975 two brothers, Philip and Paul Malone, applied to be Boston firefighters. Because their Civil Service exam scores were too low, they were denied. When the brothers reapplied in 1977, they changed their racial classification from white to black. Because the city of Boston was under a court mandate to hire more people of color as firefighters and police officers, the brothers were hired.[40] Their deception was discovered ten years later when the brothers applied for a promotion and the commissioner, who knew them personally, was puzzled by their racial classification. The brothers were fired for racial fraud, and an investigation found eleven other firefighters who fraudulently listed themselves as Hispanic.[41]

Another possible case of soulmaning involves Mark Stebbins, who ran for a city council seat in Stockton, California, as a black candidate since the district was heavily populated by people of color. Accused of lying about his race to get votes, Stebbins argued that "he *believed* he was black when he was growing up [and that notion] was premised on the belief that he had a black ancestor who had passed as white."[42] In addition, Stebbins himself identified and lived as a white man until moving to Stockton as an adult. His opponent pointed out that Stebbins's siblings, parents, and grandparents were categorized as, and lived their lives as, white.[43] Stebbins survived a recall election and was embraced by the black community in his district, who could capitalize on the political advantage Stebbins's seat offered. It is likely that the black residents of Stebbins's district felt a black council member would best represent their interests. As with the controversy surrounding Manley, Stebbins's situation asks the question: can a person choose his racial identification? Stebbins responded to the racial questions by stating, "Obviously I could pass as white, but there's a point where you really have to say where you stand and to stand there with your life. There's no better way to erase or eradicate racism than to deny that it's bad to be black."[44]

Literature on passing assumes that there are tangible benefits to being one race instead of another. Griffin passed for black not in an effort to gain benefits, but to perform a sociological experiment. The Malone brothers wanted to be firefighters and understood that classifying themselves as black could help them achieve their goal faster than retaking an exam, while Stebbins believed that in a district populated by people of color, being classified as black could increase his chances for election. The logical question to ask would be: what benefits did Manley gain by living as black woman? Manley was not a journalist like Griffin, so it is doubtful that Manley was eager to experience the virulent overt racism she would have encountered at that time. Manley was not that far removed from the historical moment when, in legal terms, whiteness could grant one the opportunity for property ownership while blackness would have codified a person as property. It is possible that Manley simply identified with what she was familiar with. Manley spent her youth surrounded by black family members: the two men her mother married were black, which meant that she was raised by a black father; and given the one-drop rules which were in existence at the time in most states, all of her siblings would be legally classified as black. Black communities were all that Manley knew and she was quoted as saying, "I've often wondered what it would be like to associate with white people."[45] If Manley was being truthful and her mother did not tell her that her father was white until she was an adult, then her entire reality, particularly during her formative years, was based on the assumption that she was black.

Being able to pass for black had other benefits as well. It is important to remember that Manley's husband Abe was a black man. When the Manleys were married, the nation was still a few decades away from the 1967 *Loving v. Virginia*, which overturned state miscegenation laws. That case stemmed from the 1958 marriage of Mildred Jeter, who was black, and Richard Loving, who was white. Because Virginia banned interracial marriage, the Lovings wed in Washington, D.C. Upon returning to their home in Virginia they were arrested and found guilty of violating the state's miscegenation law. The judge suspended their 25-year sentence on the condition the couple leave Virginia and never return. The Lovings sued and in 1967 the U.S. Supreme Court ruled in their favor.[46] Though New Jersey did not have a miscegenation law in place, sixteen states did, which means the Manleys would have had to traverse legal landmines whenever they engaged in interstate travel, if law enforcement authorities believed Effa Manley was white.[47] Possibly because of the legal and social barriers against interracial relationships, their marriage certificate lists both the bride and the groom as "colored" and her mother's first husband is listed as her father.[48] Whether Manley made a conscious decision to list herself as colored or the marriage official simply assumed her racial background is unknown. This uncertainly would call into question any information retrieved from census data or other government documentation. It is possible that Manley's parents as well as Manley herself were explicit in how they chose to classify themselves. It is also possible that officials looked at Manley's parents and siblings and classified her based on their assumptions.

Lastly, the Manleys entered a business enterprise that was for the most part owned, operated, and staffed by black people. Pretty much everyone from the groundskeepers, bus drivers, ticket takers, players and managers, to the sportswriters who covered the league, were legally defined as black. The most prominent white men involved with the Negro Leagues were Kansas City Monarchs owner J.L. Wilkinson, the booking agents who Manley spoke out against, and Eddie Klep, who in 1946 became the first acknowledged white player in the Negro Leagues.[49] Manley was already a minority of one as the sole woman within the league's leadership. At the time, Manley's gender was not necessarily viewed as an asset by others within baseball's establishment. At point, Art Carter characterized her by writing, "Mrs. Manley exercising her feminine prerogative to talk as much as she wanted, gained the floor and virtually beefed out her male companions in a stormy debate over election of officers."[50] Wendell Smith remarked that a charity drive was being placed "in the capable, feminine hands of Mrs. Abe Manley, wife of the owner of the Newark Eagles."[51] It is clear that gender played a role in how Effa Manley was framed by sportswriters and, more than likely, how she was treated by everyone within the Negro Leagues hierarchy. By passing for black, Manley did not have to deal with the impact a double-minority status based on gender *and* race would have had.

With all of the confusion in baseball history regarding who was passing for what and the various ramifications of those decisions, the issue of racial identification becomes a very complicated story. It becomes more complicated when a little-known player by the name of William Edward White enters the picture.

When the biographical committee of the Society for American Baseball Research (SABR) began its research on William Edward White, all they knew was that he had been a student at Brown University and had played one game for the Providence Grays in 1879, in which he got a hit, scored a run, and fielded twelve plays without an error.[52] Committee members searched through Brown University's records and found a Mr. White who was born in 1860 in Milner, Georgia, and was the son of an A.J. White. With a birthplace and father's name secured, the committee turned to the census. The 1880 census found an Andrew J. White who claimed to have no wife or children, but his household also included a Hannah White, who was described as a 35-year-old mulatto woman. Researchers tracked Hannah White through the 1870 census and found her living with her mother and three children, one of whom was named William. If this is the same William White, then under most state laws at the time he would have been classified as black, as race in the United States at the time followed the maternal line, not the paternal one. Defining race in this fashion would make William White the first black professional baseball player in the United States. There was one problem: William White was listed as white on the 1880 census.

White's identification leads to a series of interesting questions: was William White passing, simply defying the notion that one drop of black blood made a person black, or had census takers made an assumption based on pigmentation and place of residence? If, through painstaking investigation, researchers find a player who is/was passing, is it fair to classify this player as black, since he obviously went to great measures to be considered white? Do researchers abide by legal definitions provided by census data or birth certificates, or personal ones provided by the individual? What happens when legal definitions are potentially in conflict with personal identification, as in the cases of Manley and Stebbins? As more states are moving away from designating racial classifications on birth certificates, legal definitions of race are becoming even more difficult to verify and personal definitions are becoming more commonplace. That leaves an equally complicated question: on what basis do we define a person's race? As Kerry Ann Rockquermore points out in her discussion of passing, "Racial passing has a particular hold on our collective imagination because we assume that individuals belong to one, and only one, biologically defined racial group."[53] Since race is a social construct and not a biological one, can racial classifications be based on physical characteristics such as skin color or hair texture? Do researchers look at ancestry, and if so, how many ancestors does a person need to be classified as one race or another? Are racial classifications really a zero-sum game in which a person can only belong to one racial category, and if they are, should they be?

The racial categorization game has been played multiple arenas in recent years. Golfer Tigers Woods so resisted the label "black" that he coined a new term to fully describe his racial identity: Cablinasian. Because Woods is multiracial, his desire to defy singular racial categories was not without merit; however, "Woods might not regard himself as an African American, but the rest of the world apparently did and he was hailed [...] as the first black man to win a golf major"[54] when he won the Masters Tournament in 1997. Throughout Woods's career, sportswriters, and many fans, have clung to the one-drop rule and framed the golfer as black. Another public figure who could check multiple boxes on the census form is President Barack Obama. Unlike Woods, President Obama made a conscious choice to label himself as black despite or because of his biracial identity. In 2004, when Obama won the Illinois senate seat, the *Journal of Blacks in Higher Education* described him as "a self-identified African American."[55] At least in President Obama's case, journalists are adhering to the racial categorization *requested* by the *individual* instead of *imposing* a categorization because he/she needs the individual to be one race or another.

Bringing it back to baseball, how should biracial players such as Yankee shortstop Derek Jeter or Cleveland center fielder Grady Sizemore be classified? Trying to pigeonhole anyone into one racial category or another says "less about what [race the subject is] and more about the social inflexibility of racial categorization."[56] As the number of U.S.–born black players continues to decline, researchers who track the sport's domestic racial makeup are running out of players to count. Officially, MLB only tracks a player's nationality, so potentially, unless the player comes down publicly on one side of the racial fence or the other, one researcher could classify Jeter or Sizemore as black and another researcher could classify them as white. Racial classifications and the color line's fluidity continue into the present.

Most things in baseball are easily quantifiable: wins, losses, home runs, batting average, earned run averages, and so on. Unfortunately, race in the United States is not nearly as cut and dried. Effa Manley's career and life have a lot to teach fans and researchers alike about baseball, racial classifications, and passing. Her team's win-loss ratio and players' statistics are tangible and fixed. Manley's racial classification, however, is open to speculation and interpretation, and there will never be an exact answer. Since researchers know Manley's place and date of birth, it may be possible to obtain her birth certificate, which could provide an answer as to how the state defined her race, but it will not tell us *why* Manley refused to be pegged into a single racial category. In addition, as evidenced by the questions surrounding William White, birth certificates and census data only tell us how the people collecting the data defined individuals, not necessarily how the individuals defined themselves. Certainly passing for white has different ramifications from passing for black, and if it were discovered that Manley was legally defined as black, then not only did Cooperstown induct a woman, but they also inadvertently inducted a black woman! At that historic moment, the very existence of the Negro Leagues shows us how rigid the color line could be, but Manley's decision to move back and forth and to not give a definitive answer to racial inquires shows us that there was some flexibility, and suggests that race has not been, nor does it need to be, a zero-sum game.

5

Barry Bonds and the
Pursuit of Dap

*"Baseball fans love numbers. They like to swirl them around their mouths like
Bordeaux wine. Most statistics are modest, unassuming and without presumption.
Other statistics have more body, and by their richness and bite, provide a substantial addition to the satisfaction and mystery surrounding the game."*—Pat Conroy[1]

*"I gave my life and soul to that game. That's what's heartbreaking. That's the
hard part of it. My [reputation] was kind of iffy anyway. I created that guy out
there for entertainment only. Whether you hated me or liked me, you were there.
And I only wanted you there. I just wanted you to see the show. That was it. All
I ever wanted was for people to have a good time and enjoy it. It was fun to come
out and people would boo or yay or whatever. They all showed up to see whatever
would happen next and it motivated me to play hard."*—Barry Bonds[2]

As discussed in Chapter 2, when Roger Maris set a new single-season
home-run record in 1961, professional baseball had been a reintegrated space
for just three years: the Red Sox were the last team to sign a U.S.–born black
player, in 1959. Major League Baseball (MLB) seemed to reach a ceiling during
the 1970s, when approximately 25 percent of major league players were black.[3]
Since then, there has been a steady decline of U.S.–born black players, who
made up 8.5 percent of the rosters during the 2011 season.[4] To highlight the
continued decline in numbers, during the 2005 season, the Houston Astros
became the first World Series team in over fifty years to not have a single
U.S.–born black player on its roster. It is ironic that at a time when Major
League Baseball is trying to figure out why the number of U.S.–born black
players has reached its lowest point in almost thirty years, one of the most
dominant players in the game, who is black himself, is often shunned by the
media. Former San Francisco Giants outfielder Barry Bonds was also one of
the most well-known MLB players in the game though some would describe
the slugger as being more infamous than famous.

For almost 60 years, much of which were during the Jim Crow era, the undeniable king of statistical dominance was Babe Ruth. During his twenty-two-year career (1914–1935), Babe Ruth placed his mark on baseball immortality, holding seven major league records. Though several of these records eventually fell, Ruth set the bar for offensive dominance and is considered by many to be the best baseball player in history. However, as the cliché goes, records were made to be broken, and in 2001, Barry Bonds's career became a statistical marvel. Beginning in that year, Bonds challenged Ruth's statistical domination and began making the case that he is, in fact, the most dominant baseball player in history by breaking six major league records, in addition to becoming the charter member of the 500–500 club.[5] Table 1 provides a side-by-side comparison of Ruth and Bonds's statistical achievements.

Table 1
Ruth vs. Bonds Statistical Comparison[3]

Statistics	Babe Ruth (22 seasons)	Barry Bonds (22 seasons)
Games	2503	2986
At Bats	8399	9847
Single-Season Home Run	60 (1927)	73 (2001)
Career Home Runs	714	762
Single-Season Base on Balls	170 (1923)	232 (2004)
Career Base on Balls	2062	2558
Single-Season Slugging Percentage	.847 (1920)	.863 (2001)
Career Slugging Percentage	.690	.607

Given his offensive output, there were some baseball fans who argued that Barry Bonds was the best baseball player in the game at that time, maybe even the best player ever to pick up a bat and glove. However, there were others who were unwilling to give Bonds any "dap," a hip-hop term meaning proper due or respect. As the quote at the beginning of this chapter from Pat Conroy points out, "Baseball fans love numbers,"[7] which raises the question: In a sport that is obsessed with statistical analysis and comparison, why did so many sports commentators dismiss Bonds's numbers? Bonds's record-breaking home-run chase was framed in a much different way than Mark McGwire's and Sammy Sosa's chase three years prior. Arguably sportswriters adopted a guilty-until-proven-innocent posture toward Bonds where performance-enhancing drugs are concerned, when some other (white) athletes were perceived to be innocent until proven guilty. The combination of race, age, performance-enhancing drugs, and surliness intersect to frame Bonds as something other than one of the best baseball players in the history of the game.

A Family Thing

During the 1998 season, Mark McGwire and Sammy Sosa shattered Roger Maris's single-season home-run mark of 61. In the process, McGwire embodied the new prototypical slugger: a white American working or middle-class male, who was uncomfortable with the spotlight, spoke proper English, was abrasive at times, exhibited a personality flaw or two, which only made him more endearing, and had a loveable sidekick. This controlling image disempowered any non-white slugger who dared challenge the record. The image McGwire helped cultivate also obscured the MLB career home-run leader Henry Aaron, who by all accounts is one of the best players in the game, as well as being a truly courageous and classy individual. In 2001 Barry Bonds dethroned McGwire as the single-season home-run record holder, and along the way broke the record for single-season walks, single-season slugging and on-base percentage.

Barry Bonds's stature as one of the best, if not the best baseball player ever, was not an accident, nor did his relationship with the media begin when he played his first game in Pittsburgh. Bonds is baseball royalty. His father Bobby Bonds played fourteen seasons in the majors and had a lifetime .268 batting average, won three Gold Gloves, and made three All-Star appearances.[8] The elder Bonds was the first rookie in the modern era to hit a grand slam in his major league debut; sportswriters touted him as the next Willie Mays, who incidentally became Barry's godfather, but when the elder Bonds failed to live up to that label, they framed him as an underachiever despite the fact that he hit 30 home runs and had 30 stolen bases in five seasons, a feat Mays accomplished only twice.[9]

The only other player to match this feat is Barry Bonds. To say that the elder Bonds's relationship with sportswriters was acrimonious would be an understatement. Bobby Bonds was frustrated by how sportswriters discussed his career, and he was not afraid to tell reporters exactly how he felt, noting later in his life, I probably had more success than anyone they ever put that [underachiever] label on. You show me another guy who's going to do 30–30 five times. But all the writers kept talking about was potential. You haven't reached your potential yet, they say. Well, unless you win a Pulitzer Prize, you're not living up to your potential either, are you?"[10]

Despite the fact that sportswriters believed Bobby Bonds did not live up to his potential as the next Willie Mays, the elder Bonds had a productive baseball career. When the Giants traded Bonds after seven seasons, it was understood that "Bonds's reputation in San Francisco had been battered. He was not only widely known as a drunk, he was falsely rumored to be a recreational drug user."[11] Upon Bobby Bonds's death in 2003, *Sports Illustrated* writer

Ron Fimrite argued, "As the son continues to topple records, researchers have discovered that the old man was himself a superior player and that his reputation as an underachiever was unfair."[12] In fact, it is worth pointing out that only two players in baseball history have hit over 300 home runs and stolen over 400 bases, and they're both named Bonds.[13]

Another factor in the younger Bonds's popular construction was his relationship to the aforementioned Willie Mays. Considered by many to be one of the best players ever, as well as one of the last players to play on both a Negro League and a major league team (having begun his career with the Birmingham Barons), Mays won the Rookie of the Year award in 1951 and later won two Most Valuable Player (MVP) awards.[14] Mays accumulated twelve Gold Gloves, played in twenty All-Star Games, and participated in five World Series during his career.[15] Mays signed with the New York Giants and, like both Bondses, spent most of his career in San Francisco. In addition to witnessing Mays's exceptional on-field heroics, according to Jeff Pearlman, both Bonds learned from Mays "that to be a superstar, one must carry himself like a superstar. That meant being occasionally difficult with the press[,] blowing off the media, blowing off teammates; [making] sarcastic comments that stung like snakebite. Mays knew he was royalty, just as he knew those frumpy-looking [sportswriters] with inkstains on their sweaters weren't of his ilk."[16] Barry Bonds was even compared to Mays both in terms of talent and personality. As one sportswriter remarked, "Both [are] great players, of course, but both [are] mercurial characters. Both men can be a royal pain in the rear."[17] In spite of such coarse reputations, these are indeed the men who taught Barry Bonds how to play baseball and arguably taught him that sportswriters were not to be trusted.

Bonds entered the 2001 season with 494 home runs, 1405 RBI, 1547 walks, and a .567 SLG, each mark registered in the top three of the league at that time.[18] These numbers, acquired in seven seasons with the Pirates and eight with the Giants, led to three MVP, eight Gold Gloves, and nine All-Star Game appearances.[19]

The combination of Bonds's offense and defense was so impressive that *The Sporting News* named Bonds its player of the decade for the 1990s.[20] In the annual poll conducted by the *Sporting News* in 2000, Bonds was ranked the fourth best player in the majors.[21] Jeff Pearlman of *The Sports Illustrated* called Bonds one of the best all-around players in the game and described his left arm as "an assault weapon once banned by the U.S. government."[22] Clearly, before the 2001 season, Barry Bonds was already having a Hall of Fame career. To make matters more interesting, Bonds became a free agent at the end of the 2001 season, a situation that, some speculate, gives players an incentive to step their game up a notch.

Who's Afraid of the Angry Black Man/Athlete?

Despite the fact that the numbers Bonds put up during his career certainly earned him the title "one of the best in the game," the commentary surrounding Bonds's achievements during the 2001 season seemed to fall into two distinct camps. The first group recognized that personality could not/ should not trump on-field achievements. Todd Jones of *The Sporting News* relayed an impassioned plea: "Please don't lose sight of what he has done just because you don't like him. Nobody likes him."[23] The second, populated mostly by the national media, tend to couch Bonds's accomplishments in terms of his personality. Falling squarely within this group, *Sports Illustrated*'s Jeff Pearlman wrote, "For 13-plus years Bonds had an unmatched record of standing up reporters, of blowing off autograph seekers, of dogging teammates, of taking every opportunity to remind everyone that there is only one Barry Bonds —*and you're not him.*"[24] Rick Reilly began one article on Bonds with the statement: "Someday they'll be able to hold Bonds's funeral in a fitting room."[25] On ESPN's *Pardon the Interruption,* Tony Kornheiser mentioned that Bonds "has been a cold, angry, condescending person for most of his career, he's not lovable and he wants it that way and has wanted it that way."[26] Ken Rosenthal of *The Sporting News* brings up the fact that Bonds "regularly behaves like a churl with the media and elicits mixed feelings inside his own clubhouse."[27]

Barry Bonds has never been accused of having a warm and fuzzy personality; however, he was neither the first nor the last athlete to have a lukewarm relationship with media. During the 1998 season, when it seemed, as one reporter put it, that McGwire would "rather get hit in the head with a Randy Johnson fastball than answer one more question from the media,"[28] sportswriters continued to follow his every move and frame him as shy as opposed to surly. Though Bonds seemed to conform to the curmudgeon portion of the controlling image McGwire represented, it worked for McGwire and against Bonds arguably because of the latter's race. In essence, sportswriters emphasized Bonds's surliness as a means to lessen his professional achievements. This is not to say that a player's personality or off-field exploits should be completely discounted; however, the question becomes, is surliness the primary explanation for Bonds's reception?

One of Bonds's biographers, Steven Travers, points out that "there is not much that supersedes ability on the field. It is about winning, and talented players put money in their teammates' pockets. That is the real bottom line. It has been said that Stalin could have had a job in baseball if he could hit with consistent power."[29] Though it hardly seems fitting to compare Bonds to Joseph Stalin, it helps to put Bonds's supposed surliness into perspective, especially since, as one journalist notes, Bonds "has never publicly embarrassed himself, never demanded to renegotiate his contract, never given less than his best."[30] Granted, professional baseball players are not saints and should not be expected to be role models, a sentiment former NBA player Charles Barkley proclaimed in his 1993 Nike commercial; at the same time, sportswriters have historically placed on-field performance above surliness and far more serious offenses.

Marcus Henry of the *New York Amsterdam News* pointed out the hypocrisy involved in deciding whose personality traits become newsworthy: "Rarely does anyone talk about Ty Cobb's racist views. Nor do they emphasize Mickey Mantle's problem with alcohol addiction or allegations that [Atlanta] manager Bobby Cox is a wife-beater."[31] Cox, Mantle, and Cobb all have one thing in common: they are all white, while Bonds is not. Henry's examples do not even include the likes of Pete Rose, who, despite being banned from MLB and the Hall of Fame for gambling while he managed the Reds, is beloved by many sportswriters and fans. After Rose released his book *My Prison Without Bars*, in which he finally admitted to betting on baseball after fourteen years of denials, ESPN's Alysse Minkoff remarked, "To many die-hard baseball fans nothing Pete Rose will ever do or say will be enough. To others, Rose can do no wrong. Remember that moving three-minute ovation when Rose was named to the All-Century Team at the 1999 All-Star Game?"[32] When NBC reporter Jim Gray asked Rose about the gambling allegations after the All-Century Team ceremony, the reporter was lambasted by fans and later had to apologize for even asking the questions.[33] The adoration Rose received comes despite being accused of, denying, and later admitting to doing something expressly prohibited by MLB guidelines. The fact that sportswriters continue to "e-race" Cobb and Cox's actions reflects the hierarchical power structure that frames white men as "beyond reproach."[34]

At the same time, framing black athletes in general, and Bonds specifically, as angry black men/athletes can be described as an attempt "to demonize black people, to label them as somehow peculiarly possessed of an unwarranted ungratefulness for what our country offers. These athletes are angry about racism, they're angry about the unfair treatment they are receiving."[35] By demonizing Bonds for his surly attitude while ignoring the offenses of white players and managers, sportswriters highlight the notions that "whiteness is the most subsidized identity in our society [and] the most powerful identity politics are those that protect the value of whiteness.[36] In essence, Cobb, Cox, Mantle, and Rose receive a free pass for their behavior that protects "the value of whiteness," while Bonds, because of his race, does not. In light of *The Sporting News*'s Michael Knisley's assertion that "there can be no disparagement of the feat, no mandatory points deduction for Bonds's sometimes-churlish personality or self-imposed distance from his teammates,"[37] the question becomes: what must Bonds do to get some dap?

The racial component of mostly white sportswriters critiquing a black athlete was barely discussed by these sportswriters even at a time when the percentage of U.S.–born black baseball players hovers around the single digits. In fact, focusing on Bonds's attitude deflected attention away from any discussions of racism: if racism was brought up as a rationale for any differential treatment, sportswriters could simply deny the charge and point to Bonds's attitude. When an AP writer asked Bonds whether or not racism played a part in his lukewarm reception, Bonds replied, "Does the KKK exist? Sure. Probably. I don't know. [Racism] hadn't changed drastically [since 1974]."[38] Even Bonds himself is at a loss to explain the treatment he received. This was not the first time that the racial quagmire was brought up where Bonds was concerned. In 1990 Bonds referred to one of his Pirates teammates, Andy Van Slyke, as "Mr. Pittsburgh" and the "great white hope."[39] The racial gauntlet was thrown down after the Pirates signed Van Slyke to a 3-year deal worth $12.5 million, while at the same time both John Smiley and Doug Drabek won their arbitration cases.[40] It was simply a coincidence that both Bonds and Bobby Bonilla, who are black and both in their fifth year of service, lost their arbitration cases that same year. Ulish Carter from the *New Pittsburgh Courier* agreed with Bonds that being a financial winner or loser that season was not a case of luck. Carter argued, "The fans, local media and Pirates treated him as if he was some kind of villain because he wanted to be paid close to what the market would bear.... The treatment of Bonds was no exception; it was the rule for Pirate fans toward Black superstars, starting with Roberto Clemente and continuing with Dave Parker, Al Oliver, and even Willie Stargell."[41]

Despite a history of "playing the race card," few speculated that racism was at the root of the animosity between Bonds and sportswriters. The *New York Amsterdam News*, a black newspaper that did consider racism as one of reasons for the ill will, likened the press treatment of Bonds to "the racist attacks on Hank Aaron when he was in full pursuit of breaking Babe Ruth's all-time home-run mark, which he did."[42] It is ironic that a few months after the 2001 season ended, the public learned that Bonds received death threats similar to Aaron's, though sportswriters failed to give the issue much attention.[43] When Aaron received death threats during his quest to break the career home-run record, sportswriters did not shy away from reporting the issue. One sportswriter remembered, "Last summer the hate mail made a good story. When the epistolary Klansmen took up their pens armed with malevolent rhetoric about a black man surpassing Babe Ruth, it was a grand focus[...]. Even Richard Nixon said on film that Aaron is what this country's all about. One thing sportswriters agreed upon was that what this country was not about was calling Hank a nigger."[44] The use of racial slurs, particularly in public settings, is tolerated less now than it was during Aaron's time, as racism is expressed less explicitly. What is interesting about Conroy's observation is that while hate mail made a good story in 1974, it did not even warrant mention in 2001.

In a radio interview Bonds talked about the threats: "I kept that completely secret from everyone.... When they told me, I was like, "you have to be kidding me. All this for a record?" I was more concerned about my children and keeping them at home or something. I didn't want anyone else on the team to know about this. And then, I didn't really want my wife to know about. But I had to tell her for my little girl's sake."[45] Bonds did not disclose whether or not the threats were racially motivated, or whether he believed they were racially motivated, and significantly, sportswriters failed to give the issue much attention. It is difficult to believe that sportswriters reversed their position on what America does and does not stand for in the intervening twenty-seven years: arguably, threatening Bonds's life would/should still rate high on the list of things the United States is not about. There has been no evidence to suggest that Mark McGwire or Sammy Sosa received death threats during their home-run chase three years earlier. As mentioned in Chapter 2, the idea of unconscious racism hypothesizes that since racism played a large part in America's shared past, all Americans unconsciously harbor negative opinions about nonwhites. Because society no longer tolerates overt racism the way it once did, the negative attitudes created by the shared racist history will find an alternative outlet.[46] In the case of the 1998 home-run chase, sportswriters manifested this unconscious racism through the seeming ease with which they framed Sosa as McGwire's sidekick, a controlling image that reaffirms the racial hierarchy within the United States with the white male at the top and "the other" at the bottom. Since Bonds was alone in his quest for the record, sportswriters framed Bonds as a malcontent who was somehow unworthy to break McGwire's record, an image that helped create an atmosphere in which some see death threats as understandable and acceptable. Is it possible that sportswriters did not report on the threats Bonds received because they would have to accept some responsibility for those threats?

Whether or not sportswriters intentionally helped create a hostile environment for Bonds is debatable; however, media representatives do have the power to frame the debate: regardless of what Bonds achieved on the field, sportswriters had the power to frame the discussion in such a way that it diminished or shifted the focus away from his professional achievements. If that is the case, and we believe that "Entertainment is not simply the expression of eternal needs — it responds to the real needs *created by society*,"[47] then what societal need is being fulfilled or created by framing Bonds in this manner?

Bonds's biographer Steven Travers argues that "the reality is that most whites love to like blacks. It makes them feel good. It helps convince them that racism is not what it used to be. What is not on the surface, however, is that most whites love to like *certain kinds* of blacks. Barry Bonds has not always been the kind of black athlete that they love to like."[48] For Travers, it is not that Bonds is a black athlete that causes problems, it is that Bonds refuses to *be a particular type* of black athlete. Journalist Dave Zirin agrees as he notes "the media have been crushing Bonds without evidence because he has never played their game. If Michael Jordan was the Tom Hanks of the professional sports world, Bonds is Sean Penn, beating down the paparazzi and challenging their self-importance."[49] Though Bonds could not be described as radical in a political sense, his relationship with the media symbolizes a power shift as Bonds forces sportswriters to meet him on his own terms: regardless of whether or not sportswriters like Bonds, his continued dominance forces those same writers to deal with him. On the other hand, by framing Bonds as a malcontent, sportswriters attempted to put the slugger "in his place," which sends a message to other black athletes: be the type of black athlete white America wants you to be or your image will be ruined. If Bonds behaved more like Sammy Sosa, whose persona in 1998 was more of a happy-go-lucky sidekick, or a Michael Jordan/Tiger Woods type, who was "perceived as both black and not black, as a superior athlete and an all–American clean-cut young man who transcended race and yet was obviously an African American,"[50] the commentary would have been different.

If ever there was a black athlete who seemingly "transcends" race it was Chicago Bulls basketball player Michael Jordan. In a similar manner, golfer Tiger Woods "embodies the imagined ideal of being and becoming American."[51] Until recently, both Jordan and Woods were framed as examples of "black buddies" who can be "physically black yet lacking a racial identity. [Their] phenomenal success points to the lucrative benefits for those black buddies who manage to develop personas as 'raceless' individuals."[52] Sportswriters and marketing executives can frame athletes such as Jordan and Woods in direct contrast to athletes like Bonds so mainstream society can have the "certain kinds" of black athlete available for adoration. On the other hand, Bonds's status as a professional athlete in and of itself reinforces a racial hierarchy, since "the typical image of blacks in the media is that of a violent physical people, habitually involved in criminal activity, entertainment or sports."[53] If that is the case, even as Bonds attempted to challenge the controlling images via his continued dominance, which shifts the flow of power from the writer → athlete dynamic to an athlete → writer one, Bonds's status as an athlete still reinforced the controlling image of black males as athletes. In other words, Bonds was in a no-win situation.

It is interesting to note that even athletes who embody society's notion of what a black athlete should be are not protected from hostility. After winning the 1997 Masters, golf's golden boy Tiger Woods began receiving death threats, though, like Bonds, he would not discuss how serious they were or if they were racially motivated.[54] And in the case of Michael Jordan, as documentary filmmaker Michael Moore points out, when Nike encourages consumers to "be like Mike," "the operative word there is *like*, because no matter how many millions he makes, to *be* Mike would mean spending an awful lot of time pulled over on the New Jersey Turnpike."[55] As transcendent as Woods appears to be, the speed with which the transcendent label was revoked after his infidelities became public, shows that transcending race has its limits. Framing Jordan and Woods as transcending race makes the racism they suffer invisible to their fans.

Then again it is possible that race alone does not tell the whole story. There have been other curmudgeonly black athletes over the years who did not incur the media's wrath (e.g. Reggie Jackson, Charles Barkley). On the other hand, there are a few unruly white players, such as former MLB pitchers David Wells and Kenny Rogers, who are shunned by the media. Wells experiences problems due to his outspoken nature and a penchant for being involved in bar fights, while Rogers physically assaulted not one but two cameramen before the Rangers released him in 2005. Clearly race alone does not dictate how unruly players will be framed. If race does not tell the entire story, what other intersecting factors are at work in Bonds's narratives?

What's Up, Old Man?

While Bonds's race was rarely brought up to explain either his accomplishments or his reception by fans and sportswriters, age was ever present in the discussion. One thing sportswriters were reasonably consistent with in terms of writing about Bonds's offensive assault was the importance of his age. Up to this point in history, it has been generally assumed that baseball players reach their peak around the age of thirty and start to decline around age thirty-five. As Pat Conroy noted, "In baseball time [a man of Bonds's age] should be caring for his sores and drooling in his spikes."[56] Since Bonds turned thirty-seven during the 2001 season, it seemed inconceivable that instead of thinking about retirement, Bonds continued to produce at such an astounding level. The idea that Bonds should be walking away from the game at this age instead of dominating it can be seen as "an expression of ageist society, in which ageist norms and assumptions govern ideas about fitness to work."[57] As Bonds moved closer to McGwire's home-run record, *Sports Illustrated* columnist Tom Verducci pointed out that "what makes no apparent sense about this career-best power display is that on July 24 [2001] Bonds will turn 37, an age when Mickey Mantle, his closest statistical twin, was finished and most players' best years are well behind them. The average age of the sixteen other 500-home run hitters when they belted their career high in homers was 29."[58] Because of its unusual timing, some interpreted Bonds's dominance as a product of performance-enhancing drugs, assuming no baseball player could perform at such a high level at such an "old" age. However, there was one problem with this line of thinking: Bonds was not the only dominant "senior citizen" in the game at that time.

In 2001, then Arizona Diamondbacks pitcher Randy Johnson, who is one year older than Bonds, won his fourth Cy Young Award by having the lowest earned run average (ERA) in the majors as well as leading the majors in strikeouts; he pitched a perfect game in 2004. At the same time, then New York Yankees pitcher Roger Clemens, who, at age 39, is two years older than Bonds, earned his sixth Cy Young Award by leading the American League in strikeouts. Despite the fact that half of the players suspended for steroid use during the 2005 season were pitchers, it was never suggested at that time that Johnson or Clemens, who are considered two of the best pitchers ever, resorted to performance-enhancing drugs to perform at such a high level at such an old age. It must be noted that pitchers tend to have longer careers than everyday players since they are only required to work once every four or five days. Therefore, the comparisons between Bonds, who is not a pitcher, and Clemens and Johnson are not entirely symmetrical. On the other hand, given the extremely small number of U.S.–born black pitchers in MLB, the fact that batters have been disproportionately targeted as part of the steroid debate has racial implications as well. It is also interesting to note that the two "elderly" pitchers have behaved curmudgeonly and sometimes violently during their careers: Clemens has a history of hitting batters and, as mentioned in Chapter 3, once threw a broken bat at Mets catcher Mike Piazza, while Johnson physically assaulted a cameraman before his first press conference in New York in 2005. Despite this history, the two pitchers are revered by most sportswriters.

In one article discussing how Clemens has remained dominant for such a long time, ESPN's Bob Klapisch remarks that Clemens "is in the weight room, consumed by a four-day ritual that he's convinced has kept his elite-caliber fastball in the mid to upper 90s, and has actually prolonged his career. When Andy Pettitte says Clemens is 'a freak of nature' it is not meant as a joke or even a figure of speech. That's because Clemens doesn't just work out; he's obsessed with exercise, and proudly says, 'My only day off is the day I pitch.'[59] If this article had been written about Bonds, who was younger and just as dominant, the discussion probably would have at least hinted at the possibility of performance-enhancing drugs. When discussing Clemens's surliness, sportswriters oftentimes joke about his exploits, explaining that Clemens is a "thrower of balls. And sometimes of bats. Both of which may be aimed at an opponent at any time."[60] The confrontations with Piazza are reduced to a punch line instead of being framed as potentially serious assaults. The joking strategy works for Johnson as well, as is evident from ESPN's Jayson Stark's comments after the pitcher assaulted a cameraman: "No cameras got mauled. No questioners got stared down. No voices were raised. This was Randy Johnson at his friendliest, most congenial, most amusing best."[61] As with Clemens, Johnson's physical assault of a cameraman was reduced to a joke. Though past surliness is alluded to, Johnson's new demeanor was welcomed instead of being criticized for being insincere, as it undoubtedly would have been with Bonds. In a manner similar to McGwire's 1998 situation, Johnson and Clemens were able to cash in on their white privilege, which shielded their violent behavior from public criticism and reframed it as an endearing personality quirk. In addition, much like McGwire before he retired, that same privilege protected Johnson's and Clemens's continued dominance from the steroid shadow — at least for a while.

Bonds, Johnson, and Clemens are not the only players in baseball's history to remain dominant after age thirty-five. Negro League pitcher Satchel Paige did not enter the majors until 1948 at the age of forty-two and went on to win the Rookie of the Year award. Henry Aaron broke Babe Ruth's career home-run record at the age of forty. Forty-three-year-old Ricky Henderson stole 25 bases in 2001 and holds the all-time stolen base record.[62] Finally, one must not forget that Mark McGwire was thirty-five when he broke the home-run record in 1998. Granted, players like Paige and Aaron were exceptions to baseball's aging rule; however, with more players staying in the league and remaining productive longer, it seems that the time span when players are considered at their peak needs to be re-evaluated. Bonds's agent Scott Boras points out, "Clemens and Bonds have taught us the book is being rewritten In the modern game [...] they are highly conditioned athletes. You can't look at the 1960s and '70s as a template for when optimum performance ends and mediocrity begins."[63] What Boras noticed is that sportswriters who do not expect these "old men" to perform at such high levels are using an outdated model of the typical baseball player. It is possible that instead of being exceptions to baseball's aging rule, players such as Bonds and Clemens are just the first prototypes in a new type of baseball player, one whose dominance and overall career can last longer. Though players such as Bonds, Clemens, and Johnson are prolonging the career span of a dominant major league baseball player, it is Bonds alone whose age seems to work against him in the eyes of the press. Unlike his fellow senior citizens, Bonds has the added burden of race to complicate the age issue. Intersectionality dictates that Bonds would experience ageism differently than Clemens or Johnson, and would experience racism differently than younger black players because of his age.

He Looks Up; You Can Put It on the Board, Yes!

Though there was not much discussion on the ways in which racism and ageism framed the discussion on Bonds, one thing that most sportswriters did discuss was the fact that the 2001 home-run chase was framed differently than the 1998 Mark McGwire and Sammy Sosa home-run chase. According to Bonds's biographer Josh Suchon,

> America loved it in '98 when Mark McGwire and Sammy Sosa put on a home-run derby for the ages. They went mano y mano [sic] through the heart of the summer. It no longer became a sports story. It was national news. Now, just three years later, Bonds was alone in the national spotlight. You couldn't help but feel sorry for Bonds. Here he was, producing the finest offensive season in baseball history, and it was as if the nation yawned.[64]

Though Bonds's achievements still warranted some national attention, the level of attention was more restrained. In fact, the number of journalists assigned to cover Bonds's quest, 350, was about half the number assigned to cover McGwire.[65] A variety of different explanations for the disparity emerged. There were some who argued Bonds's record-breaking season came too soon after the McGwire/Sosa chase,[66] and others who, as previously mentioned, blamed Bonds's attitude. Bonds himself blamed the media for the differential treatment and still others blamed the nation's ambivalence in the wake of the terrorist attacks on September 11.[67] In the eyes of San Francisco journalists, however, these were just excuses designed to hide the fact that Bonds's 2001 campaign was worthy of more praise than the McGwire/Sosa race.

It is interesting that the San Francisco media, who are arguably more familiar with Bonds and conceivably would be subjected to more of his curmudgeonly behavior had a completely different view of Bonds's 2001 season from that of the national media. Bruce Jenkins of the *San Francisco Chronicle* observed, "For his supreme, otherwordly accomplishment, Bonds got a shrug. He got Page 5 in sports sections around the nation as he edged closer to Mark McGwire. [It seems that] we're the only ones who get it. We're watching Michael Jordan at the top of his game, Jim Brown reducing massive would-be tacklers to small children, Tiger Woods on the back nine at Pebble Beach."[68] It is ironic that Jenkins would compare Bonds's accomplishments to Jordan and Woods, the very same racially transcendental figures Bonds could not or would not emulate. Others in San Francisco pointed out that when doing a direct comparison, Bonds was a better player, and deserved the home-run record more, than McGwire:

> There are two reasons I hope Barry Bonds breaks Mark McGwire's home-run record: (1) Bonds is a better player. (2) Bonds is a better person. McGwire is a one-trick pony, a weak defender, poor baserunner and a below-average percentage hitter[...]. Meanwhile, Bonds has been an eight-time Gold Glove winner, he is approaching 500 stolen bases for his career and he has hit .300 or better seven times; this year almost assuredly will be his eighth.[69]

Describing Bonds as a better person than McGwire was not a concept national media representatives would ever fathom. As mentioned in Chapter 2, though it took some time for McGwire to warm to the increased media scrutiny, his evasiveness was framed as shyness. Bonds, who displayed similar behavior, was framed as a churl. Describing Bonds as a better player did have merit, as Bonds accumulated better offensive and defensive numbers. By all statistical measures, Bonds's 2001 season far exceeded McGwire's 1998 totals, as shown in Table 2.

Table 2
Home-Run Season Statistical Comparison[70]

	McGwire (1998)	Bonds (2001)
Home Runs	70	73
At Bats	509	476
At Bats Per Home Run	10.61	6.52
Batting Average	.299	.328
Base on Balls	162	177
On-Base Percentage	.470	.515
Slugging Percentage	.752	.863
Stolen Bases	1	13
Strikeouts	155	93

Every record McGwire broke in 1998, Bonds broke in 2001 and then some. Although Bonds had a better statistical season than McGwire, this did not help move him into the spotlight.

When comparing the two seasons, statistical dominance is not the only place where Bonds excelled. Some sports journalists reminded their readers that in the midst of his home-run chase, Bonds had to "help provide entertainment for a nation in dire need of diversion; lead the San Francisco Giants in a come-from-behind drive for a playoff berth; smile and expound for a vast press corps that he usually shunned; watch ball four after ball four after ball four after...; play while mourning the death of a friend and former bodyguard Franklin Bradley [and] worry about his impending free agency."[71] While McGwire and Sosa could bask in the national glow of their achievements,

Bonds's accomplishments hung in the shadow of September 11, a far more somber backdrop than the White House sex scandal from which McGwire and Sosa diverted attention. Despite the fact that President George W. Bush urged professional sports to play their regularly scheduled games, following the NFL's lead, baseball suspended games for one week.[72] Commissioner Bud Selig released a statement that read: "Our game, besides being a national pastime, is a social institution with social responsibilities that include responding to an unimaginable crisis such as this in a timely and significant manner."[73] Even with the pause, it would be misleading to argue that the ambivalence toward Bonds's season was due entirely to the terrorist attacks. On the contrary, when New York hosted its first home games after the attacks, then Mayor Rudolph Guiliani stated that one of the few things that got his mind off the terrorist attacks was baseball, and to that end, despite being a rabid Yankees fan, Guiliani attended a Mets game.[74]

Following that game, which was the first large-scale public gathering in New York since the attacks, newspapers ran stories titled "Baseball Helps Heal Stricken City" and "Through the Tears, Let's Play Ball," so clearly baseball could and did have a place after September 11. According to Rebecca Kraus, "Baseball provided an emotional release, a sense of hope, and a place for the community to gather in its time of need, thus fulfilling its role as the national pastime."[75] However, instead of playing up Bonds's quest for the record, and the fact that he pledged $10,000 to the United Way for every home run he hit for the rest of the season, sportswriters shifted their focus to the New York Yankees, a team headed, as usual, for post-season play. While some sportswriters maintained a "been there, done that" attitude toward Bonds's home-run chase, the same ambivalence was not levied toward the Yankees, who were making their fourth straight World Series appearance. It is interesting to point out, as former Yankees first baseman Scott Brosius remembered, "For the rest of that year anyway we weren't the hated New York Yankees."[76]

The continued framing of Bonds as the angry black man/athlete seems to go against interest convergence theory, which argues that "the interests of blacks in achieving racial equality will be accommodated only when it converges with the interests of whites."[77] As mentioned in the introduction, interest convergence in a baseball context hypothesizes that professional baseball did not reintegrate because it had the best interests of black players in mind: it was the financial gains and the prospect of winning that fueled desegregation efforts. In the case of Barry Bonds, it would seem that it would have been in sportswriters' best interests to frame Bonds's chase as a unifying force for the nation to rally behind. In the wake of national tragedy and the cusp of his historic achievement, Bonds's personality seemed to soften. As Bruce Jenkins of the *San Francisco Chronicle* observed, Bonds "readily accepted the media's need for interviews, revealed more of his gentle side than anyone thought possible and showed a rare glimpse of emotion, crying at the podium, during the postgame ceremony of his record home run. His reward: 'Yeah, whatever.'"[78] It was clear that nothing Bonds did was going to be enough to repair his reputation and shift the focus to his work instead of his personality. While the spirit surrounding 9/11 was enough to reform the image for the entire New York Yankees roster, it was not enough to reform Barry Bonds's image. Sportswriters had framed Bonds in such a way that no amount of good deeds or need for national unity could alter that image.

Performance-Enhancing Drugs Redux

Though, as mentioned in Chapter 2, the discussion of steroids in MLB began after McGwire's admitted use of androstenedione (andro) during the 1998 home-run chase, it was Bonds's offensive surge that heightened the debate. Throughout the early 1990s, baseball experienced a surge in offensive numbers as, starting in 1993, "the rate of home runs per game jumped 24 percent from 1.44 to 1.78. Homers and muscles have kept growing since then."[79] A variety of explanations was offered to explain the increased offense, including, according to Tom Verducci of *Sports Illustrated*, "an unprecedented boom in the building of ballparks, many with reduced foul territory, closer outfield fences and improved lighting — each a condition that improved hitting. There's also better manufacturing of equipment (making for harder baseballs and bats), a tighter strike zone, four expansion teams and continued advances in nutrition and training."[80] Despite the fact that any of the factors Verducci presents might help explain the increased offensive numbers, it was the revelation that Mark McGwire used a performance-enhancing drug during the 1998 home-run race that caused steroids to become the preeminent factor. McGwire continued to insist that andro had no effect on his performance, stating the substance "has nothing to do with you hitting home runs. [It's about] hand-eye coordination and God-given talent."[81] It got to the point where *Chicago Tribune* columnist Rick Morrissey suggested, "From about 1993 on, it was like the Wild West of performance-enhancing drug use out there, and we have no earthly idea what was real and what wasn't, in terms of records. So we're putting a big, fat asterisk over the whole era. That asterisk would say: Records are in question because of widespread use of anabolic steroids."[82]

However, despite the information surrounding McGwire's use of performance-enhancing drugs, MLB did not institute any drug testing or prohibit the use of performance-enhancing drugs until 2003. Unfortunately, the instituted policy did not test all players, and there were no penalties for a positive test. Under the Collective Bargaining Agreement, if more than five percent of the players on any 40-man roster tested positive, MLB would move to more stringent testing. Not all players were happy with the toothless drug policy. In fact, sixteen members of the White Sox were poised to refuse to take the drug test. Because not taking the test would be labeled as "failing" the test, MLB would be forced to institute a stronger policy. When the MLBPA heard of the protest, the union pressured the players to comply with the existing drug policy.[83] In the end the planned protest became a moot point because more than five percent of the players tested in 2003 had positive results anyway, which meant every player was randomly tested during the 2004 season and there were mild disciplinary measures in place for positive results.

Most of Bonds's steroids-related troubles began in September 2003, when federal investigators seized anabolic steroids from the home of his friend and personal trainer Greg Anderson. Anderson worked for Victor Conte's Bay Area Laboratory Cooperative (BALCO), which supplied nutritional supplements and strength training advice to professional athletes. The federal government began investigating BALCO after it received reports that the company was providing illegal steroids to their customers. During the raid, authorities also seized names and drug intake schedules from Anderson's home. Bonds, former New York Yankees stars Jason Giambi and Gary Sheffield, and over thirty additional athletes were called to testify in front of a grand jury regarding their involvement with BALCO.

Despite the fact that grand jury testimony is sealed, several athletes' testimony was leaked to *San Francisco Chronicle* journalists Lance Williams and Mark Fainaru-Wada, who later published it in their book *Game of Shadows*. Since Bonds was arguably the most dominant player in the game at the time, if not ever, it was to be expected that his relationship with BALCO would raise a few eyebrows. Despite the fact that Bonds repeatedly denied taking performance-enhancing drugs and never failed a drug test, sportswriters took a guilty-until-proven innocent posture toward the slugger. Skip Bayliss of ESPN remarked,

> The feds have decided their evidence will get them no farther than the court of public opinion. And in that runaway jury of an arena, Bonds quickly was convicted and sentenced to life in baseball's Hall of Shame. Surely the feds knew exactly what they were doing. They tossed a match in a bone-dry forest of squawk-show hosts and fans dying to bury Bonds. Within hours, most people had leaped, or been yanked, to this conclusion: Bonds finally admitted he uses steroids![84]

In 1998, when Mark McGwire admitted to using andro during part of his record-breaking season, there was no discussion of placing an asterisk next to his mark. This was certainly one instance where Bonds's race worked against him. The sad fact is that even if Bonds never tests positive for any performance-enhancing drugs, there is no way for him to prove he did not take any steroids in 2001.

Stories alleging that Bonds took illegal steroids were widely published despite the continued assertions made by Anderson's lawyer that Bonds "never took anything illegal."[85] This statement did not satisfy sportswriters because steroids were completely acceptable within baseball's rules. The story became such a national firestorm that President George W. Bush took time in his 2004 State of the Union Address to admonish MLB and their weak testing policy: "Athletes play such an important role in our society, but, unfortunately, some in professional sports are not setting much of an example. The use of performance-enhancing drugs like steroids in baseball, football, and other sports is dangerous, and it sends the wrong message — that there are shortcuts to accomplishment, and that performance is more important than character."[86] As a former MLB team owner, President Bush arguably had firsthand knowledge of how common steroid abuse was among players. In fact, José Canseco, who is considered the Typhoid Mary of steroids in MLB, was a member of the Rangers when Bush owned the team; however, there is no evidence to suggest that Bush addressed the steroids issue while he owned the Rangers. At the same time, some questioned why, in the midst of the War on Terror, baseball warranted special attention. It could be argued that President Bush tried to use the steroid scandal to divert attention from the war in much the same way that the McGwire-Sosa home-run chase provided a diversion from President Clinton's sex scandal as discussed in Chapter 2.

Guilty Until Proven Innocent

Despite the denials, it seemed that every discussion regarding Bonds's achievements ended with an asterisk and a question mark. In June 2004, the *San Francisco Chronicle* obtained grand jury testimony from Olympic sprinter Tim Montgomery in which Montgomery admitted that he used an undetectable steroid supplied by Victor Conte and that Bonds was supplied with the same substance.[87] The report was published and circulated despite the fact that there is no legal way to access grand jury testimony and it contradicts Conte's own repeated public assertion that he never supplied Bonds with anything. The overall steroid issue took a dramatic turn that October when former National League MVP Ken Caminiti, who two years prior had admitted using steroids during his career, died of a drug overdose.

In December 2004, New York Yankees first baseman Jason Giambi's grand jury testimony was leaked to the *San Francisco Chronicle*. Though Bonds was not implicated in that testimony, Giambi allegedly admitted to using testosterone and human growth hormones, which he received from BALCO, in addition to steroids he took for years prior to meeting Greg Anderson. Bonds's troubles intensified shortly thereafter when the *San Francisco Chronicle* printed excerpts from his sealed grand jury testimony, in which he allegedly admitted to using cream and clear substances. Anderson told him they were flaxseed oil and a rubbing balm for arthritis,[88] but federal prosecutors believe they were designer steroids. Despite discussions surrounding the morality of taking performance-enhancing drugs, there was no discussion as to how the *San Francisco Chronicle* illegally obtained the grand jury testimony. By focusing on Bonds, sportswriters and commentators could divert attention from any unethical and illegal practices journalists employ to get a story. There are some who argued that the testimony leaks may not have been an accident. Skip Bayless of ESPN argued, "From the start, it was as clear as "the clear" that the feds were only after one man. It was obvious the Bush administration wanted to slap one big, bad face on its campaign to clean up steroid abuse in sports."[89] Was the Bush administration after Bonds because he was the most visible and dominant player in baseball? Or did Bonds's race and age effectively place a bulls-eye on his back? The racial angle would not be unheard of in the Bush family as the elder Bush had utilized the Willie Horton ads, thought by some to be racially inflammatory, during his 1988 presidential campaign. The ad highlighted the story from Massachusetts, the state of presidential challenger Michael Dukakis, of a black convicted felon who, when released on a weekend furlough, murdered a young white couple after raping the wife. Some have speculated that the racially charged ads cost Dukakis the election. However, racism would not explain why Jason Giambi's testimony was leaked, since Bonds was not implicated in Giambi's testimony to the grand jury.

Few believed that Bonds would unknowingly take steroids. One ESPN writer urged his readers, "Don't believe Barry Bonds, who says he didn't know what he was taking. Don't believe Jason Giambi, at least not completely, because he says he didn't think the stuff worked all that well. (Bonds, by the way, is a much better liar than Giambi. Bonds looked people square in the face and lied, even after his grand jury testimony.)"[90] What got lost in the ensuing discussion was the fact that Bonds allegedly admitted to unknowingly using what may have been a performance-enhancing drug during the *2003* season, not the 2001 season when he broke the single-season home-run record. Despite the gap, sportswriters still discussed whether or not Bonds's record should be preceded by an asterisk.

As mentioned earlier, investigating Bonds's link to BALCO was certainly fair game. However, other players who were linked to BALCO, specifically Giambi and Gary Sheffield, both of whom played for the revered New York

Yankees, seem to have earned a free pass despite some suspicious activity during the 2004 season. The free pass was issued in that year when Giambi arrived at spring training visibly thinner and proceeded to miss half of the season due to unspecified health reasons.[91] Those unspecified health reasons were later revealed to be an intestinal parasite and a benign pituitary tumor, the former being a known side effect of steroid use. With Giambi's obvious physical change, there was some speculation, albeit muted, that the weight loss and physical ailments were due to steroid abuse. Bonds, whose physical appearance and professional aptitude remained the same, continued to be the poster child for suspected steroid abuse. McGwire and Giambi benefited from the differential treatment their white privilege afforded them where steroid allegations were concerned.

As mentioned in the introduction and discussed again in Chapters 2 and 4, Peggy McIntosh defined white privilege as "an invisible package of unearned assets which I can count on cashing in each day, but about which I was 'meant' to remain oblivious."[92] Granted, the fact that Giambi's testimony was leaked is one instance when white privilege did not work to his advantage. However, the different treatment Bonds and Giambi received after their testimony was leaked could be attributed to white privilege. Though not present in McIntosh's original list of white privileges, has the assumption of innocence until proven guilty moved from constitutional right to white privilege? Is it possible that Giambi's whiteness protected him from the hostility leveled at Bonds? Is the very ability to pronounce guilt or innocence itself an aspect of white privilege, as a large number of sports reporters are white, while a substantial portion of athletes are black and Latin? To further these questions, McIntosh states later in her essay, "Whiteness protected me from many kinds of hostility, distress, and violence which I was being subtly trained to visit in turn on people of color."[93] Are sportswriters imposing the very hostility and violence they are protected from because of their racial identity upon Barry Bonds? It is telling that even after MLB instituted more stringent drug testing, the skepticism remained.

It got to a point during the 2004 season that when Bonds was randomly tested for steroids he announced it to the media and stated the test would clear his name. ESPN's Tony Kornheiser responded to Bonds's assertion by saying, "I think a lot of people think that Barry Bonds *used* steroids. Fewer people think he *uses* steroids."[94] Despite his continued exceptional performance, which included breaking the single-season walk record again and becoming only the third member of the 700-home-run club, Bonds still seemed to be guilty until proven innocent in the eyes of the sports media. As Kornheiser implies, even if Bonds's tests are negative, there is no way for him to prove he did not take performance-enhancing drugs during the 2001 season.

Level Playing Field?

When Bonds's grand jury testimony was leaked, the skepticism intensified. The firestorm surrounding the revelation was more contained than one would expect, arguably because more racially incendiary sports stories were breaking at the time. In the weeks preceding Bonds's revelation, the sports world was embroiled in two major controversies, both of which had race at the center. The first involved a brawl between players (who were predominantly black) and fans (who were predominantly white) during a Detroit Pistons–Indiana Pacers game. The second involved the premature firing of Notre Dame's first black head football coach, Tyrone Willingham, before his contract had expired. Despite Willingham's 21–15 record, this was the first time in the school's history that a coach was not allowed to finish out his contract. Given what was going on in the sports world and MLB's own racial history, the context within which sportswriters framed the steroids discussion was questionable.

On the December 5, 2004, edition of ESPN's *The Sports Reporters*, John Saunders, Mitch Albom, Mike Lupica, and William C. Rhoden discussed the use of steroids by Bonds and Giambi in terms of violating the ethos of fair play and the notion of a level playing field. The *Detroit Free Press*'s Mitch Albom made the analogy of one player having a rocket pack on his back while the other players merely relied on their two feet to run from base to base.[95] What the writers failed to recognize was that professional baseball in the United States has never existed on a level playing field. This history should not be used to condone the use of performance-enhancing drugs; however, it must be pointed out that the use of the level playing field argument to condemn steroid use is inherently flawed. For over fifty years MLB effectively barred U.S.–born and non–U.S. born black players from the league. It is only in the last few years that Asian players have further integrated the majors. It was during this segregated time that Babe Ruth set his offensive records; however, sportswriters do not question whether Ruth would have hit 60 home runs during a single season or 714 career homers if he had had to face the likes of Satchel Paige or Willie Foster on a regular basis.

At the same time, the "World Series" was played for several decades before MLB played a single game outside the United States. The financial obstacles one faces in terms of equipment and facilities can impede players from lower socioeconomic classes from participating and competing effectively in the sport. And, to date, with the exception of the All-American Girls Baseball League and the Negro Leagues, no women can be seen on a major league roster. In fact, the entire discussion surrounding home-run records is evidence of baseball's exclusionary history. What gets lost in the discussions surrounding the single-season home-run record is the distinct possibility that neither Bonds, McGwire, Maris, nor Ruth may in fact hold that record. There is evidence to suggest that Negro League star Josh Gibson hit 84 homers as a member of the Pittsburgh Crawfords in 1936.[96] Because the record cannot be concretely confirmed, as few mainstream white newspapers followed Negro League games, Gibson's accomplishment is rarely mentioned in the record books. The all-time home-run record also highlights the game's exclusionary history. Baseball statisticians know that Sadaharu Oh hit 868 career home runs in the Nippon Professional Baseball League in Japan, which dwarfs the MLB record.[97] In essence, baseball has never operated on a level playing field as the game and its record books have historically excluded more people than they have included. The controlling image of baseball's alleged level playing field allows sportswriters and fans to ignore the sport's historical and contemporary inequalities and allows those same sportswriters to frame Bonds as a cheater despite a lack of credible evidence (and an effective drug policy).

While condemning Bonds's alleged use of what may have been performance-enhancing drugs and questioning the validity of his testimony, sportswriters continued to discuss the veracity of Bonds's offensive records. As previously mentioned, Bonds allegedly admitted to unknowingly using what may have been performance-enhancing drugs during the 2003 season, two years after breaking the single-season home-run record. Despite the time difference, there were some who asked whether Bonds's record should be accompanied by an asterisk, though former ESPN columnist Ralph Wiley asserts, "It's not like you can all of a sudden sneak up and have 700 home runs in the big leagues. There is nothing, absolutely nothing on this green earth that you can eat, drink, sniff, inject or rub on yourself that can make you hit 700 home runs in the Show. That product exists only in our collective imagination."[98] In 1998, when Mark McGwire admitted to using andro during part of his record-breaking season, there was no discussion of placing an asterisk next to his mark. Is it possible that this is an instance where Bonds's race worked against him? Given the fact that McGwire was thirty-five when he broke the record, age bias may not enter the discussion at this point. However, as with the previous discussion comparing Bonds to Roger Clemens and Randy Johnson, Bonds would experience age bias differently from McGwire because of the added burden of race. In addition, the controlling images surrounding Bonds effectively guaranteed that he would not receive the benefit of the doubt where asterisks were concerned, unlike McGwire.

Bonds's Continued Dominance

After Barry Bonds's record-breaking 2001 season it seemed inconceivable to many that he would continue to perform at such a high level because he was still getting older. Though Bonds did not have another 70 home-run season, it was arguably due less to a lack of ability than to a lack of hittable pitches. In 2002 Bonds tallied 198 walks, breaking the single-season walk record he had established the year before. In 2004 when MLB instituted a new, albeit toothless, steroid testing policy, many expected Bonds's performance to drop even further. On the contrary, though his home runs remained the same, Bonds's other offensive numbers in many instances surpassed his 2001 totals.

Bonds once again broke the single-season walk record with an astonishing 232 BB. The frequency with which Bonds was walked caused San Francisco fans to play "The Chicken Dance" whenever opposing teams would not pitch to him, especially after Bonds was once intentionally walked while the bases were loaded. While most interpret walking a player as high praise, some see the practice as more of an insult. Sports economist Andrew Zimbalist noted, "It was unlikely that Barry Bonds would break his new record of seventy-three home runs because pitchers had taken to walking him with such frequency that if one didn't know better one might suspect he were a 5th Avenue poodle."[99] Howie Evans of the *New York Amsterdam News* hypothesized that the increased number of walks was not designed to prevent Bonds from potentially hitting a game-winning home run but to "keep Bonds from breaking the [all-time home-run] record. And if it means making him the poster boy for BALCO [Bay Area Laboratory Cooperative], or sending his Black butt directly to first base without an opportunity to swing the bat, then the game plan is working, just as he walks his way to the Hall of Fame to the detriment of baseball and the fans who want to see him swinging for the record without a biased agenda."[100] Granted, since the goal of any team is to win, it is understandable for an opposing team to walk Bonds. Few pitchers want to be featured on *SportsCenter* for giving up a home run to Bonds. On the other hand, when McGwire and Sosa were chasing home-run history, they received 162 and 73 walks respectively — markedly fewer than Bonds's 232.

At the same time, there is another consideration: baseball's entertainment value. San Francisco fans were not the only ones upset at the number of walks Bonds received. In fact, fans at ballparks across the country began the practice of booing their own pitchers when they walked Bonds. This prompted sportswriters to ponder the ethics of continuously walking Bonds, a practice that ESPN's Stephen A. Smith vehemently argued against on *Pardon the Interruption*:

> With the regular season about a month from expiration, the Colorado Rockies are 20 games below .500, 21 games out of first place, invisible in the post season picture, already planning their fall and winter vacations, yet here they are, walking Barry Bonds three times yesterday, two intentionally, obviously showing no interest what-

so-ever in entertaining fans with some semblance of suspense. I'm a New York Yankees fan [...] and I went to Yankee Stadium, got stuck in traffic, paid thirty dollars for parking to see Bonds get walked. It is frustrating [and] that is why baseball suffers. You come to the park to see Barry.[101]

As Smith points out, continuously walking Bonds cheated fans who paid money to see Bonds jog around the bases after hitting a home run, not walk to first after being given a free pass. The 232 BB, 120 of which were intentional, contributed to Bonds's .609 OBP, which, of course, broke the existing MLB record.

In addition to the increased statistical records, Bonds made three more All-Star appearances after 2001, bringing his total to thirteen. Finally, Bonds was voted MVP three more times for a career total of seven. He became the only player in history to win four consecutive MVP Awards — no other player has ever won more than three total. This feat prompted the normally critical Tom Verducci to ponder, "Someday they'll name the award after him. Would next week be too soon?"[102] Though many were in awe of Bonds's continued statistical dominance, the reverence was tempered by steroid allegations.

Here We Go Again

It was inevitable — though not entirely welcomed. As long as Barry Bonds remained healthy and pitchers threw pitches in the general vicinity of the strike zone, Bonds would break Hank Aaron's all-time home-run record. There were a few other predictable certainties to the 2007 season: despite the fact that Bonds had not failed a drug test, the issue of performance-enhancing drugs would dominate the discussion; the media response to Bonds's breaking the record would range from benign indifference to outright hostility; and race would remain just below the surface of the discussion but rarely be talked about. Wisdom would dictate that in a sport that is obsessed with statistics, a player who holds the record for career home runs, single-season home runs, career walks, single-season walks, single-season on-base percentage, and single-season slugging percentage, in addition to winning seven Most Valuable Player awards and eight Gold Gloves, would be praised in every ballpark in the nation. Instead, Bonds was framed as, and by extension viewed as, a pariah. Merely mentioning the slugger's name engendered the type of passion and hostility usually reserved for corrupt politicians or terrorists.

The year 2007 was a banner year for race in sport — in both good and bad ways. The year began on a hopeful note when the Chicago Bears' Lovie Smith and the Indianapolis Colts' Tony Dungy became the first African American head coaches in the National Football League to reach the Super Bowl.[103]

Unfortunately it only took two months for the glow of Smith and Dungy's accomplishment to fade. On April 3, 2007, while the Rutgers women's basketball team was playing its first championship title game, radio talk show host Don Imus and his producer Bernard McGuirk referred to the team as "nappy-headed hos."[104] Less than two weeks later, MLB celebrated the 60th anniversary of Jackie Robinson's first regular-season game with the Brooklyn Dodgers. Many players, coaches, and managers opted to wear the number 42, including the entire Houston Astros team, which did not have any U.S.–born black players on its roster.[105] MLB began the anniversary season by holding an inaugural Civil Rights Game between the Cardinals and Cleveland, the first American League team to sign a U.S.–born black player in the 20th century. Despite the franchise's history, the inclusion of the Cleveland Indians, whose name and mascot are an affront to many people of color, was viewed by some as hypocritical and disingenuous in terms of honoring civil rights. The disturbing saga surrounding Atlanta Falcons quarterback Michael Vick's involvement in dog fighting produced its own racial commentary. Lastly, Detroit Tigers DH Gary Sheffield created quite a stir when he not only claimed that the increasing number of Latin players had to do with their pliability, but also charged Yankees manager Joe Torre with racial bias against black players. Though sport often frames itself as a bastion of fair play and equality, according to ESPN. com columnist Pat Forde, "You'd have to go straight ostrich to escape the current crossfire over race, race relations, racial dynamics and racial viewpoints in sports."[106]

When the 2007 season began, Barry Bonds was second on the MLB career home-run list with 734 and was a mere stone's throw away from Henry Aaron's hallowed 755. The fact that Bonds pushed Babe Ruth to third on that list was disturbing to many sportswriters, and those sentiments not only produced their own racialized commentary but fanned the flames of steroid discussion. After three years of trying, in July 2006 a grand jury failed to indict Bonds on charges of perjury, tax evasion, or any steroid-related matter. Jason Whitlock of the *Kansas City Star* made an intentional Freudian slip when he remarked, "Federal persecutors, oh, I mean federal prosecutors announced today that they will continue their grand jury witch hunt to put Bonds in jail for passing Babe Ruth on the home-run chart."[107] The zeal with which the authorities pursued Bonds is not surprising; as Patricia Hill Collins points out, "Since 1980, whatever measures are used — rates of arrest, conviction, jail time, parole, or types of crime — African American men are more likely than White American men to encounter the criminal justice system."[108] This means that despite the fact that white sluggers like Mark McGwire and Jason Giambi and white pitchers like Grimsley admitted using performance-enhancing drugs during their careers, authorities would focus solely on a black Barry Bonds.

Though many bemoaned Bonds's passing of Ruth and denounced the slugger's "tainted" record, the fact that Ruth's record is tainted by his having played during the Jim Crow era was rarely mentioned.

Lies, Damn Lies, and Statistics

Though race was hardly mentioned by mainstream reporters as an explanation for the ways Bonds was framed, the aforementioned incidents brought race to the forefront in 2007. Fan reaction to Bonds's feats are usually measured by the boos leveled at the slugger in every National League ballpark that wasn't in San Francisco; and in May 2007 sports fans chimed in on Bonds's quest. An ESPN/ABC poll found that 37 percent of fans wanted Bonds to break the record and 73 percent of fans believed that Bonds used steroids.[109] But those statistics only tell part of the story. The poll also found a drastic difference in the responses along racial lines: 74 percent of black fans wanted Bonds to break the record, only 37 percent believed that Bonds used steroids, and black fans were nearly twice as likely as white fans (46 percent vs. 25 percent) to believe that Bonds was being treated unfairly.[110] When asked for the reasons behind Bonds's treatment, 41 percent of black fans blamed steroids and 25 percent blamed race, while "virtually none" of the white fans attributed Bonds's treatment to race.[111]

Methodologically the poll is problematic because it perpetuates the myth that race in the United States is simply a black/white issue by not including Latina/o, Asian American, or Native American fans as part of the sample. However, in all honesty, no one should have been surprised that black fans are more likely than white fans to support Bonds. What was surprising was the fact that over one third of the total respondents actually *wanted* Bonds to break the record, which raises the question of whether or not sportswriters and commentators were doing fans a disservice by framing Bonds in such a negative manner. Equally startling was the fact that *none* of the white respondents who stated that Bonds had been treated unfairly believed that race had anything to do it. ESPN's Jayson Stark responded to the poll results when he wrote, "For nearly all white fans who think Bonds has been treated unfairly to say race has nothing to do with it is stunning. We say to those fans: You're kidding yourselves if that's what you truly think."[112] Author Dave Zirin points out, "To argue that race has nothing to do with the saga of Barry Bonds is to embrace ignorance frightening in its Rocker-esque grandiosity."[113] As previously noted, the poll results were not that much of a surprise — it simply provided the most recent evidence that blacks and whites often view the world differently.

At the same time, the inability or unwillingness of white fans to even entertain the possibility that race could have anything to do with the way Bonds had been framed highlights Kimberlé Crenshaw's notion that there is a "deep dissonance between conventions built on the fantasy that racism is a thing of the past or the preserve of the crazies, and the reality that racist influences are as enduring as Old Glory."[114] People who believe that racism no longer exists in the United States or who define racism in terms of the most egregious acts (e.g., racial death threats against Henry Aaron) would have no reason to suspect that race affected how Bonds was framed. On the other hand, the very notion of unconscious racism supposes that people will not recognize the role race plays in their everyday lives. It stands to reason that unconscious racial attitudes influence the ways in which sportswriters discuss sports issues involving race or ethnicity generally, and the ways Bonds's home-run chase had been framed more specifically. When MLB began the reintegration process in the 1940s and sportswriters began paying attention to athletes of color, racist attitudes were the norm and could be expressed freely. Since overt racism is supposedly no longer tolerated, the negative attitudes created by the shared racist history will find an outlet; and in this case, the ways in which Bonds's pursuit of Aaron's record was framed provided such an outlet.

Because this type of racism is unconscious, most will not even recognize it. ESPN.com's Gene Wojciechowski wrote, "While I hate to disappoint the racial-conspiracy theorists, this isn't about his being an African-American. If this were the very freckled and very white Mark McGwire in Bonds's cleats, I'd be saying the very same thing: that you can't celebrate the accomplishments of someone who allegedly used illegal performance enhancers."[115] One only has to go back to the 1998 home-run chase to see that McGwire's public acknowledgment that he used andro did little to damper sportswriters' enthusiasm. *The Sporting News*'s Steve Marantz and Michael Knisley were explicit about their support of McGwire when they wrote:

> Not that [McGwire's] perfect. His use of the over-the-counter supplement, androstenedione, makes us wonder about his judgment. A substance incompletely researched, banned from the NFL, NCAA and Olympics, barred from the shelves of major dietary supplement chains, is dubious. We question that blind spot, yet perversely, find him more appealing because of it, in the way Cindy Crawford's mole accents her beauty.[116]

Sportswriters cannot claim ignorance of McGwire's andro usage. But even with McGwire's legal yet potentially unethical use of performance-enhancing drugs, the slugger was revered by fans and journalists alike. Was McGwire's acceptance because andro was legal, because everyone within the baseball establishment wanted the sport to recover following the 1994 strike, because McGwire is white, or some combination of the three? To be fair, McGwire is certainly being punished now for using performance-enhancing drugs by being denied entry into the Hall of Fame during his first few years of eligibility. Wojciechowski is correct to a certain extent: as with any other issue, the subject of what role race plays in the Bonds story does not have a simple answer. On the other hand, framing those who suggest that race could play a role in the Bonds as "racial conspiracy theorists" is telling and highlights the fact that many sportswriters, like fans, are reluctant to at least acknowledge the *possibility* that race played a role in how Bonds was framed and perceived.

I'm the King of the World

As mentioned earlier, Bonds certainly could not be described as having a warm and fuzzy persona. To say that Bonds's relationship with sportswriters was acrimonious would be kind. Robert Miles of *ESPN The Magazine* remarked, "Your image rivals Mel Gibson's post–DUI rant. You're in a worse spot than a couch-jumping Tom Cruise or a crotch-flashing Britney Spears. Thing is, people don't think you're crazy, they think you're just mean."[117] Bob Hertzel of *The Sporting News* claimed "Bonds is smog.... Bonds is a sneer."[118] Even people outside of sports writing circles have commented on Bonds's persona. In the *Chronicle of Higher Education,* Warren Goldstein commented that Bonds "appears to be a genuinely unpleasant human being, who reserves special hostility for the reporters charged with covering his exploits."[119] Todd Boyd, professor of critical studies at the University of Southern California wrote on ESPN.com:

> There has long been a notion among certain members of the African-American community that once a successful black person manages to make it to the top of his respective field, there is a vested interest among other people outside of the community to see this person fall. Barry Bonds is only the most recent example of such a notion. The vehemence with which these outside forces seem aligned in their interest to go after Bonds has helped to fuel such thinking.[120]

Regardless of whether anyone actually wanted to see Bonds break the record and irrespective of whether people believed he deserved the record, on August 5, 2007, Bonds tied Aaron's mark. Commissioner Bud Selig was in PETCO Park in San Diego, during the game and his reaction was puzzling. As the ball flew out of the park, Bonds was greeted with more cheers than boos; however, Selig had to be prodded to his feet by Rangers owner Tom Hicks. Once Selig rose to his feet, he promptly placed his hands in his pockets and looked on with disgust. Reports indicated that Selig did not even speak to Bonds personally when the slugger tied the record, so it was hardly surprising that he was not in attendance when Bonds broke the record.[121]

On August 7, 2007, when Bonds came up to bat in the bottom of the fifth inning, he was given an enthusiastic standing ovation by the hometown fans. Bonds was already 2 for 2, having doubled, singled, and driven in two of the Giants' four runs in the tied game. Flashbulbs erupted every time Bonds swung the bat, and once the count moved to 3–2, the crowd chanted, "Barry, Barry...." The chanting must have helped, as Bonds sent the next pitch over the right field wall for number 756. Bonds was met at home plate by his son while an emotional Bonds pointed in the air as a tribute to his late father Bobby. The entire stadium erupted in cheers as Bonds hugged his teammates and his family and waved to the crowd. After a taped message from Henry Aaron was played on the scoreboard, Bonds thanked the fans, his teammates, his family, the opposing team, and he broke into tears as he thanked his father.

Jim Reeves from the *Fort Worth Star-Telegram* arguably had the most extreme reaction when he wrote, "It is now officially a national day of mourning. Black bunting should hang from every ballpark in America. A riderless black horse, its saddle empty, its stirrups filled by a pair of Hank Aaron's cleats turned backward, should be led around every warning track tonight. The greatest record in sports has fallen to a liar and a cheat."[122] On his ESPN television program, Jim Rome began his show by saying "congrats on the asterisk,"[123] and Gene Wojciechowski wrote on ESPN.com, "Bonds and his career numbers are a fraud," said the slugger was "as embraceable as a cactus," and called the entire evening "a make-believe piece of baseball drama."[124] Mike Lupica proclaimed on ESPN's *The Sports Reporters* that in light of Bonds's accomplishment, Joe DiMaggio's 56-game hit streak was now the greatest record in sports.[125] Lupica failed to remember or neglected to mention that DiMaggio's streak is tainted by the fact that it was accomplished in 1941, which places it firmly within baseball's Jim Crow era. Dave Zirin observed the visceral reaction to Bonds's and wrote, "Nothing is off-limits. I've seen it all: comparing [Bonds] to O.J. Simpson? Sure. Comparing him to a child molester? Sure. Call for a lynching? These are the words of John Seibel on ESPN radio: 'If [Bonds used steroids], hang him. Now I'm not saying hang him. I'm saying hang him from a tree. I'm not saying strap him to a gurney and inject poison in his veins.'"[126]

The response to Bonds's accomplishment was not surprising despite the fact that Bonds never tested positive for performance-enhancing drugs and never admitted to knowingly taking steroids. Many sportswriters point to Lance Williams and Mark Fainaru-Wada's *Game of Shadows* as gospel for the steroid era though the authors included sealed grand jury testimony in their work. Despite discussions surrounding the morality of athletes' taking performance-enhancing drugs, there was no discussion surrounding the ethics of using illegally obtained evidence.

Because an overwhelming majority of sportswriters and sports reporters are white, 90 percent and 87.5 percent respectively, while players of color make up approximately 40.5 percent of MLB's rosters, the selective reporting illustrates George Lipsitz's concept of the possessive investment in whiteness.[127] Lipsitz argues that "racial injuries [...] originate from the indirect, inferential, institutional, and systemic skewing of opportunities and life chances along racial lines. Whiteness is the most subsidized identity in our society; the most powerful identity politics are those that protect the value of whiteness. White advantages come from favoritism, not fitness, fortitude, or family formations."[128] By focusing on Bonds, sportswriters diverted attention from any unethical or illegal practices their fellow journalists employed to get the story. This diversion perpetuates a racial system where mostly white sportswriters can frame issues about athletes, the majority of whom are men of color, without equitable accountability.

Playing While Black

The issue of race and records did not formally enter into the mainstream discussion until a February 22, 2005, press conference in which Bonds "played the race card" and stated, "Babe Ruth ain't black either. I'm black ... we go through a little bit more."[129] Though the majority of sportswriters framed Bonds's comment as simply deflecting attention away from steroids, ESPN's *Outside the Lines* discussed the matter with White Sox General Manager Ken Williams and writer Howard Bryant, the latter of whom remarked that Bonds

> is the third generation descendant of the forefathers of integrated baseball. I mean the stories that you and I had learned in the history books he learned at his dinner table from his father, from Willie Mays, Jackie Robinson, and Hank Aaron and I think that when you watch him play he's playing to erase a lot of slights. He's playing to erase the slights that his father went through, he's playing to erase the double standards that Willie Mays and these great, great superstars had to endure, and let's face it, when I, one of the things that I took from listening to him at that press conference was when he was talking about asterisks and steroids and cheating and all these other things I heard him say, "Now wait a second. Babe Ruth and the rest of these stars had to play 60 years not playing against black competition or Latinos." So I mean, why wouldn't you put an asterisk on that? I mean, how unfair is that? I saw a guy who was very very driven by what he considers to be a historical inaccuracy.[130]

Bryant places Bonds's thought process squarely within the boundaries of his family's history and MLB's historical racial dynamics.

While mainstream white sportswriters did not raise the issue of race, black newspapers had been discussing the issue for quite some time. In 2003,

Marcus Henry of the *New York Amsterdam News* wrote, "There are some in the media who choose to emphasize his sometimes surly attitude as opposed to his skill as a baseball player. But that shouldn't be a shock when one considers how much different black and white athletes are treated in the media."[131]

Marvin Wamble wrote in a 2005 *New Pittsburgh Courier* article that Bonds "had to be respected because of his skill, but sports reporters in general do not like athletes who display a hint of arrogance. This dislike is especially evident for African-American millionaire athletes who refuse to bow down to the Holy Pen."[132] In a 2006 piece published in the *Los Angeles Sentinel*, Maulana Karenga wrote:

> Certainly, at the heart of the hatred and hostility directed toward Barry Bonds now and Hank Aaron earlier are the issues of race and racism, summed up in [W.E.B.] DuBois' cogent and compelling category, "unforgivable Blackness." Indeed, in a racist society, being Black in itself is unforgivable; being Black and excellent is intolerable, and being Black, excellent and defiant is outrageous. Hank Aaron is the first two; Barry Bonds is [...] all three.[133]

Earl Ofari Hutchinson, writing for the *Chicago Defender* in 2007, argued, "Bonds has run neck in neck [*sic*] with O.J. Simpson as the man much of the public loves to loathe for two tormenting reasons. One is race, and the other is Bonds. The two are not inseparable. A big, rich, famous, surly, blunt-talking Black superstar who routinely thumbs his nose at the media sets off all kind of bells and whishes [*sic*] in the public mind."[134] Clearly the black press saw a racial component to the ways in which Bonds was being framed long before his accomplishments approached those of Aaron or Ruth, calling into question whether Bonds's "playing of the race card" was either new or completely unheard of.

Despite the denials and Bonds's continued dominance even after a steroid testing policy was in place, it seemed that every discussion regarding Bonds's achievements ended with an asterisk and a question mark, especially when he returned to full form in 2006 after an injury-prone 2005. Soon it became clear what lengths sportswriters and federal investigators would go to in order to get Bonds. In June, federal prosecutors attempted to pressure Diamondbacks pitcher Jason Grimsley to wear a wire in an effort to gain incriminating evidence against Bonds.[135] This move came despite the fact that Grimsley and Bonds had never been teammates, and, according to Grimsley, he did not know Bonds very well.[136] Until federal agents searched Grimsley's home, forcing him to admit that he used performance-enhancing drugs, most of the steroid discussion in baseball centered around batters rather than pitchers. The singular focus on batters certainly has racial connotations since the vast majority of U.S.–born black baseball players are position players, while the number of U.S.–born black pitchers hovers in the single digits.

There's No Need to Fear: A-Rod Is Here

One person who unexpectedly benefited from the ways in which Bonds's record-breaking has been framed is Yankee third baseman Alex Rodríguez. On the August 5, 2007 edition of *The Sports Reporters,* John Saunders, Michael Kay, William C. Rhoden, and Mitch Albom contemplated the fact that Bonds tied Aaron's record. Mitch Albom argued, "The saddest part is on the same day that Bonds ties this record, A-Rod hits his 500th and half the country is going 'hit 'em faster A-Rod, hit 'em faster.'" Rhoden replied, "And the strange thing is that Bonds has turned a guy like A-Rod into a hero."[137]

The embracing of A-Rod's quest for baseball immortality brings up an important point. As previously mentioned, there are those sportswriters who argue that Bonds's perceived link to performance-enhancing drugs is the only reason why his accomplishment is being framed as tarnished. If that is the case, then it stands to reason that A-Rod's record should be viewed as tainted as well. Atlanta third baseman Chipper Jones expressed a similar sentiment when he noted, "All of us who did something great in this era are in effect suspects."[138] If we define the steroid era as being from the 1980s through 2005, then any and all offensive and defensive numbers gained during that era are suspect, including Roger Clemens's and Greg Maddux's wins, Craig Biggio's hits, and home runs from a variety of players including Sammy Sosa, Ken Griffey, Frank Thomas, Jim Thome, and Alex Rodríguez. Sportswriters who frame Bonds's record as tainted are rather disingenuous in their pleas for A-Rod to break the record and hypocritical for not calling attention to other "tainted" records. In order for the home-run record to be framed as "pure," it would take the heroics of someone who matriculated into the majors after steroid testing was implemented — for instance, the Brewers' Prince Fielder or the Phillies' Ryan Howard, though the latter began his career in 2004.

Parting Shots

Pat Conroy reminds us that "baseball fans love numbers."[139] There are volumes of books dedicated to the study of baseball statistics that fans use to compare and contrast their favorite players both past and present. By all statistical measures, Barry Bonds is one of the best, if not the best offensive player in the history of the game. The problem Bonds encounters is that despite the numbers, some sportswriters refuse to give him some dap. Barry Bonds is a complex human being and the issues that surround his all-time home-run record are complicated. There are a myriad of different reasons why some sportswriters and fans have not embraced Bonds and the record. Perceptions about steroids, the impact of age on performance, race, and the fact that Bonds has never seemed to care about what people thought of him, influence the way fans and sportswriters think, talk, and write about Barry Bonds. No one is going to be able to point to one factor and say that is the single reason why sportswriters frame Bonds in the ways they do.

However, sportswriters and fans should be willing to admit the possibility that race plays a part in how athletes are perceived. Race permeates every aspect of United States history, institutions, politics, economy, and culture. Regardless of whether people choose to admit it, race influences our perceptions and seeps into sports culture as well. By framing Bonds as a surly, doping curmudgeon, sportswriters obscured the role that the intersection of race and age play in how some media representatives discussed Bonds's accomplishments. Characterizing Bonds in this manner also guaranteed that "no matter how many home runs he hits, if he hits 780, [Bonds is] never going to be recognized as the greatest home-run hitter in the game. He may not like that, it may not be fair, but that's the reality."[140] The reality is that because Bonds does not have the warm and fuzzy personality sportswriters seem to require from black athletes, the steroid clouds that follow Bonds, despite the fact that he has never failed a drug test, and the racial smog which permeates everyone's actions and perceptions, Bonds will never be given the professional respect his on-field performance deserved. As Ralph Wiley pointed out, "What Barry Bonds has done is show great merit in the game. Unfortunately when you are what is called 'black,' that can be inconvenient; often when you show merit, the rules on merit are changed to make them more obtuse."[141]

Despite how sportswriters framed Bonds, in 2013, when he is eligible for the Hall of Fame, there will undoubtedly be sportswriters who hold his surliness against him. Others will finally give him the dap he deserves as they remember that "Bonds didn't just have a brush with greatness, he knocked down the door, plopped down on the sofa and put his feet up."[142]

6

It's the End of the World as We Know It: Race and Forgiveness in the Era of Performance-Enhancing Drugs

"Baseball will survive this latest crisis, just as it survived the Black Sox scandal, racial discrimination, labor strife, a canceled World Series, mushroom cloud-sized salaries and Pete Rose's lies.... Somehow baseball keeps shooting itself in the foot, but never seems to run out of toes. It's the Wile E. Coyote of sports; it prospers in spite of itself."— Gene Wojciechowski[1]

"Leak the names that leaked the names. [...] People are obviously breaking the law acquiring those names, and it's not the agreement the federal government had with Major League Baseball. Those names were court-sealed. For crying out loud, you can't release them, period." Jimmy Golen[2]

Steroids and other performance-enhancing drugs have a public and storied history in Major League Baseball (MLB). Arguably, baseball's steroids era publicly began in 1998 with the discovery of Mark McGwire's androstenedione (andro) use and ended in 2005 when MLB instituted what many believed to be a strong steroid policy. During the steroids era, there have been clouds of suspicion, congressional hearings, prolonged investigations, one tragic death, and a flurry of denials and semi-apologies. While baseball became "a pharmacological trade show,"[3] and performance-enhancing drugs became so prevalent that "even pitchers and wispy outfielders are juicing up — and talking openly among themselves about it,"[4] sportswriters largely ignored the issue. After 2003, when Barry Bonds, Jason Giambi and Gary Sheffield were called to testify about their connection to the Bay Area Laboratory Cooperative (BALCO), sportswriters changed their approach from indifference to outrage, and in some cases, as time went on, back to indifference.

The previous chapter on Barry Bonds discussed how race, among other factors, influenced how sportswriters reviewed the slugger's alleged steroid use.

117

Unfortunately, Bonds's acrimonious relationship with media representatives has obscured the racial aspect of how he is perceived. Some sportswriters point to performance-enhancing drugs as the sole reason for Bonds's treatment; however, alleged steroid usage did not permanently tarnish Jason Giambi's image. In theory, sportswriters could also point to a combination of surliness and performance-enhancing drugs to explain Bonds's treatment, but at the same time, these two factors only heightened Mark McGwire's image during the 1998 home-run chase. It could also be said that neither Giambi nor McGwire was as talented as Bonds and the latter's excellence heightened the scrutiny. Unfortunately there would be no way to test that theory because there were no other big-name players associated with performance-enhancing drugs to provide a comparison. Since Bonds's exile from professional baseball at the end of the 2007 season, a number of potential future Hall of Fame players have been associated with or "admitted" to using steroids, including Roger Clemens, Andy Pettitte, Manny Ramírez, David Ortiz, and Alex Rodríguez. Media representatives have responded to these steroid allegations with disbelief, anger, and indifference. With such a range in responses, baseball fans wonder: what accounts for the different ways suspected steroid users have been treated by sportswriters? Does race and/or ethnicity help explain the different responses?

The New Face of Steroids?

In 2006, after the book *Game of Shadows* was released, Commissioner Bud Selig asked former Maine Senator George Mitchell to conduct an investigation into steroid use in MLB. Upon hearing about Mitchell's involvement, many suspected that the investigation was simply a ploy for MLB "to formally distance itself from Bonds's accomplishments."[5] After twenty months and an undisclosed amount of money, Mitchell issued his report, which began with the assertion:

> For more than a decade there has been widespread illegal use of anabolic steroids and other performance enhancing substances by players in Major League Baseball, in violation of federal law and baseball policy. Club officials routinely have discussed the possibility of such substance use when evaluating players. Those who have illegally used these substances range from players whose major league careers were brief to potential members of the Baseball Hall of Fame. They include both pitchers and position players, and their backgrounds are as diverse as those of all major league players.[6]

Instead of hanging Bonds out to dry by himself, like many suspected the Mitchell Report would, Mitchell implicated almost everyone within MLB from the top down. In addition, the report gave Bonds a new accused steroid-user friend, equal in stature and curmudgeonly behavior: Roger Clemens.

Given the similarities between Clemens and Bonds, it stands to reason that sportswriters would treat the two superstars in a similar fashion. Fortunately or unfortunately, depending on the point of view, that was not the case. In terms of talent, if Barry Bonds is considered the best batter of his generation, then Roger Clemens is certainly its best pitcher. Clemens boasts seven Cy Young Awards, is eighth on the all-time wins list, and ranks second in career strikeouts. If Bonds has been framed as being less than civil towards sportswriters, teammates, and fans, then it would not be an exaggeration to say that Clemens is not an Eagle Scout either.

Because of a plea agreement with federal authorities, Clemens's trainer Brian McNamee cooperated with Mitchell's investigation. According to McNamee, he "injected Clemens approximately four times in the buttocks over a several-week period with needles [containing Winstrol] that Clemens provided."[7] McNamee claimed that in 2000, he injected Clemens multiple times with testosterone and human growth hormones; and in 2001, he injected Clemens with "Sustanon or Deca-Durabolin on four to five occasions at Clemens's apartment."[8] McNamee provided George Mitchell with firsthand accounts of Clemens's steroid use from 1998 through 2001. Since Clemens is equal to Bonds in terms of talent, age, and surliness, if race is not a factor in how Bonds has been framed, then Clemens should receive similar treatment from sportswriters.

When Mitchell's report was released and fans everywhere learned that Clemens's name was included, ESPN commentators and sportswriters afforded Clemens a privilege that was not given to Bonds: the benefit of the doubt. As mentioned in the discussion of Mark McGwire, the idea of innocent-until-proven-guilty was a form of white privilege handed out by sportswriters to McGwire, and now Clemens, but denied to the likes of Barry Bonds. In the case of Clemens, the innocent-until-proven-guilty privilege manifested itself with an extensive discussion regarding evidence in terms of how it is collected and whether or not it could be corroborated. Mitchell did not have any subpoena powers and could not compel any players, past or present, to cooperate with the investigation. During the *SportsCenter* special immediately following Mitchell's press conference, Karl Ravech, John Kruk, and Steve Phillips expressed concern regarding the burden of proof and the use of hearsay evidence within the report.[9] ESPN.com's Jason Stark added, "There is clearly more skepticism about the accuracy, or at least the provability, of the allegations about Clemens and McNamee."[10] According to Howard Bryant, "Short on access and information, Mitchell's investigators aggressively pressured team trainers, managers and strength coaches to speculate about players and their possible use of performance-enhancing drugs."[11] Jonathan Littleman feigned concern that Mets clubhouse employee Kirk Radomski was "Mitchell's A-No. 1 source—a towel boy handed to him on a silver platter. That's it? One towel boy, one strength and conditioning coach, and existing government investigations out of Albany, N.Y., and BALCO. Not exactly Sherlock Holmes. Or Sam Spade."[12] ESPN.com's Lester Munson expressed similar apprehension when he wrote, "The tough issue is what constitutes reliable information.... He is dealing with information and possibly some people involved in the sale or delivery of drugs."[13] Even super-agent Scott Boras chimed in just prior to the report's release with the statement, "I'm going to assume that a lot of the basis for this is hearsay information.... It's not based on any kind of clinical testing, so it is widely a product of hearsay testimony. Without clinical testing or hard evidence, any report like this has to be reviewed with great scrutiny."[14] In essence, while sportswriters ignored the illegal nature of using sealed grand jury testimony to convict Bonds in the court of public opinion, they found the use of testimony from federal snitches, who would be prosecuted to the full extent of the law if they lied, to be egregiously troublesome.

What is interesting about the sudden respect for the letter of the law in Clemens' case is the complete lack of coverage given to abuses in Bonds's ongoing legal entanglement. On MSNBC's *The Rachel Maddow Show*, Dave Zirin discussed the most recent postponement of Bonds's trial when he noted:

> The Justice Department wins 95 percent of the time when they bring these cases to trial. This was going to be one of those five percent, because Judge Susan Illston—she struck down most of the prosecution's case because she saw the prosecution as having used the Bill of Rights basically as dental floss during the whole process of trying to gather evidence.... I mean, you had the IRS agents walking into a continental drug testing lab with warrants that said, we can get 10 people's results and they leave with 4,000—4,000 people's results. And a three-judge panel judging the actions of this particular agent, a man named Jeff Novitsky, and what they said was, "Gee, I didn't know the Fourth Amendment was repealed. No one told us about that."[15]

It is not surprising that this information was not widely discussed on ESPN. This lack of interest could have something to do with the fact that ESPN hired *Game of Shadows* writer Mark Fainaru-Wada as a commentator. As discussed in the previous chapter, the authors of this book included sealed grand jury testimony in their work despite the fact there is no legal way to obtain that testimony. Even though the inclusion of such testimony should have raised legal and ethical questions, the issue did not garner a lot of public discussion. Because of the likelihood that a prolonged discussion about legal and constitutional abuses in the Bonds investigation could bring up grand jury testimony, ESPN probably would not want to touch any discussion of "tainted" information with a thirty-nine-and-a-half foot pole.[16]

In the same way that Bonds's Hall of Fame chances have been called into question because of his association with BALCO, sportswriters chimed in on whether or not they would vote for Clemens in five years, and the responses were mixed. Steve Krasner proclaimed, "Yes, I would vote for him on the first ballot. If, as Brian McNamee says, he started using steroids in 1998, he already had 213 wins, four Cy Young Awards and a 3.00 ERA at the time. Without the steroids he wouldn't have won 350 games, but I do think he would have been a double-digit winner for many seasons."[17] Mike Antonen, harking back to the viability of federal snitches, argued, "At this point, I would vote for Clemens to go to Cooperstown. I know what is in the Mitchell report, but I wouldn't hold him out of the Hall of Fame until there is stronger evidence against him and more of the story is heard."[18] Joe Crowley of the *Chicago Sun-Times* placed the whole issue of whether to allow performance-enhancing drug users into Cooperstown in perspective when he remarked, "God forbid we mix the guys rubbing cream on their body with the racists, wife beaters, bat-corkers, adulterers and murder suspects that currently reside in a collection of dust and baseballs that is the Baseball Hall of Fame."[19]

The five-year waiting period between retirement and induction is designed so that voters can place a player's career in the proper context. In essence, Clemens was being treated exactly as all players are supposed to be treated: sportswriters are supposed to wait for more complete information before making a final judgment on induction. This is in direct contrast to sportswriters who made up their minds regarding Bonds's induction before the slugger had even "retired." Again the question must be asked: why the difference in treatment? Jayson Stark discusses the difference when he acknowledges that

> the perception of those stories hasn't been similar. And we can't escape the notion
> that that might be due in part to how those tales have been reported and told.
> There is almost universal acceptance of the guilt of Bonds and Anderson. There is
> almost unanimous agreement in the court of public opinion, in fact, that those
> two did everything they're alleged to have done. But there is clearly more skepticism
> about the accuracy, or at least the provability, of the allegations about Clemens and
> McNamee. Full disclosure: There is certainly more skepticism on the part of this
> reporter, anyway. And there are plenty of others out there like me.[20]

The skepticism highlights George Lipsitz's possessive investment in whiteness, which "creates the racialized hierarchies of our society."[21] This possessive investment "accounts for advantages that come to individuals through profits made from housing secured in discriminatory markets, through the unequal educational opportunities available to children of different races, through insider networks that channel employment opportunities to the relatives and friends of those who have profited most from present and past racial discrimination,"[22] and apparently, it also determines which players are given the benefit of the doubt when steroid allegations are released, and which are just guilty. Predominantly white sportswriters had invested an immense amount of time and energy during the previous five years painting Bonds as the boogieman of performance-enhancing drugs in MLB, and having a new (white) face of steroids was inconceivable. Add to that effort the fact that "race and drugs are so inextricably linked in U.S. culture that ... the black body becomes the narrative replacement for drugs,"[23] and Bonds fit the profile of the perfect villain. White sportswriters had no incentive to revoke the "benefit of the doubt" they had conferred upon Clemens because of his race.

Some might ask if engaging in a possessive investment in whiteness by bestowing white privilege on Roger Clemens and other white athletes makes all sportswriters racist. That is a far too simplistic and inaccurate analysis of the situation. According to Tim Wise, "One can hate Barry Bonds and also spend Sundays singing 'We Shall Overcome' with the Harlem Boys Choir before reading select passages from *Go Tell It on the Mountain*."[24] It simply means that white sportswriters can and do confer white privilege on Clemens, and benefit from it themselves, whether or not they openly exhibit any racist tendencies.

Even as the Mitchell Report gave baseball a "white Barry Bonds,"[25] the role that race plays in how sportswriters frame Bonds is as clear as mud. As the late Ralph Wiley argued, "What Barry Bonds has done is show great merit in the game. Unfortunately when you are what is called 'black,' that can be inconvenient; often when you show merit, the rules on merit are changed to make them more obtuse."[26] While many white journalists seemed shocked, shocked, to find that people thought that that race was a factor in how Bonds was framed, more sportswriters were at least willing to acknowledge that race may play a role in how they treat Clemens. Dan Wetzel pointed out, "For years Bonds supporters have pointed the finger at Clemens as a sign of a media (and racial) double standard. Their guy was getting crucified daily, while Clemens was getting standing ovations and new contracts.... Anyone who spent years spewing contempt at Bonds needs to do the same to Clemens, because there is no difference between them."[27] The previously quoted Jayson Stark compared Bonds and Clemens by writing, "Some will say there's a racial component to those perceptions. It's tempting to say that's a bunch of baloney, but for a long time now, surveys have shown that race is a major factor in how Bonds is perceived. So there's no reason not to think race shows up in the perceptions of Clemens, as well. We'd be naive to think otherwise."[28] Bill Plaschke of the *Los Angeles Times* highlighted the difference between Clemens and Bonds when he wrote, "America does not want to believe the dirt on Clemens because he is a nice guy, a family guy, a good ol' guy and, let's be honest here, a Caucasian guy. America likes its sport villains dark and moody and everything that has always been Bonds."[29] While the influence of race in sports discussions is no longer a taboo subject for sportswriters, it is difficult to say what caused the change. It is possible that sportswriters learned from the backlash their coverage of Bonds generated and are trying to be more racially aware in their analysis.

Another plausible explanation has to do with then presidential candidate Barack Obama. It had been almost twenty years since the United States had seen an African American run for president. While Obama and his staff did their best not to make race a central theme during the campaign, there is no doubt that his candidacy put race on the table. *Orlando Sentinel* columnist Mike Bianchi went so far as to make the argument that sport was one of the reasons why Obama was successful in his candidacy. According to Bianchi, "If you're searching for tangible reason why it became possible for Barack Obama to make his historic run at the presidency of the United States, then look no further than the golf course, basketball court or football field. Obama may have emerged from the partisan political arena, but it was the nonpartisan athletic arena that opened white America's eyes and minds to the amazing potential and personalities of black America."[30]

Bianchi failed to notice that the black athletes who get the fame and the attention are the ones who distance themselves as far from politics as humanly possible. In a rebuttal, Dave Zirin pointed out:

> For more than a century, masses of white audiences have cheered black entertainers and athletes. And for most of that time, blacks struggled mightily to climb the corporate or political ladder. Why? Because being wowed by the ability of blacks to perform on a field or stage is not in the same ballpark as accepting their political leadership. Not even close. More to the point, the rare black athletes who have dared to make waves have been pilloried for not knowing their place. After men like Jack Johnson, Muhammad Ali, Tommie Smith and John Carlos got too political, the phrase "just shut up and play" emerged — to smack down future jocks for trying to do more than entertain.[31]

It was admirable that Bianchi initiated a discussion regarding race, sport, and politics; it was his conclusion that was problematic. Because the nation was already embroiled in an albeit muted conversation about race in terms of presidential politics, it is possible the discussion spilled over into the sporting realm. In the end, the acknowledgment does not change the fact that race *continues* to play a role in how sports stories are framed, but it appears to be a step in the right direction because, as Michael Wilbon points out, "It ain't just black folks who need to write about this. White men specifically do not get absolved of the responsibility of writing about race in this culture, race and sports, it's an obligation to engage the reader."[32]

What is interesting about Clemens's case is that while sportswriters were initially skeptical about the Mitchell Report and the evidence against the former Yankee pitcher, that benefit of the doubt did not last very long. In the aftermath of the Mitchell Report and the repeated denials, Clemens was granted the opportunity to discuss performance-enhancing drugs in front of Congress. Baseball fans and sportswriters would finally have an opportunity to hear Clemens's and McNamee's stories at the same time and decide for themselves who was telling the truth. Given McNamee's status as a drug dealer and federal snitch, most believed that Clemens would easily clear his name during the hearings; however, the pitcher ran into a small problem. Prior to those hearings, Yankee pitcher Andy Pettitte provided a sworn deposition in lieu of testifying in front of the full committee. In his deposition, Pettitte admitted that McNamee injected him with Human Growth Hormones (HGH); that Clemens told him he was taking HGH; and that Clemens's wife was taking HGH as well.[33] Pettitte's deposition corroborated what McNamee told Mitchell. Subsequently, Chuck Knoblauch came forward and admitted that McNamee provided him with HGH, as was stated in the Mitchell Report.[34] When presented with this information during the hearing, Clemens proceeded to throw Pettitte, McNamee, and his own wife under the proverbial bus. Clemens claimed that Pettitte "misremembered" the conversations in which Clemens admitted to using steroids and that he had no knowledge that McNamee injected Debbie Clemens with steroids in their own bedroom until after the fact.[35] Essentially Clemens wanted people to believe that McNamee told the truth about having provided steroids to everyone *except* him, and that did not go over very well.

During ESPN's *Mike and Mike in the Morning* following the hearings, Mike Greenberg had the following reaction before playing a clip from Clemens' testimony: "On some level, as you listen to this, it's so physically painful that I can barely stand to hear it again."[36] When asked who was more credible, Tim Kurkjian stated, "There were too many inconsistencies in Clemens's account, too many points that were too difficult to believe." Peter Gammons acknowledged, "Clemens had to prove his innocence. He did not."[37] Unfortunately for Clemens, he may have talked himself into even more trouble, since the committee recommended that the Justice Department investigate whether or not Clemens lied under oath.

In August 2010, the Justice Department announced that they were charging Clemens with "one count of obstruction of Congress, three counts of making false statements and two counts of perjury,"[38] and the trial began less than one year later. After only two days of testimony, the trial judge declared a mistrial. Federal prosecutors introduced video of Clemens's testimony before Congress where Representative Elijah Cumming referred to Laura Pettitte's sworn statement that her husband Andy Pettitte told her about Clemens's performance-enhancing drug use. Unfortunately Laura Pettitte's statement is considered double hearsay and is not admissible in court, a fact the prosecutors were well aware of since the issue came up during pretrial hearings.[39] Given the nature of the mistake, many wondered out loud if the federal prosecutors included the evidence on purpose in an effort to force a mistrial. This argument is what Clemens's attorneys used to try to stop a new trial, but the judge rejected that notion. Much like McGwire's taking the 4½ Amendment during his congressional testimony, and Rafael Palmeiro wagging his finger and swearing he did not take steroids five months before testing positive for performance-enhancing drugs, Roger Clemens managed to erase any goodwill he had left with fans, and the white privilege sportswriters bestowed upon him was unceremoniously revoked. Instead of endearing himself to the public, Clemens landed himself in the same purgatory as Bonds. It would seem that in the beginning, when white players were entangled with performance-enhancing drugs, their white privilege shielded them from some of the venom; however, those privileges can and will be revoked at any time if the benefactor proves to be a liability.

Andy Pettitte, You're My Hero?

While sportswriters were dismissing Clemens and federal prosecutors were deciding whether to press charges against him, one person managed to escape the Mitchell Report and congressional hearings completely unscathed: Andy Pettitte. Pettitte spent twelve seasons with the Yankees and three with the Astros. While he is not in the same league in terms of quality as Roger Clemens, he has a lifetime ERA of 3.91 and 229 wins, and has managed to pitch in eight World Series (his teams won five of those Series). After the Mitchell Report was released, Pettitte did something that no player had done before: he unequivocally admitted to using performance-enhancing drugs and apologized. And with that apology came forgiveness. Joel Sherman of the *New York Post* wrote, "I so badly want to be angry at Andy Pettitte. Yet, I cannot sustain it. I am mad at Pettitte, not for the drug taking, but for lying to my face about it, multiple times over the years.... So why do I find myself so forgiving? There is something gentle and, yes, sincere about Pettitte that makes him so likeable."[40] Richard Justice of the *Houston Chronicle* went so far as to write, "Andy Pettitte became a role model Monday afternoon. In the end, it's that simple."[41] ESPN's Mike Golic opined, "As far as Congress was concerned, if Andy Pettitte walked into that room they would have all genuflected. I mean they were treating him as the choir boy, the do-gooder, the halo around the head guy."[42] Following the Yankees' 2009 World Series victory, Tony Kornheiser and Michael Wilbon pondered whether Pettitte would be inducted into the Hall of Fame; performance-enhancing drugs received only a cursory mention at the very end of the discussion.[43] Despite the fact that Pettitte admitted to using an illegal substance, lied to the Mitchell Commission, and lied to MLB about using HGH, Pettitte has not been suspended, has not been arrested, and was called a "role model both on and off the field" by Congressman Henry Waxman.[44]

It is safe to say Pettitte's apology went a long way to acquiring a Teflon uniform, so that even admitting to using performance-enhancing drugs won't stick. Instead of being labeled a cheater and a steroid user like Bonds or Clemens, Pettitte was cheered during his first regular-season start in Yankee Stadium.[45] Would Clemens have had his white privilege card revoked if he had simply admitted to using performance-enhancing drugs and apologized? Would Bonds be in the media's good graces and still be playing today if he had admitted to using steroids and apologized? Is an apology all that is necessary for redemption? If Pettitte's case is any indication, then players who use performance-enhancing drugs and apologize should get a free pass, right?

Baseball's Second Favorite Villain

As discussed in Chapter 3, when Alex Rodríguez signed the largest contract in sports history in 2000, he was lambasted from every direction. Despite his being one of the best players in the game, it was said that he was not "worth" $25 million per season—a framing that has racial connotations as well. When he was traded to New York, Yankee fans and the New York media were less than hospitable. Granted, Rodríguez's lackluster playoff performances did not help matters at all, and *Sports Illustrated*'s Tom Verducci points out:

> A-Rod routinely is treated like the guy in the dunk tank at the county fair, even, most incriminating of all, by his peers. In the past two years he's been called out by Boston pitcher Curt Schilling ("bush league"), Red Sox outfielder Trot Nixon ("He can't stand up to Jeter in my book, or Bernie Williams or Posada"), Chicago White Sox manager Ozzie Guillén ("hypocrite") and New York Mets catcher Paul Lo Duca (who accused him on the field of showing up the Mets by admiring a home run too long).[46]

When it seemed that the only thing that could redeem Rodríguez was carrying the Yankees to another World Series title, Barry Bonds's breaking of Henry Aaron's all-time home-run record came along. On the August 5, 2007, edition of *The Sports Reporters,* John Saunders, Michael Kay, William C. Rhoden, and Mitch Albom contemplated the fact that Bonds tied Aaron's record. Mitch Albom argued, "The saddest part is on the same day that Bonds ties this record, A-Rod hits his 500th and half the country is going: 'hit 'em faster A-Rod, hit 'em faster.'" Rhoden replied, "And the strange thing is that Bonds has turned a guy like A-Rod into a hero."[47] If Rodríguez continues his current pace, and does not suffer any serious injuries, he is on pace to hit well over 800 home runs.

Of course, those sportswriters who were secretly, or publicly, wishing for A-Rod to break the record ran into a problem. In February 2009, *Sports Illustrated* writer Selena Roberts broke the story that Alex Rodríguez tested positive for performance-enhancing drugs in 2003. In an interview with ESPN's Peter Gammon, A-Rod admitted, "I was young. I was stupid. I was naive. And I wanted to prove to everyone that, you know, I was worth being one of the greatest players of all time. And I did take a banned substance. You know, for that I'm very sorry and deeply regretful."[48] If the response to Andy Pettitte's admission is any indication, A-Rod should escape without any permanent damage to his career, right? Yes and no. When Roberts's story initially broke, the response was predictably hostile. He was called "A-Fraud" by the *New York Daily News.*[49] Jayson Stark opined that Rodríguez "has destroyed [baseball's] history" and committed "a crime against the once-proud history of his sport."[50] According to Steve Politi of the *New Jersey Star-Ledger,* A-Rod's admission was "unprecedented. Rodríguez has trampled over the most storied franchise in sports like Godzilla in downtown Tokyo."[51] Never mind that Rodríguez was not the only Yankee who admitted to using performance-enhancing drugs. Like Bonds and Clemens, Rodríguez had the misfortune of being a truly great player, and as Buster Olney pointed out in his discussion of A-Rod, "record-holders, however, are simply held to a different standard, because they have performed at a different standard."[52] Though Rodríguez does not hold any records yet, as previously mentioned, he was the player who was going to save baseball from the dreaded Barry Bonds. Because A-Rod was viewed as baseball's savior, much like Mark McGwire had been ten years previously, Rodríguez wasn't able to simply fly under the radar as Pettitte did despite his public apology.

While Rodríguez was supposed to be haunted by his steroid admission for the rest of his career, the reality of the situation looked a little different. Much like Pettitte, the brouhaha surrounding Rodríguez's performance-enhancing drug use died down after the prolific slugger returned to form. Though A-Rod missed part of the 2009 season due to a hip injury, he still managed a .286 BA and a .532 SLG. While Rodríguez had historically performed horribly during the postseason, in '09 his performance was nothing short of spectacular. He hit .365 with 6 home runs, 16 RBI and helped the Yankees win their 27th World Series.

The short-term memory loss exhibited by fans and sportswriters when it comes to A-Rod and performance-enhancing drugs has a few possible explanations. First, like Pettitte, Rodríguez's apology went a long way in placating fans. The forgiveness just took a little longer to arrive for A-Rod than it did for Pettitte. Second, the hostility toward A-Rod when the story first broke could have had more to do with personal baggage (i.e., his contract, his off-field personal issues, etc.) and less to do performance-enhancing drugs. In much the same vein as Bonds, and as discussed in previous chapters, the relationship between Rodríguez, sportswriters, and fans has not always been harmonious, which certainly affects reactions to the slugger's performance-enhancing drug use. Third, until Bonds's trial is finished, and possibly even after it has been concluded, no one whose name is not Barry Bonds will take over as baseball poster child for performance-enhancing drugs. Fourth, and the most likely possibility, the public's attitude has very little to do with race and everything to do with a growing indifference to the subject. Given the Mitchell Report's findings that performance-enhancing drugs were pervasive, fans are no longer surprised when names are released. Sportswriters have ceded that every great player in this era is under suspicion and every record broken is "tainted." Baseball, sportswriters, and fans might display an initial shock at the news, as seen with Pettitte and Rodríguez, but they will move on fairly quickly.

Bush League Justice

While Rodríguez may have redeemed himself in the eyes of fans, and even some sportswriters, the performance-enhancing drugs revelation was problematic for reasons having nothing to do with A-Rod. According to Selena Roberts, Rodríguez tested positive for performance-enhancing drugs in 2003. As mentioned in the previous chapter, MLB did not test for steroids or any other substances until 2004. The previous year, MLBPA had agreed to a pilot test program which did not include penalties and was supposed to remain anonymous. Clearly, the word anonymous does not mean what it used to mean. Since the tests were supposed to remain anonymous, there should not have been any way to link a positive or negative test to a particular player. In addition, if officials truly wanted to avoid this situation, the samples and the results should have been destroyed once MLB had the information it required.

This is the second time there has been a breach in baseball's confidentiality protocols: when it was revealed that Rafael Palmeiro tested positive for performance-enhancing drugs in 2005, the type of drug he used was also revealed. Under the terms of MLB's drug policy, only the player's name and the date of his suspension was supposed to be made public.[53]

Violation of MLB's drug policy is not the only problem with Rodríguez's revelation because, once again, there are also questions surrounding the legality of this leaked information. In 2004, as the Justice Department was investigating BALCO, federal authorities obtained a search warrant for certain players' drug-testing records. Though the authorities only had a warrant for ten records, they seized a spreadsheet containing the drug-testing records of "all baseball players, mixed in on a computer with those from other sports and businesses."[54] In August 2009, the California Appeals Court ruled that federal authorities illegally seized players' test results, concluding: "This was an obvious case of deliberate overreaching by the government in an effort to seize data as to which it lacked probable cause."[55] While this ruling certainly helped Barry Bonds's legal team, since anything the authorities seized is inadmissible, as a lawyer for the players' union also pointed out, "If the government had never unconstitutionally seized the test results, there would never have been any leaks."[56] In essence, Roberts would not have had the evidence to out Alex Rodríguez if federal authorities had not executed an illegal search and seizure. Not only do players have to deal with the backlash associated with using performance-enhancing drugs, but there is every indication that these players' civil rights have been violated — a story that did not receive much attention in the sports world.

To be fair, these players would not be in a position to have their civil rights violated if they hadn't taken performance-enhancing drugs in the first place. However, that does not change the fact that players like Bonds and Rodríguez have had their reputations destroyed by a Justice Department willing to violate their civil rights in an effort to make their case, and by journalists willing to ignore the unconstitutional way the evidence was obtained. According to Michael Butterworth, "The discourse opposed to steroids cannot be viewed in isolation. Instead, it serves as a complement to President Bush's self-declared 'war on terror.'"[57] The violation of players' civil rights points to an ends-justify-the-means mentality within George W. Bush's Justice Department, which manifested itself not only in illegal seizures of drug information, but also in the political firing of attorneys and existence of torture memos. While violating the civil rights of rich athletes who were taking illegal substances seems like a trivial matter, particularly in light of other Justice Department abuses during the same time period, former MLBPA Executive Director Donald Fehr summed the matter up perfectly when he stated, "I worry that what we accept one day in sports ... makes it that much easier to apply it to the rest of the world."[58]

MLB is not the only sport having legal issues concerning performance-enhancing drugs. In 2009 the NFL suspended two New Orleans Saints and two Minnesota Vikings players after they tested positive for bumetanide. All of the players stated they took an over-the-counter weight-loss supplement, StarCaps, which did not state on the label that it contained bumetanide. According to the NFL players' union, "Dr. John Lombardo, who oversees the league's steroid policy, learned that StarCaps contained bumetanide but did not inform the players."[59] A federal judge issued an injunction preventing the NFL from suspending the players pending the trial outcome. What is new about this case is that the two Vikings players argued that the policy violated Minnesota state law, not federal laws, and the U.S. Court of Appeals agreed that their case could go forward. While this litigation is pending, what is interesting to note is that NFL Commissioner Roger Goodell was not interested in whether or not the league's doctor withheld vital medical information from his patients and essentially set them up to be suspended. Instead, Goodell went to Congress and asked for legislation that would allow Collective Bargaining Agreements to supersede state law because, as he put it, "Professional athletes and their collective bargaining representatives should not be permitted to manipulate state statutes as a means to gain a competitive advantage."[60]

While MLB has had its share of legal mishaps and entanglements when it comes to steroid testing, surprisingly, it did not side with the NFL on this issue. Michael Weiner, general counsel for MLBPA, testified before the subcommittee hearing on this matter and stated unequivocally that not only should Congress not interfere in the StarCaps case, but placed the blame squarely on the NFL's shoulders for not informing their players of the problem with the supplement, and with the FDA which allowed the substance to be sold in the first place.[61] It is difficult to believe that professional sports leagues and players' unions can negotiate collective bargaining agreements covering all manner of minutiae, but cannot conceive of a testing policy that does not violate state laws and protects the rights of the players, the vast majority of whom are men of color. Unfortunately, no matter what sort of testing and penalties the leagues come up with, players will undoubtedly still fail drug tests.

Just Manny Being Manny?

Because Alex Rodríguez and Andy Pettitte admitted to using performance-enhancing drugs before MLB tested for and banned these substances, there was very little Commissioner Bud Selig could do in terms of sanctions. In fact, with the exception of Rafael Palmeiro, the vast majority of drug suspensions were of players who were not household names. This changed during the 2009 season. As Alex Rodríguez was returning from hip surgery, a new player joined the performance-enhancing drugs club: Manny Ramírez. Unlike Pettitte, who was mentioned in the Mitchell Report, or Rodríguez, who admitted to using performance-enhancing drugs before there was official testing, Ramírez knew he was going to be tested, knew there were going to be penalties for a positive test, and still failed a drug test. In April of that year, MLB and Ramírez were informed that the slugger's urine showed an elevated level of testosterone, which leads to a 50-game suspension.[62] Ramírez argued that he was under a doctor's care for a personal issue and the doctor corroborated his story. The medical records showed the doctor prescribed human chorionic gonadotropin (HCG), a female fertility drug which does have legitimate uses to combat a male reproductive disorder. Unfortunately for Ramírez, HCG is also commonly used when someone is cycling off steroids.[63] Because of the latter connection, and the fact that HCG is specifically named on the banned substances list, Ramírez became the first superstar to be suspended for using performance-enhancing drugs. Not only did Ramírez face a 50-game suspension, but he also had to forfeit over $7 million in salary. As noted in the previous section, the disclosure of which substance Ramírez tested positive for is still a violation of MLB's drug policy; however, that did not stop the name of the drug from being widely publicized.

In a similar vein as Pettitte and Rodríguez, Manny Ramírez immediately issued a statement that read, "Recently I saw a physician for a personal health issue, he gave me a medication, not a steroid, which he thought was okay to give me. Unfortunately, the medication was banned under our drug policy. Under the policy, that mistake is now my responsibility. I have been advised not to say anything more for now."[64] Because the statement wasn't a full-on apology, the response to Ramírez's suspension was interesting. Jeff Jacobs of the *Hartford Courant* wrote, "The initial thought is he's just stupid enough to be telling the truth. The initial reaction is that Manny Ramirez is so flighty, such a carefree goofball, that he isn't focused enough for a dedicated regimen of performance enhancing drugs."[65] Ken Fedlin of the *Toronto Sun* surmised, "Until today, Manny was an interesting knucklehead. Now he's just another cheat."[66] Beverly Ford of the *New York Daily News* began her column by writing, "It's just Manny being Moronic."[67] Other *New York Daily News* writers noted, "Ramírez now joins some of the greatest players in recent baseball history — Barry Bonds, Mark McGwire, Roger Clemens and Rodríguez — in his link to pharmaceutical cheating."[68] Surely the exclusion of Andy Pettitte from this list is simply an oversight on the writers' parts. Unfortunately, when discussing Ramírez and other players associated with performance-enhancing drugs, the vast majority of writers excluded Pettitte from their discussion.

Much like Alex Rodríguez, something besides anger and disappointment seems to be fueling how sportswriters responded to the news. The words "stupid," "moronic," and "knucklehead," though not applied to any other players associated with performance-enhancing drugs, have less to do with a failed drug test and more to do with the "Manny being Manny" persona, and all of its racial connotations, that sportswriters and Ramírez have cultivated over the past seventeen years. During his time with Cleveland, Ramírez had "picked up a reputation for flighty, lackadaisical play."[69] Steve Herrick of *The Sporting News* devoted an entire article to "The wacky world of Manny Ramírez" which recounted when Ramírez would lose track of balls and strikes, lose track of balls in the sun, incur driving citations, and accidentally hugging a teammate who had recently had an appendectomy too hard.[70] When Ramírez signed with the Red Sox in 2000, the "Manny being Manny" routine only intensified with the increased media attention associated with Boston. In an article for the *New Yorker*, Ben McGrath wrote:

> Manny Ramirez is a deeply frustrating employee, the kind whose talents are so prodigious that he gets away with skipping meetings, falling asleep on the job, and fraternizing with the competition.... Ramírez's appearance — he styles his hair in dreadlocks, wears a uniform cut for a sumo wrestler, and smiles broadly and indiscriminately — hints at this extracurricular flakiness, and even gives off a whiff of pothead.... In the outfield and on the base paths, Ramirez can seem oafish and clumsy, and many of the baseball-related incidents for which he is best known reflect a chronic absent-mindedness.[71]

As discussed in Chapter 1 concerning Sammy Sosa's happy-go-lucky persona, it is impossible to know whether the "Manny being Manny" persona is a way for sportswriters to impose stereotypes onto a player, or a calculated façade created by Ramírez, or some combination of the two. Regardless, it is difficult to ignore the racial connotations associated with the way Ramirez has been and continues to be framed by sportswriters. The ways in which Ramirez is being described comes dangerously close to the racist attacks Latin players like Roberto Clemente and Orestes Miñoso endured in the 1950s (i.e., being labeled "moody," "not a team player," or "troubled").[72]

One the other hand, having a reputation for not being the sharpest tool in the shed helped Ramírez during the initial firestorm as well as when he returned to baseball following his suspension. Like Pettitte and Rodríguez, Ramírez was greeted with open arms by Dodgers fans when he returned from his suspension. Bob Padecky was incensed that "Ramirez returned not to ostracism but to love and affection from teammates [and] to standing ovations."[73] The love was short-lived, as Ramírez was placed on waivers but picked up by the Chicago White Sox in 2010. After a disappointing season on the South Side, Ramírez signed with the Tampa Bay Rays for the 2011 season.

Shortly after the season began, Ramírez abruptly announced his retirement. The league released a statement that read: "Major League Baseball recently notified Manny Ramirez of an issue under Major League Baseball's Joint Drug Prevention and Treatment program. Rather than continue with the process under the program, Ramirez has informed MLB that he is retiring as an active player. If Ramirez seeks reinstatement in the future, the process under the drug program will be completed. MLB will not have any further comment on this matter."[74] Ramírez would have faced a 100-game suspension if he had failed another drug test. The news of his retirement was unexpected, though many sportswriters did not act at all surprised. MLB.com's Anthony Castrovince wrote, "Manny's sudden, surprising retirement was a fitting finale to a circus-like career.... he played the game of baseball and the game of life by his own rules. And Manny's rules didn't always mesh with reality."[75] Though most sportswriters hypothesized that a second failed drug test would certainly prevent Ramírez from being inducted into Cooperstown, there wasn't any hint of animosity toward the slugger. When Ramírez was cleared for reinstatement in December 2011, the news was met with shrugged shoulders.

Again, a pattern seems to be emerging: the initial report that a player used performance-enhancing drugs is met with varying degrees of anger based primarily on the player's previous relationship with the press, and after a brief mourning period, the entire sport moves on. While race and/or ethnicity may play a role in how players are perceived prior to their admission, race does not seem to play as prominent a role in the severity or the duration of the player's public shaming after the fact.

I Love It When You Call Me Big Papi

Red Sox fans were feeling quite smug when Manny Ramírez was caught using performance-enhancing drugs after he left for the Dodgers. Unfortunately, Boston could not avoid the spotlight when it was revealed that David Ortiz tested positive for performance-enhancing drugs in 2003. For a third time, the "anonymous" testing turned out to be anything but anonymous. Unlike with Palmeiro and Ramírez, the terms of the collective bargaining agreement were honored, and the substance Ortiz tested positive for was not revealed because, according to the *New York Times* article that broke the story, "the testing information was under seal by a court order."[76] While A-Rod and Manny Ramírez had plenty of excess baggage which hampered their forgiveness, Ortiz is loved by everyone in baseball circles, with the possible exception of Yankee fans.

In the same vein as Andy Pettitte, Big Papi, as Ortiz is affectionately known, should have been able to come clean, apologize, and move forward. Ortiz immediately released a statement that read in part:

> I want to talk about this situation and I will as soon as I have more answers. In the meantime I want to let you know how I am approaching this situation. One, I have already contacted the players association to confirm if this report is true. I have just been told that the report is true. Based on the way I have lived my life, I am surprised to learn I tested positive. Two, I will find out what I tested positive for. And, three, based on whatever I learn, I will share this information with my club and the public. You know me — I will not hide and I will not make excuses.[77]

Like Manny Ramírez, Ortiz did not issue a full-on, Andy Pettitte–style apology, though in this case that may not have been possible. What is interesting about Ortiz's situation is that while having the records sealed by the court did not stop his name from being leaked, it has prevented Ortiz from finding out what substance he tested positive for. In 2004 General Counsel Michael Weiner told Ortiz that he did not test positive for steroids, according to Weiner, "The union can't confirm to Ortiz that he tested positive, only that he was on the list."[78] Because Ortiz did not have access to complete information, he was left to speculate that legal over-the-counter supplements accounted for the possible positive test, which places him in a similar situation as the previously discussed NFL players.

While Ortiz was understandably eager to get to the bottom of the situation, sportswriters and fans did not seem interested in placing the slugger's head on a platter. Joe Posnanski of *Sports Illustrated* opined, "Big Papi is something new in this endless rerun of drug charges: He is baseball's first cuddly steroid user. Yes, all the players who have been named, implicated or linked to steroids had their passionate fans. But, mostly, they did not generate love. Papi did."[79] When discussing that matter on ESPN's *Pardon the Interruption*, Tony Kornheiser and Dan Le Batard discussed why very few people seemed fazed about Ortiz's situation:

> KORNHEISER: Dan, it's almost like nothing happened, did nothing happen?
> LE BATARD: I'll tell you what happened, some guys that we liked ended up on that steroid list and we decided to stop paying attention. It wasn't A-Rod, it wasn't Barry Bonds, it wasn't the polarizing guys anymore ... some other guys ended up on the list and we just changed our minds. We just said you know what? I'm tired of this steroid story.[80]

While cuddly was not the word used to describe Andy Pettitte, David Ortiz seems to be following in his footsteps as far as responses to performance-enhancing drugs is concerned. Bob Raissman of the *New York Daily News* noticed the discrepancy when he wrote:

> When it comes to ESPN fleshing out anything on Ortiz [...] the Worldwide Leader is not hitting on all cylinders. Especially when compared to the way ESPN feasted

on the Alex Rodríguez story. Maybe this is all about a growing sense, expressed by a variety of pontificators, that the public has become tired of PED coverage. It's also worth noting that Ortiz's popularity, manifested through his engaging personality, has earned him major goodwill style points from not only ESPN, but those in the business of covering baseball.[81]

In that same vein, *Newsday*'s Ken Davidoff opined, "It doesn't matter who was doing what and when. It doesn't matter what the profoundly conflicted George Mitchell discovered en route to his 'report,' or what some lawbreaking attorney is leaking.... Go ahead, Yankees fans, take tonight to pepper Big Papi. Take the whole weekend, if you'd like. Then move on."[82] In the end, all of the goodwill Papi had garnered over the years with sportswriters and fans, in addition to a general desire to close the book on the steroid era, lessened the leak's impact.

He's Back

Given the fact that Hall of Fame voters did not come close to inducting Mark McGwire during his first four years of eligibility, it was assumed that McGwire's association with professional baseball was over. Apparently the St. Louis Cardinals had other plans. In January 2010, the Cardinals announced that McGwire would be the team's new hitting coach. As discussed in Chapter 1, McGwire became persona non grata after he invoked his 4½ Amendment right to "not talk about the past" during his congressional testimony. It was inevitable that sportswriters would question McGwire about performance-enhancing drugs once he was back in baseball. On January 11, 2011, in what can only be categorized as a preemptive strike, McGwire issued a statement that read in part: "I used steroids during my playing career and I apologize. I remember trying steroids very briefly in the 1989/1990 off-season and then after I was injured in 1993, I used steroids again. I used them on occasion throughout the '90s, including during the 1998 season. I wish I had never touched steroids. It was foolish and it was a mistake. I truly apologize. Looking back, I wish I had never played during the steroid era."[83] Later that same day, McGwire sat down for a live interview with Bob Costas on the MLB Network. He tearfully explained that injuries led to his use of performance-enhancing drugs and denied that the drugs had any effect on his ability to hit home runs.[84]

The reactions to McGwire's admission were mixed yet muted. According to ESPN's Gene Wojciechowski, "McGwire owed baseball an apology. Apology accepted."[85] The Cardinals' players had nothing negative to say about McGwire, and in his first public appearance in St. Louis after the admission, fans gave the slugger a standing ovation.[86] Though some sportswriters were displeased by the inconsistencies in McGwire's statements, once the 2011 season began, the steroids issue faded away. McGwire's trajectory seems to mirror Andy Pettitte's: as long as the player admits to using performance-enhancing drugs and is sincere in his apologies, all will be forgiven.

In Chapter 1 the question raised was whether or not McGwire's white privilege kept steroid allegations from sticking. In 2011, ESPN's Howard Bryant subtly asked a similar question about forgiveness when he wrote, "While Bonds can't get a phone call returned, Palmeiro is invisible and Miguel Tejada can't get a job, McGwire is trading on good will not afforded his former colleagues even though he is the one who has done the most damage to the sport." Whether it was intentional or not, all of Bryant's examples of steroid outcasts are men of color.[87] Again, it is difficult to know whether the forgiveness is a product of sportswriters' possessive investment in whiteness which would allow them to continue bestowing white privileges upon McGwire, or whether forgiving and forgetting stems from simple exhaustion with the whole steroid era.

Our Long National Nightmare Is Over

It took four years, but the case of *United States vs. Barry Lamar Bonds* finally began on March 21, 2011. The trial itself lasted for only twelve days and the jury deliberated for only four. Though the defense did not call a single witness, the judge was forced to declare a mistrial on the four perjury charges; Bonds was found guilty of obstruction of justice. In an interesting turn of events from Bonds's playing days, most of the venom about the verdict was not directed at the slugger, but at federal prosecutors. Michael Wilbon of the *Washington Post* and ESPN's *Pardon the Interruption* reacted to the verdict by saying it was "a giant waste of time and money."[88] ESPN's Jayson Stark remarked, "So let's get this straight. The only thing we've learned about Barry Bonds is that he was evasive. The government could have assembled a panel of distinguished baseball writers to convict him on that charge, like, 15 years ago. So THAT'S what The Trial of the Home Run King has taught us? I've never felt prouder of the fine work my tax dollars have been doing all this time."[89] Jemele Hill argued, "The federal government wasted a lot of time and taxpayer money, and Bonds's place in history is just as confusing to some as it was before."[90] Jeff MacGregor ranted, "Those unreckoned millions spent chasing the shadows cast by [Bonds's] giant noggin could've sent a few hundred thousand poor kids to school [with] a hot, healthy breakfast for a year or two, I'm sure."[91]

While Barry Bonds is still considered the boogieman of performance-enhancing drugs, sportswriters' mood about Bonds's case has shifted. This change of heart is partially due to the fact that the Justice Department was unable to prove that Bonds lied under oath, and partially due to the estimates that the trial cost an estimated $6 million[92]—which, even when the nation is not in the midst of an economic downtown, is a lot of money. It is not just Bonds who is benefiting from the nation's battered economy: financial considerations are also being used to argue against federal prosecutors' retrying Roger Clemens. After Clemens's mistrial, Representative Ted Poe from Texas argued, "We've got more than 100 terrorists in Guantanamo who need to be prosecuted, and they're wasting their time on a case that never should have been filed.... We had no business investigating steroids in baseball, it was a complete waste of time and money."[93] As pointed out throughout this chapter, it seems that both baseball fans and sportswriters are tired of Bonds and the entire spectacle of performance-enhancing drugs in professional baseball.

Parting Shots

The previous chapters highlighted the ways in which race permeated discussions surrounding Barry Bonds, the home-run records, and performance-enhancing drugs. As time has progressed and more players have become entangled with performance-enhancing drugs, the role race played in the discussion became less clear-cut. Though it is interesting to point out that the unconstitutional search and seizure of the 2003 drug tests and the subsequent leaks of that information have predominantly impacted players of color, and all of the blame for the steroids era continues to fall on the players and navigate away from the owners, race does not appear to play the same pivotal role in how new members of the performance-enhancing drugs club are framed. A player's prior relationship with sportswriters and fans is a better predictor of how a link to performance-enhancing drugs will be received. If a player is beloved, or has a minimal amount of acrimony associated with his name, the backlash surrounding a link to performance-enhancing drugs will be minimal. If, however, a player has a history of hostility toward fans and/or sportswriters, the backlash will be equally hostile, but may fade away. It is also true, as in the case of Bonds and Rodríguez, that race may have played a role in how a player was initially framed by sportswriters, so it would be erroneous to conclude that race has been completely "e-raced" from the discussion.

When race enters the sports arena in a major way, as in the case of Don Imus or of NFL quarterback Donovan McNabb's stating that black quarterbacks are held to a higher standard, NFL Hall of Famer Kellen Winslow, Sr., maintains, "We bring down the person who made the comment until it settles down and we go right back to where we were. We don't take advantage of the opportunity to hold those discussions and to grow from them."[94] Arguably, the firestorm surrounding Barry Bonds was one of those moments where sportswriters took advantage of the opportunity. When other players were linked to performance-enhancing drugs, race was no longer the elephant in the room that everyone refused to acknowledge. Instead, particularly with Clemens, then the role race could play in how stories were framed was then recognized and analyzed, and eventually became less of a factor in terms of forgiveness.

The fact that players have had to endure less hostility from sportswriters and fans also signals that, perhaps, baseball is ready to close the book on the steroids era. Even if that is the case, sportswriters must continue to make sure that race does not tiptoe back into the limelight. As mentioned earlier in this chapter, when the Cardinals hired Mark McGwire as a hitting coach, the news was met with shrugged shoulders. Is this also a sign that the steroids era and discussions surrounding it have run its course? Or is it a ruse, as baseball enthusiast Keith Olbermann noted when he asked, "Why is it OK for [McGwire] to just waltz back in as batting coach of the Cardinals? Would we let Bonds come back in? This is unacceptable, and it gives credence to the very disturbing claim that race is at play when it comes to the punishment of steroid cheats."[95] Is this race making a comeback or simple exhaustion on the part of fans and sportswriters? Again, the frustrating thing about race is that there are rarely any easy answers; however, the fact that people are at least asking the question and pointing out the possibility that race is playing a role, is progress of a sort.

7

Who Are We Celebrating, Anyway? Major League Baseball and the Honoring of Jackie Robinson

"Jackie Robinson had to be bigger than life. He had to be bigger than the Brooklyn teammates who got up a petition to keep him off the ball club, bigger than the pitchers who threw at him or the base runners who dug their spikes into his shin, bigger than the bench jockeys who hollered for him to carry their bags and shine their shoes, bigger than the so-called fans who mocked him with mops on their heads and wrote him death threats."— Henry Aaron[1]

"I once put my freedom into mothballs for a season, accepted humiliation and physical hurt and derision and threats to my family in order to do my bit to help make a lily white sport a truly American game. Many people approved of me for that kind of humility. For them, it was the appropriate posture for a black man. But when I straightened up my back so oppressors could no longer ride upon it, some of the same people said I was arrogant, argumentative and temperamental. What they call arrogant, I call confidence. What they call argumentative, I characterize as articulate. What they label temperamental, I cite as human."— Jackie Robinson[2]

When most people think about race and baseball, the first thing that comes to mind is the name Jackie Robinson. Even people who do not follow and know absolutely nothing about the sport can recite the history of Robinson's entry into Major League Baseball (MLB). According to the late Jules Tygiel, "The Jackie Robinson story is to Americans what the Passover story is to Jews: it must be told to every generation so that we never forget. But if this is true, and it most assuredly is, what is it that we must not forget?"[3] In the last few years, MLB has taken these words to heart and staged elaborate celebrations to commemorate Robinson's breaking the color barrier. Beginning with the 60th anniversary of Robinson's achievement, MLB began playing a Civil Rights Game, which included panel discussions on race in baseball.

In addition, MLB provided players and managers with the opportunity to wear Robinson's number on April 15, which was officially designated Jackie Robinson Day. While there are very few who would argue that Robinson's accomplishment should not be shouted from the rooftops at every available opportunity, there are some problems with how Robinson is being framed, and in addition, the way MLB chooses to celebrate Robinson's legacy has become increasingly problematic. This chapter will analyze the narratives and the celebrations surrounding Robinson and what these narratives tell us in regards to issues of race, nationality, and history in the United States as a whole.

Throughout this book I have used elements of Critical Race Theory not only because sports and the legal system have always had a nasty habit of bumping into each other, but also because, while both systems claim to be based on merit and objectivity, they are based on neither. Critical Race Theory is also "characterized by frequent use of the first person, storytelling, narrative allegory ... and the unapologetic use of creativity,"[4] elements that I have not employed in this book thus far. Because this chapter is less about how sportswriters frame Jackie Robinson Day and more about the narrative MLB chooses to perpetuate Robinson's story and the ways in which the league frames Robinson, the analysis may be helped by using first-person narrative and some creativity, while obviously maintaining the same scholarly rigor employed in the previous chapters. For the purposes of this chapter it will be also be helpful to engage in what Critical Race Theorist Derrick Bell terms racial realism. According to Bell it is helpful to think of the law and arguably other institutions, including Major League Baseball, as "instruments for preserving the status quo and only periodically and unpredictably serving as a refuge of oppressed people."[5] So the primary question of this chapter becomes: how does MLB use Jackie Robinson's legacy to preserve the status quo?

That's My Story and I'm Sticking to It

The story MLB tells about Robinson, the story most casual baseball fans hear, maintains that in August 1945, Dodger executive Branch Rickey met with Robinson, who was playing for the Negro League's Kansas City Monarchs, to discuss signing a major league contract. Rickey was looking for "a ball player with guts enough not to fight back."[6] After agreeing not to fight the racism he would face for a period of three years, Robinson signed a contract with the Montreal Royals. After playing an amazing season with the Royals, Robinson was called up to the Dodgers on April 15, 1947. While this story is factually true, there is a great deal missing from this version of events.

Baseball enthusiasts have known for decades that Jackie Robinson was not the first black professional baseball player in the United States: professional baseball was an integrated space in the nineteenth century, when players such as Moses Fleetwood Walker, George Stovey, and Bud Fowler struggled for acceptance. By the time *Plessy v. Ferguson* codified the separate-but-equal doctrine throughout the United States in 1896, professional baseball had pushed the few U.S.–born black players it employed out of racially integrated teams, and baseball remained a segregated space until it was reintegrated by the likes of Jackie Robinson and Larry Doby. Arguably, MLB does a much better job than the other professional team sports in embracing its history, including the good, bad, and ugly; however, the "integration" narrative the league perpetuates leaves out a large and important portion of the story.

In the book *Lies My Teacher Told Me: Everything Your American History Textbook Got Wrong*, James Loewen discusses how history textbooks deal with baseball's integration by writing:

> Students never learn that blacks played in the major leagues until the nadir [1891–1940], so the usual textbook story line — generally uninterrupted progress to the present — stays in place.... [These textbooks perpetuate the story that] in race relations, as in everything, our society is constantly getting better. We used to have slavery; now we don't. We used to have lynchings; now we don't. Baseball used to be all white; now it isn't. The notion of progress implies that race relations have somehow steadily improved on their own. This cheery optimism only compounds the problem, because whites can infer that racism is over.[7]

Much of this argument appears on the surface to be about semantics: do we frame the events of 1947 as the integration of MLB or as the reintegration of professional baseball? Framing Jackie Robinson as the first African American to play MLB, as many history textbooks do, "e-races" (to once again use Kimberlé Crenshaw's term for the color-blind ideal that dismisses the "dynamics of racial power"[8]) Walker, Stovey, and Fowler from baseball's history; and, as Loewen argues, perpetuates the notion that race relations in the United States have always followed, and will undoubtedly continue to follow, a forward trajectory. Discussing Robinson and Doby in terms of the reintegration of professional baseball does nothing to diminish their accomplishments; it opens the door to discussing black professional baseball players in the nineteenth century, and demonstrates that racial progress is not guaranteed.

Given how much MLB has embraced its history, particularly when it comes to black baseball and the Negro Leagues, why would black players from the nineteenth century be left out of the discussion? Arguably this omission has to do with a phenomenon termed interest convergence, which argues that "the interest of blacks in achieving racial equality will be accommodated only when it converges with the interests of whites."[9] Using the landmark *Brown v. Board of Education* decision as an example, Derrick Bell argues that *Brown* had less to do with ensuring equal opportunities for black communities and more to do with enhancing the United States' credibility abroad, promoting the South's move toward industrialization, and reassuring black veterans that the goals of World War II were valid abroad and at home.[10] In this case, framing Robinson and Doby's accomplishments as the reintegration of baseball is not in the best interest of MLB. Professional baseball frames itself as a pioneer when it comes to race relations — one of the first and only industries that integrated without legal pressure. Examining baseball's racial history would point out just how agonizingly slow baseball's reintegration process was. Ten years after Robinson and Doby joined their respective teams, neither the Tigers nor the Red Sox had signed a single black player. While changing the narrative to include the earlier period of integration would be historically accurate, it also makes MLB's actions in the 1940s look less magnanimous. Many institutions within the United States, including baseball, have a "practice of accepting black contributions and ignoring the contributors."[11] The narrative will not change because it will highlight the achievements of those early pioneers; it only changes when it is in baseball's best interests.

How Many Is Too Many?

In 1982 the National League's Rookie of the Year Award was renamed for Robinson, and in honor of the fiftieth anniversary of reintegration, Robinson's number 42 was retired for every team in perpetuity. Every major league ballpark displays Robinson's number, and once New York Yankees pitcher Mariano Rivera, who already wore 42, retires, no MLB player will ever wear 42 again.

Not content to wait for an anniversary that is a multiple of ten, MLB designated April 15, 2004, as Jackie Robinson Day throughout the league. Commissioner Selig noted, "We celebrate so no generation shall forget what Jackie Robinson did. So young players not only know who Jackie Robinson was but what Jackie Robinson did for them."[12] Fast forward three years to the sixtieth anniversary of baseball's reintegration: veteran outfielder Ken Griffey, Jr., asks Commissioner Selig and Rachel Robinson if he may wear 42 on Jackie Robinson Day. According to Griffey, "I knew the [Robinson] family. It was just my way of saying thank you. I had no idea it would be something like this. I think this is a great cause. There's a lot of people in here that wouldn't be in here if it wasn't for him. The family deserves this. You never know how long it would have been if he would have failed."[13] Rachel Robinson approved of the gesture, and while originally only one member per team would have the honor of wearing 42, Commissioner Selig expanded the invitation to any player who was interested.[14] On Jackie Robinson Day, the entire Dodgers staff and many players on other teams un-retired Robinson's number. Following the games the jerseys were auctioned off with the proceeds going to the Jackie Robinson Foundation.[15]

Though many of the players who wore Robinson's number were demonstrably honored, what started as a handful of tributes turned into a mandate: starting in 2009, all players, coaches, and umpires were asked to wear 42 on Jackie Robinson Day. Pitcher CC Sabathia wondered aloud whether having so many people wearing the jersey was a good idea, saying, "It does water it down a little bit."[16] Outfielder Torii Hunter remarked, "This is supposed to be an honor and just a handful of guys wearing the number. Now you've got entire teams doing it. I think we're killing the meaning. It should be special wearing Jackie's number, not just because it looks cool."[17] Is forcing individuals to wear the number 42 a good way to honor Robinson? Even though the edict made wearing the number optional, it is difficult to imagine that any player would decline the option and then be forced to explain the decision on national television.

We would like to believe that all professional baseball players are enlightened souls when it comes to race relations, but let's imagine for a moment that John Rocker was still pitching in 2009. I do not think there is anyone who would argue that having Rocker, who demonstrated such a low opinion of anyone who was not a white heterosexual male, wear 42 would be a good idea. On the one hand, seeing all of the on-field personnel wearing 42 can be seen as a powerful gesture of honor and unity — though it certainly made life difficult for any fans scoring the game. On the other hand, the visual in some ways diminishes what Robinson and Doby experienced when they reintegrated professional baseball. We have to remember that Robinson and Doby received minuscule, if any, support from their teammates, managers, coaches, or umpires; they were, in every sense of the word, alone. While having only one player per team wear 42 (or 14 if Cleveland wanted to honor Doby) would not have the same visual impact as an entire baseball diamond full of 42s, it again would be more historically accurate and it would shift the focus of the celebration from MLB as an organization to Robinson and Doby as individuals.

What I find so interesting about the current "everyone should wear the number" approach is that this was not always the mindset baseball players had regarding Robinson's number. When Selig announced that 42 was going to be retired, several ballplayers were already wearing that number, and as such, they were all grandfathered in. One player, Marc Sagmoen, was making his Major League debut wearing 42 when Selig announced the number was being retired. Though he did not have to, the very next game, Sagmoen switched numbers, saying, "I just didn't think it would be right. I thought it would be better to retire it now. It was nice to wear it for one game, but I wouldn't have felt right to wear it every game."[18] And Rangers manager Johnny Oates maintained, "If [Sagmoen] had been in the dugout [when the announcement was made], we would've torn the jersey off his back." In the span of twenty years, Robinson's 42 went from a number so sacred and filled with meaning that no individual could ever live up to its memory, to being a commodity everyone has access to, and which is auctioned off to the highest bidder. After MLB made wearing 42 *de rigueur* for Jackie Robinson Day, only one player has ever declined the honor: in 2007, Los Angeles outfielder Garret Anderson refused to wear 42, saying simply "I just don't feel worthy of it."[19]

Divide and Conquer

Beginning with the sixtieth anniversary celebration, MLB held the inaugural Civil Rights Game, which, according to Selig, was "designed to commemorate the civil rights movement, one of the most critical and important eras of our social history.... I am proud of the role that Major League Baseball played in the movement, beginning with Jackie Robinson's entry into the big leagues on April 15, 1947, and very pleased that we have this opportunity to honor the Movement and those who made it happen."[20] Celebrating baseball's place within the larger civil rights movement is certainly a noble idea, and MLB did not stop at the Civil Rights Game: there was a round-table discussion on the diminishing number of U.S.–born black players in professional baseball held in conjunction with the National Civil Rights Museum. Filmmaker Spike Lee unveiled a short documentary piece on the Civil Rights Game, and MLB honored Lee, Vera Clemente, and the late Buck O'Neill with Beacon Awards, which were designed to honor an individual's contributions to civil rights and their link to baseball.[21]

While the thought behind the Civil Rights Game was noble, the execution is where MLB fell short in three ways. First, many wondered aloud why the game was played in March. Though the game was well publicized and carried on ESPN, if the goal was to bring awareness and to celebrate the civil rights movement, why not play the game during the regular season to maximize the audience? Not only would the game be meaningless because it took place during spring training, but also most sports fans spend the month of March engrossed in college basketball's March Madness, not baseball. The timing was rectified in 2009, when the Civil Rights Game was moved to the regular season.

While the timing of the game was a simple issue to rectify, the next two controversies are a bit more complicated. When the Civil Rights Game was announced, the two teams scheduled to participate were the defending World Series Champion Cardinals and Cleveland. It was the latter team's inclusion that raised some questions. On the one hand, Cleveland was the first American League team to sign a U.S.–born black player: Larry Doby, who unfortunately is often left out of the reintegration discussion, debuted three months after Robinson. In addition, Cleveland hired the first black manager: Frank Robinson helmed the team from 1975 to 1977. On the other hand, there are many who find Cleveland's logo Chief Wahoo offensive and demeaning, myself included; notice throughout this book that Cleveland and Atlanta are referred to by their city names while every other club is referred to by their team name. Many Native American groups have been protesting these mascots since Frank Robinson managed in Cleveland and they "see the elimination of such mascots as part of a larger agenda of reducing societal stereotyping about Native Americans (in the media, school curriculums, and so forth) and informing the public about the realities of Native American lives."[22] It is unlikely that MLB was unaware of the controversy Cleveland's inclusion would draw, since, as Filip Bondy of the *New York Daily News* remarked,

> Chief Wahoo has long been given a tacit go-ahead from Bud Selig, the same commissioner who has done so much in recognizing the contributions of African-Americans and in confessing the past exclusionary policies of baseball. Selig has embraced the legacy of Jackie Robinson and other black pioneers.... The lack of empathy on this issue is truly inexplicable. One race can't commit genocide against another, then turn that race into a mascot.[23]

The lack of empathy Bondy describes harks back to Charles Lawrence III's notion of unconscious racism, which has been discussed in previous chapters. According to Lawrence, the nation's history of racism is so engrained that all Americans unconsciously harbor negative opinions about nonwhites. Because society no longer tolerates overt racism, the negative attitudes created by the shared racist history will find another outlet.[24] While outward expressions of overt racism against African Americans may not be tolerated as they once were the same may not be true for overt acts against Native Americans. Kimberly Roppolo makes the argument that "if we had sports teams named the New York Niggers or the Jersey Jigaboos, Americans would know this was wrong."[25] But because these mascots demean Native Americans, no one seems concerned. Maybe in anticipation of the controversy Cleveland's inclusion would generate, neither team wore their official jerseys during the game; throwback Negro League jerseys, which did not feature any team logos, were worn instead. Were the changed jerseys the only way to honor Doby's and Cleveland's contributions to baseball's reintegration without promoting Chief Wahoo? It is a complicated problem, to be sure.

To make matters even worse, the selection of teams was not the only way the Civil Rights Game pitted African American and Native American communities against each other. MLB chose Memphis, Tennessee, as the official home of the Civil Rights Game. According to Selig, this location was chosen in honor of the Rev. Dr. Martin Luther King, Jr., and because the National Civil Rights Museum is located just blocks from the ballpark. Much like the inclusion of the Cleveland team, the location, on the surface, seems like a good idea. Unfortunately while MLB seemed focused on Memphis's significance during the 1960s, they missed the city's significance during the 1830s: Memphis is along the route of the infamous Trail of Tears, where thousands of Cherokees died and were buried in shallow graves. Because Memphis has a sizable Native American population, due partially to the forced relocation, adding Chief Wahoo to the relative silence on the Trail of Tears issue was the straw that broke the camel's back. Alice Gwin Henry, president of the Faraway Cherokees in Memphis, lambasted the debacle by saying, "It's disgusting. It tells you where they're coming from. We try not to be overbearing when it comes to the use of names, but nobody has addressed the Trail of Tears as it's associated with an abuse of civil rights."[26] One blogger summed up the baseball's epic fail in this regard noting, "MLB invited the St. Louis Cardinals and the Cleveland Indians, of the Chief Wahoo Indians, to a city that was on the Trail of Tears, with people in and near Memphis that are ancestors of that particular genocidal event, to a game that is supposed to commemorate one race's struggle for equality and acceptance, with a team that sports, to a good chunk of the people that matter, a logo and name that are inherently offensive."[27]

As expected, MLB was completely silent on the Trail of Tears issue, and only a minuscule number of sportswriters had anything critical to say about the game's location or Cleveland's inclusion. In this case the ignorance of this history renders racism not simply unconscious but invisible — or perhaps, given the lack of attention this issue generated, simply "an open secret, which everyone has agreed upon."[28] Whether or not the silent backlash had anything to do with the fact that the Civil Rights Game left Memphis after two years is unknown.

My Aren't We Plural Lately

One of the key questions that has to be asked about MLB's celebrations of Jackie Robinson is who or what exactly is being honored. I have always assumed that since the celebration is billed as Jackie Robinson Day that the person being honored would be Jackie Robinson; however, that does not seem to be the case. In discussing the Civil Rights Game, Commissioner Selig commented, "We did things that led people to believe that you could have black and white getting together, living together, working together, and enjoying each other, so the Civil Rights Game I think without question is a manifestation of how proud we are of what we've done and more importantly what we should do in the future."[29] The word that stands out in Selig's comments is the proverbial we. Who is the "we" Selig is referring to? Selig could not have been referring to himself since, as he mentioned later in the interview, he was a child when Robinson signed with the Dodgers. Context clues lead us to the probability that Selig is talking about Major League Baseball, and if that is the case, it might be helpful to analyze the league's role in reintegration. *We* expelled the few black players it had in the late nineteenth century and perpetuated segregation, whether de jure or de facto is still not completely clear, while touting itself as the national pastime. *We* raided the Negro Leagues for its best players with complete disregard for the players' contracts. *We* forced Robinson to endure verbal and physical abuse from teammates and fans and did not let him defend himself. *We* took well over ten years to completely reintegrate, and *we* did nothing for almost two decades when black players were forced to stay in separate hotels and eat in separate restaurants than their teammates. Finally, *we* "made no efforts, and apparently gave minimal thought, to bring blacks into coaching, managing, front office, or ownership roles."[30]

Selig's statements remind me of a sequence from Rob Reiner's 1987 film *The Princess Bride*. In the film the character Vizzini continuously refers to events as being inconceivable: it is inconceivable that Westley is following their boat, but he is; it is inconceivable that Westley is climbing the rope faster than they are, but he is; it is inconceivable that Westley does not fall to his death when his rope is cut, but he doesn't. After the third inconceivable occurrence, Inigo Montoya turns to Vizzini and says, "You keep using that word. I do not think it means what you think it means."[31] Commissioner Selig continues to use the word *we* to describe the reintegration process: I do not think the word "we" means what he thinks it means. In reality, "we" treated Robinson, Doby, and the first two generations of black players as second-class citizens, while framing ourselves as a bastion of integration and equality. Former sportswriter Ed Sullivan framed Jackie Robinson Day in a very different way than Commissioner Selig when he noted, "I think that even [though this] is called one of the finest days in baseball, I think it is also one of its most disgraceful days.... I think baseball, organized baseball, should be issuing an apology for the 50 years of de facto segregation."[32] Again, the notion that MLB played an equal role in the reintegration process perpetuates the myth that the league has done and will continue to help its players and to help the nation move forward where race relations are concerned. If MLB truly embraced the narrative it perpetuates about itself, then it stands to reason that the league would continue its commitment to racial justice.

Divide and Conquer Redux

In April 2010, Arizona Governor Jan Brewer signed one of the toughest immigration laws in the nation. The controversial SB 1070 made it a crime to not carry immigration documents, it required law enforcement officials to "detain people they reasonably suspect are in the country without authorization," and it allowed citizens to sue law enforcement officials who they felt were not enforcing the legislation.[33] The reactions to the law were swift and decisive: President Obama publicly criticized the bill, Mexico's President Felipe Calderón not only condemned the law, but also issued a travel advisory to Mexican nationals traveling to Arizona. Arizona Congressman Raúl Grijalva called for a boycott of his own state in protest of the law. One of the main criticisms of the legislation was the question surrounding what criteria law enforcement officials would use to decide who they suspected to be an undocumented immigrant. Because no one could describe what they thought an undocumented immigrant looked like, most suspected the law could result in racial profiling. Even though officials were loath to admit it, that when they think of an undocumented immigrant they are thinking of someone who looks like Alex Rodríguez, who is a U.S. citizen, as opposed to someone who looks like Justin Morneau, who is not a U.S. citizen.

Given the large number of non–U.S. born players in the league, many people looked to MLB to take a stand against the law, especially given the fact that half of the League holds spring training in Arizona and the 2011 All-Star Game was scheduled to be held there. Janet Murguía, President and CEO of the National Council of La Raza, authored a plea to Bud Selig that read in part: "We are asking the league to take a stand against bigotry and intolerance. Selig should stand up for the hundreds of players who form the backbone of today's game but whose last names and appearances put them at risk of being stopped by law enforcement every time they happen to play the Diamondbacks at Chase Field. He should stand up for the millions of Latino fans who fervently support the teams that make up the league."[34] Padres first baseman Adrian Gonzalez and White Sox manager Ozzie Guillén both said they would not play in the All-Star Game if it were held in Arizona.[35] The Players' Association issued a strongly worded statement in opposition to the law, which clearly stated: "If the current law goes into effect, the MLBPA will consider additional steps necessary to protect the rights and interests of our members."[36] It seemed as though everyone was making statements regarding what came to be known as the "Papers Please" law, except representatives of MLB. Moving the All-Star Game would not have been unprecedented: in 1993 the Super Bowl was scheduled to take place in Tempe, Arizona, but the NFL Players' Association voted to move the game because the state refused to recognize Martin Luther King Jr. Day. Arguably due to the negative publicity and the millions of dollars the state lost due to the NFL's decision, Arizona voters later approved the holiday. No one is ever going to confuse the NFL with the NAACP or Amnesty International, but in this case, the NFL is a far more progressive organization than MLB. Selig's silence was puzzling: if Selig is as enthusiastic about baseball's link to civil rights and, as he phrased it, the work MLB will do in the future in terms of civil rights, then why not take a stand?

From a practical standpoint, it makes more sense to be concerned about the well-being of Latin players, since they make up 27 percent of the League, while African American players make up approximately 10 percent.[37] Taking a stand against the Papers Please law would also be in the best interests of the League: no one wants to turn on *SportsCenter* and see a list of Latin players who were on their way to a spring training game and got arrested because they didn't have their work visas handy. Proponents of moving the All-Star Game tried to make the decision as easy as possible for Selig by invoking Jackie Robinson's legacy and by appealing to the civil rights legacy Selig claims to cherish. New York Congressman José Serrano wrote an open letter to Selig that read, "Major League Baseball is a standard bearer for diversity and tolerance — it should not tacitly support Arizona's immigration policy by holding such a prestigious event there."[38] The Rev. Jesse Jackson urged players and management to "follow the example set by Jackie Robinson"[39] and speak out against the Papers Please law. Most players followed Selig's lead and said nothing. In some ways, Selig was saved from having to defend his avoidance: the Justice Department sued Arizona over the law and a federal judge blocked key parts of the law including the provision that many believed would lead to racial profiling. The judge's decision seemed to deflate much of the urgency surrounding the law, and the protest calls decreased, though there were still some protests during the All-Star Game. What is especially odd about that particular All-Star Game is that despite the lack of a player-organized boycott, many of the biggest stars, including Derek Jeter, Alex Rodríguez, and CC Sabathia declined to attend. Possibly as a result, the TV ratings dropped eight percent from the previous year, marking a new low for viewership.[40]

It would seem that even though MLB takes pride in its connection to the Civil Rights Movement, it does not actually practice what it preaches. For Dave Zirin, "Selig clearly loves the symbolism of civil rights more than the sacrifice."[41] ESPN.com's Jeff MacGregor argued, "Whenever it's safe and convenient ... Major League Baseball can always be counted upon to take as much reflected credit as possible for the courage of individuals such as Jackie Robinson or Branch Rickey or Curt Flood [but otherwise the League] is as hidebound and reactionary as any institution in America, and something of a stooge for the status quo."[42] Apparently a commitment to civil rights is to be commended among players of the past, but it's horribly inconvenient when people expect results in the present. That raises the question, regardless of the league's past affiliation with civil rights, is it realistic to expect MLB to actually advocate for anyone's civil rights? If Bell's theory of racial realism is correct, then MLB will always preserve the status quo, and any gestures toward justice and equality are purely self-serving.

On the surface it seems logical that immigration reform, or at least less hostile anti-immigration laws, are in MLB's best interests given the international nature of the league; but in reality, it does not matter. As discussed in Chapter 1, teams have been operating under the boatload mentality when it comes to Latin players for almost two decades. As harsh as it sounds, and Critical Race Theorists are all about being blunt, if the boatload mentality is your starting point, then that means every Latin player from Albert Pujols down to the ubiquitous "player to be named later" is infinitely expendable. If Johan Santana does not have his papers in order and is arrested on his way to pitch against the Diamondbacks, there are twenty other players waiting to take his place, and the Mets won't have to pay any of them the same $21 million annual salary. On second thought, maybe advocating for less hostile anti-immigration laws is not in MLB's best interests; the status quo makes better economic sense.

Oh the Irony

After a rough start with the first few Civil Rights Games, MLB was hoping for a nice and quiet event in 2011. Held in Atlanta, the Civil Rights Game featured the home team versus the Phillies. Both teams wore 1974 throwback uniforms as homage to Henry Aaron's breaking the all-time home run record. Once again, we have a problem with location, location, location. Much like Cleveland, Atlanta finds itself on the wrong side of the Native American mascot issue. While Atlanta thankfully does not have a grinning Chief Wahoo as their logo, the fans are notorious for the "tomahawk chop" they perform in unison. As mentioned in Chapter 2, in the discussion of Mike Piazza, it was one month prior to the Civil Rights Game that Atlanta pitching coach Roger McDowell was suspended without pay for yelling a homophobic slur and simulating an explicit sex act in front of fans. Undeterred by these minor controversies, Selig once again made the argument that "baseball is a social institution, and it has really important social responsibilities. I really believe that in every way. This event symbolizes what we should do, and frankly, what we want to do more of."[43] Unfortunately for Selig, the theory of baseball as a social institution bumped up against the practice of baseball as a social institution — again.

In May 2011, the Georgia legislature followed Arizona's lead and passed an immigration law that empowered law enforcement officials to check an individual's immigration status. The bill was decried by civil rights groups across the nation and the Justice Department almost immediately filed suit to prevent implementation of the law. As mentioned earlier in this chapter, prior to the game, MLB selects three recipients for a Beacon Award, given to honor the individual's commitment to civil rights. Whether Selig realized it at the time or not, this year's award winners actually took their awards seriously. Upon receiving his award, Grammy-award winning musician Carlos Santana took the microphone and said, "The people of Arizona, and the people of Atlanta, Georgia, you should be ashamed of yourselves."[44] The fun did not end there. After being booed by Atlanta fans, Santana held a press conference and continued to do exactly what you would expect a person being honored with a Beacon of Change award would do: he spoke out, saying: "This law is not correct. It's a cruel law, actually, This is about fear.... I am here to give voice to the invisible. Most people at this point, they are either afraid to really say what needs to be said, this is the United States, the land of the free. If people want the immigration law to keep passing in every state then everybody should get out and just leave the American Indians here. This is about civil rights."[45] Now, I'm almost willing to give MLB the benefit of the doubt in terms of the All-Star Game, though I boycotted every single moment of it. Moving the game would have been expensive and probably would have incurred a very loud backlash. But this is the Civil Rights Game, whose expressed purpose is to link baseball and civil rights, so this is a perfect time to make a statement about the rash of anti-immigration laws sweeping the nation, or at the very least to admonish the fans who booed Santana for trying to get the Civil Rights Game to live up to its name. That did not happen. Fans were spared Selig's comments on the matter since he left the game early; whether he had a prior engagement or was actively trying to avoid grappling with Santana's comments is unknown.

Remarks by one Beacon Award winner could be dismissed as an aberration, but when fellow Beacon Award recipient Morgan Freeman chimed in saying the laws were "absolutely un–American, completely, that's the kind of discrimination that's going to be our next civil rights struggle,"[46] you would think it would be even more difficult for MLB to ignore. Yet again, the only things heard from the Commissioner's office were crickets. the *Nation* columnist Dave Zirin blasted Selig's inaction on his blog:

If Selig really gave a damn about Civil Rights, he would heed the words of Carlos Santana.... He would recognize that the sport of Jackie Robinson, Roberto Clemente and Curt Flood has an obligation to stand for something more than just using their memory to cover up the injustices of the present. If Bud Selig cared about Civil Rights, he would above all else, have to develop something resembling a spine. But if Bud is altogether unfamiliar with the concept of courage, he received one hell of an object lesson from Carlos Santana.[47]

If nothing else, MLB's actions surrounding the Civil Rights Games highlight Derrick Bell's theory of racial realism: regardless of what Selig says, MLB will always be less concerned with justice and more concerned with protecting the status quo.

Parting Shots

Peggy McIntosh and Tim Wise talk about white privilege. Those privileges have to come from somewhere: they come from people and organizations in higher positions of power that have a vested interest in protecting whiteness. In previous chapters I've discussed sportswriters engaging in a possessive investment in whiteness by bestowing white privileges, such as framing a white player as innocent until proven guilty when it comes to performance-enhancing drugs while immediately throwing players of color under the bus, or ignoring the vast wealth accumulated by team owners while at the same time bemoaning player salaries. Having the power to frame a narrative, to mold how we view Jackie Robinson, is a manifestation of white privilege, and Major League Baseball is choosing the image of Robinson they want to perpetuate based on self-interest (i.e., a possessive investment in whiteness). Tim Wise makes the argument that progressive activists and groups exercise white privilege through "the favoring of white perspectives over those of people of color, the co-optation of black and brown suffering to score political points, and the unwillingness to engage race and racism even when they are central to the issue being addressed."[48] This is exactly what MLB has done when it comes to Jackie Robinson: it has favored the narrative that Robinson was the first black player, thereby "e-racing" nineteenth-century black baseball players from the sport's history; it proclaims to honor Robinson's achievements while ignoring the institutional and systemic racism he had to endure in order to obtain those achievements; and it has completely ignored the racial issues involving Native American mascots and immigration laws even when they are brought up during a Civil Rights Game. Organizations can and do have a possessive investment in whiteness and do perpetuate white privilege.

When Jackie Robinson was elected into the Baseball Hall of Fame in 1962, his plaque mentioned batting averages, stolen bases and double plays.

There was no mention of the reintegration of professional baseball. When the plaque was rededicated in 2008, the final line was revised and included the statement, "Displayed tremendous courage and poise in 1947 when he integrated the modern major leagues in the face of intense adversity."[49] Major League Baseball has tried its best to honor Jackie Robinson's memory and has, unfortunately, come up embarrassingly short. In many ways it seems that Major League Baseball is comfortable with a certain version of Jackie Robinson: MLB prefers the quiet version of Robinson, the version that turned the other cheek and did not speak out against the verbal and physical abuse he encountered. In essence, Major League Baseball pays homage to a "safe" version of Robinson. Unfortunately for Major League Baseball, the safe version leaves out entirely too much because, as Steve Wisensale points out, "Although remembered primarily for integrating baseball and for his athletic skills in a Dodger uniform, Robinson always appeared to be someone who was on a much broader and more important mission in life."[50] As the quote from Robinson at the beginning of this chapter states, that version of Robinson is seen as the "appropriate posture for a black man."

If Major League Baseball were truly committed to the idea that baseball and civil rights are linked, no matter how dubious that idea might be, it would honor the less safe version of Robinson. It would honor in both words and actions the Robinson who was court-martialed and later exonerated for refusing to sit in the back of a bus; it would honor the Robinson who spoke out against the reserve clause at Curt Flood's trial even though he was retired and the outcome did not affect him in the least; it would honor the Robinson who, during one of his rare baseball appearances after retiring, chastised the league for not having any minority managers. Wearing the number 42 and simply playing the game wasn't enough for Mr. Robinson and it should not be enough for Major League Baseball. Maybe Major League Baseball is just like any other sport or any other business venture and expecting it to live up to past ideals is an exercise in futility. Maybe Major League Baseball is simply playing lip service to Robinson's memory in an effort to appear far more enlightened than it actually is or to cover up the rapidly diminishing number of U.S.–born black players in the league. For Doug Battema, we have two options when it comes to framing Robinson: "We can view Robinson as an agent for positive change in the present, or as a symbol of a status quo for which we can be content."[51] Clearly, the powers that be are going with option two. Unlike Major League Baseball, I prefer option one: if I see something wrong I feel the need to speak out about it. As Mr. Robinson once stated, "I love baseball and — even though I do, in fact BECAUSE I do — I will continue to criticize it."[52] Major League Baseball can honor Robinson their way, and I'll honor him in my way. This is my way.

Conclusions

"This is a simple game. You throw the ball. You hit the ball. You catch the ball. You got it?"—Bull Durham[1]

"The one constant through all the years, Ray, has been baseball. America has rolled by like an army of steamrollers. It has been erased like a blackboard, rebuilt and erased again. But baseball has marked the time. This field, this game: it's a part of our past, Ray. It reminds us of all that once was good and it could be again."—Field of Dreams[2]

Major League Baseball presents an interesting conundrum: as the *Bull Durham* quotation illustrates, it is a very simple game; however, as the *Field of Dreams* quotation points out, it is a simple game fraught with historical meaning and national resonance. At first glance, this book may appear to be an amalgam of baseball events that have little if anything to do with one another. But what these incidents illustrate is a pattern of behavior that occurs when uncomfortable topics such as race, class, nationality, and sexual identity enter the sports discussion. White privilege can be conferred upon baseball personnel by sportswriters when there is a lack of diverse voices framing these race and sport discussions.

Sportswriters bestowed white privilege upon Mark McGwire when they ignored suspected drug use throughout the 1998 season; relegated Sammy Sosa, who had similar accomplishments, to the role of a sidekick; admonished Sosa for a corked bat while still side-stepping McGwire's use of performance-enhancing drugs; and allowed McGwire to return to baseball without much fanfare after admitting drug use. White privilege reared its head again when Roger Clemens was initially given the benefit of the doubt about performance-enhancing drugs and Andy Pettitte was forgiven and cheered, while Barry Bonds remains the poster-child of baseball's steroid era. Of course the most puzzling example of white privilege and baseball's steroid era is how the commissioner's office, team owners, managers, not to mention the sportswriters themselves, have seemingly been absolved for any culpability from allowing performance-enhancing drugs to flourish.

Privileges are not given out based solely on race: gender, class, sexual identity, and nation of origin are all identities where privileges and disadvantages are distributed. Alex Rodríguez's initial contract worth $1.3 million highlights how U.S.–born players can capitalize on the privileges based on their national origin. If Rodríguez had been raised in the Dominican Republic, his initial contract would have more closely resembled that of players like Sammy Sosa, whose $3,500 signing bonus in 1986 was the same amount the Dodgers paid Jackie Robinson in 1947.[3] Despite being considered one of the best players in the game, A-Rod's contract drew outrage that was swift, decisive, and hostile, considering that no one was concerned about the massive fortunes that the predominantly white team ownership have accumulated. Unfortunately for Mike Piazza, who represented the elite white males, whiteness proved to be less than beneficial because it ensured that any questions surrounding his sexual identity would be more damaging to the elite white, heterosexual, male power structure and therefore would be extremely newsworthy. At the same time, stereotypes about Asian masculinity which relegate Asian men broadly, and Asian players specifically, to the bottom of American masculinity and sexual identity hierarchies, were some one of the reasons why stories surrounding Kazuhiro Tadano's sexuality were downplayed by sportswriters.

Peggy McIntosh makes the argument that "white privilege is like an invisible weightless knapsack of special provisions, maps, passports, codebooks, visas, clothes, tools and blank checks."[4] This definition raises the question: Where do these special provisions and blank checks come from? By providing players and other members of baseball's power structure with privileges based on race, the predominantly white sportswriters and editors are engaging in a possessive investment in whiteness which creates advantages based on "favoritism, not fitness, fortitude, or family formations."[5] As long as sportswriters give white players a free pass for the same sins that players of color commit, the cycle of white privilege will continue. Logically, as long as 97 percent of sports editors and 86 percent of sports columnists are white, the people framing the stories will continue to have a possessive investment in their whiteness and bestow privileges to people who share their racial background. The same holds true for gender, class, and sexual identity. It stands to reason that if sports news environments become more diverse, racial bias should decrease. At the very least, the discussions surrounding race will become more complex.

This is not to say that athletes are victims who are powerless against sportswriters' racial whims. On the contrary, this text highlights ways that baseball players have exercised some semblance of agency even if the choices available to them were limited. Sammy Sosa made the choice to play the sidekick to Mark McGwire. If non–U.S. born black players like Roberto Clemente demanded that sportswriters respect his language, culture, and talent in the 1970s, Sosa could have made similar demands in the 1990s. At the same time, Sosa had to be aware of the fact that the accolades would certainly be greater if he happily let McGwire be "The Man." Alex Rodríguez could have spent his entire career in Seattle; however, like the overwhelming majority of people in the United States who subscribe to capitalism, A-Rod made the choice to take a job with higher pay and more benefits. Instead of ignoring the rumors about his sexual identity, Mike Piazza chose to perpetuate the idea that even being framed as gay would be detrimental to his career. This choice led Piazza to literally hold a press conference where he could assert his heterosexual identity. Perhaps because of his father's interactions with sportswriters and the mistaken notion that on-field talent should trump personality, Barry Bonds made the choice not to be the type of black athlete sportswriters were used to dealing with. Bonds has on occasion shown himself to be a warm and generous person. When for instance, Giants fan Bryan Stow was viciously beaten on Opening Day at Dodger Stadium in 2011, Bonds offered to pay for Stow's children to attend college.[6] Years after being unceremoniously released by the Giants, Bonds remained loyal to a fan in need. Because Bonds chose not to bill himself as a pre-infidelity Tiger Woods or a pre–Miami Heat LeBron James, sportswriters balked and framed him as an angry black man. Effa Manley had a choice in terms of her expressed racial identity. Manley could, and sometimes did, pass for white and at the same time could, and did, pass for black. She also made the decision to deliberately obfuscate efforts to pin down her racial identity.

Jackie Robinson exercised agency at every turn, beginning with the choice not to express his anger and frustration during the first few years of his career. After he had the ability to fight back, Robinson could have remained silent and kept his head down but chose not to. After he left the baseball spotlight, Robinson could have settled into a quiet retirement, but he chose to actively engage with the civil rights struggles of the time. The combination of these choices turned Robinson into one of the most influential people of the twentieth century and ensured that the world was a better place because he lived in it. The choices are not always pretty, but they are choices, and athletes have the agency to make those choices. The problem occurs when sportswriters do not respect the players' agency and use their considerable voice or column inches to show disrespect for those choices.

Ultimately, how an event is discussed by media representatives is as important as the event itself. Sports are pervasive in American culture, and sportswriters have a tremendous amount of power to shape how and what we think about individuals and sporting events. Given the role that sportswriters play, it is the job of fans and commentators to keep them honest, especially since, as William Zinsser points out, "Sport is now a major frontier of social change, and some of the nation's most vexing issues are being played out in our stadiums, grandstands and locker rooms. If you want to write about America, this is the one place to pitch your tent."[7]

Chapter Notes

Preface

1. Patricia Hill Collins, *Black Sexual Politics; African Americans, Gender, and the New Racism* (New York: Routledge, 2004), 153.

2. Jackie Robinson, "Letter to Michael Hamilburg," in *First Class Citizenship: The Civil Rights Letters of Jackie Robinson* edited by Michael G. Long (New York: Times Books, 2007), 302.

3. Kyle McNary, *Black Baseball: A History of African-Americans & the National Game* (New York: Sterling, 2003), 12.

4. Mary G. McDonald and Susan Birrell, "Reading Sport Critically: A Methodology for Interrogating Power," *Sociology of Sport Journal* 16, no. 4 (1999): 284.

5. Ibid., 290.

6. Susan Birrell and Mary G. McDonald, "Reading Sport, Articulating Power Lines: An Introduction," in *Reading Sport: Critical Essays on Power and Representation*, edited by Susan Birrell and Mary G. McDonald (Boston, Northeastern University Press, 2000), 4.

7. Josh Suchon, *This Gracious Season. Barry Bonds & the Greatest Year in Baseball* (Los Angeles: Winter Publications, 2002), 20.

Introduction

1. John Thorn, "Why Baseball," in *Total Baseball: The Ultimate Baseball Encyclopedia*, ed. John Thorn, Phil Birnbam, and Bill Dean (Wilmington, DE: Sport Media, 2004), 3.

2. "The First Inning: Our Game: 1840s–1900," *Baseball*, dir. Ken Burns (1994; PBS Distribution, 2010), DVD.

3. Ibid.

4. Leonard Koppett, *Koppett's Concise History of Major League Baseball* (New York: Carroll & Gaf, 2004), 460.

5. Richard Lapchick, Eric Little, Ray Mathew, and Jessica Zahn, "The 2008 Racial and Gender Report Card of the Associated Press Sports Editors" (Orlando, FL: The Institute for Diversity and Ethics in Sport, 2008), 2.

6. Ibid., 5.

7. Derrick Bell, "The Racism Is Permanent Thesis: Courageous Revelation or Unconscious Denial of Racial Genocide," *Capital University Law Review* 22, no. 1 (1993): 586.

8. Ibid., 573.

9. Fred L. Pincus, "Discrimination Comes in Many Forms: Individual, Institutional, and Structural," in *Readings for Diversity and Social Justice*, edited by Maurianne Adams, Warren J. Blumenfeld, Rosie Castañeda, Heather W. Hackman, Madeline L. Peters, and Ximena Zúñiga (New York: Routledge, 2000), 31.

10. G. Jarvie and I. Reid, "Race Relations, Sociology of Sport and the New Politics of Race and Racism," *Leisure Studies* 16,4 (1997): 216.

11. Collins, *Black Sexual Politics*, 153.

12. Ibid., 350.

13. Patricia Hill Collins, *Black Feminist Thought: Knowledge, Consciousness, and the Politics of Empowerment*, Revised Tenth Anniversary Edition (New York: Routledge, 2000), 69.

14. Ibid., 72.

15. Kimberlé Crenshaw, "Demarginalizing the Intersection of Race and Sex: A Black Feminist Critique of Antidiscrimination Doctrine, Feminist Theory, and Antiracist Politics," *Feminist Legal Theories*, ed. Karen J. Maschke (New York: Garland, 1997), 24.

16. Peggy McIntosh, "White Privilege: Unpacking the Invisible Knapsack," *White Privilege: Essential Readings on the Other Side of Racism*, 3rd Edition, edited by Paula Rothenberg (New York: Worth, 2002), 97.

17. Patricia Hill Collins, *From Black Power to Hip Hop: Racism, Nationalism, and Feminism* (Philadelphia, Temple University Press, 2006), 180.

18. Stephanie M. Wildman and Adrienne D. Davis, "Language and Silence: Making Systems of Privilege Visible," *Critical Race Theory: The Cutting Edge*, ed. Richard Delgado and Jean Stefancic (Philadelphia, Temple University Press, 2000), 658.

19. George Lipsitz, *The Possessive Investment*

in *Whiteness: How White People Profit from Identity Politics* (Philadelphia, Temple University Press, 2006), vii.

20. Richard Delgado and Jean Stefancic, "Introduction," *Critical Race Theory: The Cutting Edge*, edited by Richard Delgado and Jean Stefancic (Philadelphia, Temple University Press, 2000), xvi.

21. Ibid., xvii.

22. Charles R. Lawrence III, "The Id, the Ego, and Equal Protection: Reckoning with Unconscious Racism," in *Critical Race Theory: The Key Writings That Formed the Movement*, edited by Kimberlé Crenshaw, Neil Gotanda, Gary Peller, and Kendall Thomas (New York: The New Press, 1995), 237.

23. Peter Monaghan, "'Critical Race Theory': Some Startling Analyses," *The Chronicle of Higher Education*, June 23, 1993, A7.

24. Kevin Hylton, "'Race,' Sport and Leisure: Lessons from Critical Race Theory," *Leisure Studies* 24, no. 1 (2005): 92.

25. "The First Inning: Our Game: 1840s–1900."

Chapter 1

1. Tom Verducci, "Making His Mark," *Sports Illustrated*, September 14, 1998, 30.

2. Edward Said, "The President and the Baseball Player," *Cultural Critique* 43 (Autumn 1999): 136.

3. Johnny Mize (1947), Willie Mays (1955), Ralph Kiner (1947), and Cecil Fielder (1990) each hit 51 homers. McGwire (1996), Mays (1965), Mickey Mantle (1956), and George Foster (1977) each hit 52. Ruth (1920; 1928), Mantle (1961), and Kiner (1949) hit 54. Hack Wilson (1930) and Griffey (1997) hit 56, while Hank Greenberg (1938) and Jimmie Foxx (1932) hit 58. Ruth belted out 59 homers in 1921 and his historic 60 in 1927. As previously mentioned, Maris hit 61 in 1961.

4. Collins, *Black Sexual Politics*, 350.

5. Collins, *Black Feminist Thought*, 69.

6. Ellis Cashmore, *Making Sense of Sports*, Third Edition (London: Routledge, 2000), 126.

7. Collins, *Black Sexual Politics*, 152–3.

8. John Hoberman, *Darwin's Athletes: How Sport Has Damaged Black America and Preserved the Myth of Race* (Boston: Houghton Mifflin, 1997), xviii.

9. "#6: McGwire and Sosa Chase Maris," *The Headliners* (Bristol, CT: ESPN, 2004).

10. Tim McCarver, *The Perfect Season: Why 1998 Was Baseball's Greatest Year* (New York: Villard, 1999), xii.

11. Verducci, "Making His Mark," 32.

12. Said, 136.

13. Ibid., 137.

14. Harvey Araton, "Why Three Is Better Than One," *New York Times*, August 14, 1998, C1.

15. David C. Ogden and Michael L. Hilt, "Collective Identity and Basketball: An Explanation for the Decreasing Number of African-Americans on America's Baseball Diamonds," *Journal of Leisure Research* 35 (2003): 216.

16. Richard E. Lapchick, "1998 Racial and Gender Report Card" (Boston: The Center for the Study of Sport in Society, 1998), 7.

17. Lapchick, "2004 Racial and Gender Report Card" (Orlando, FL: The Institute for Diversity and Ethics in Sport, 2005), 35.

18. Brooks Boyer, "2005 Chicago White Sox Advertising Campaign," *Chicago White Sox*, http://chicago.whitesox.mlb.com/NASApp/mlb/cws/fan_forum/campaigns/television/index.jsp (accessed October 25, 2005).

19. Enid Trucios-Haynes, "Why Race Matters: LatCrit Theory and Latina/o Racial Identity," *Berkeley La Raza Law Journal*, 11/12 (2000): 8.

20. William A. Henry III, "Beyond the Melting Pot," *Time* April 28, 1990, 28.

21. Gary Smith, "Home Run Fever," *Sports Illustrated*, August 3, 1998, 40.

22. Joel Stein, Dan Cray, Maureen Harrington, Staci D Kramer, and Romeh Ratnesar, "The Fun Is Back," *Time*, July 27, 1998, 46.

23. Smith, "Home Run Fever," 42.

24. "#6: McGwire and Sosa Chase Maris."

25. Pedro Gomez, "Latin Players Could Use More Support," *The Sporting News*, June 2, 2002, 30.

26. Ibid., 30.

27. Douglas S. Looney, "Sosa: Big Home Runs, Bigger Smiles," *Christian Science Monitor*, July 2, 1999, 12.

28. Marcos Bretón and José Luis Villegas, *Away Games: The Life and Times of a Latin Baseball Player* (New York: Simon & Schuster, 1999), 35.

29. Joel Stein and Julie Grace, "Grand Slam," *Time* September 28, 1998, 76.

30. Marcos Bretón, "Fields of Broken Dreams: Latinos and Baseball," *ColorLines* 3, no. 1 (2000), http://search.proquest.com/docview/215541421?accountid=14925 (accessed September 3, 2011)

31. Steve Rushin, "Sam the Ham," *Sports Illustrated*, September 14, 1998, 35.

32. Tom Verducci, "Sosa: So, So Fun," *Sports Illustrated*, September 7, 1998, 21.

33. Collins, *Black Sexual Politics*, 155.

34. McIntosh, 97.

35. Ibid., 99.

36. Dave Kindred, "The Class of '98," *The Sporting News*, December 21, 1998, 14.

37. Bob Ley, "Language Barriers," *Outside the*

Lines Nightly (Bristol, CT, ESPN, June 12, 2003).

38. Rick Reilly, "The Magical and Mysterious Oz," *Sports Illustrated*, April 24, 2005, 86.

39. Tim Wendel, *The New Face of Baseball: The One-Hundred Year Rise and Triumph of Latinos in America's Favorite Sport* (New York: HarperCollins, 2003), 11.

40. Collins, *Black Sexual Politics*, 166–7.

41. "#6: McGwire and Sosa Chase Maris."

42. Michael Knisley and Steve Marantz, "A Finish with a Flourish," *The Sporting News*, October 5, 1998, 48.

43. Collins, *Black Sexual Politics*, 170.

44. bell hooks, *Killing Rage: Ending Racism* (New York: Henry Holt, 1995), 114.

45. Bretón, "Field of Broken Dreams."

46. Bill Dedman, "It's a Race for the Record, But Is It Also About Race?" *New York Times*, September 20, 1998, 3.

47. Berta Esperanza Hernandez-Truyol, "Borders (En)Gendered: Normativities, Latinas, and a LatCrit Paradigm," *New York University Law Review* 72 (1997): 907–9.

48. "#6: McGwire and Sosa Chase Maris."

49. Dedman, 3.

50. Ibid,, 3.

51. David W. Chen, "Dominicans' Favorite Son: Sammy Sosa, Homerun Hitter," *New York Times*, September 5, 1998, B3.

52. Rick Reilly, "Pride of the Yankees," *Sports Illustrated*, September 28, 1998, 102.

53. Lawrence III, "The Id, the Ego," 237.

54. Gary Smith, "The Race Is On," *Sports Illustrated*, September 21, 1998, 50.

55. Mark Fitzgerald, "All's Quiet When Sosa Smacks 62nd," *Editor & Publisher*, September 19, 1998, 37.

56. Trucios-Haynes, 8.

57. Stein and Grace, 77.

58. Ibid., 77.

59. Jane Juffer, "Who's the Man?: Sammy Sosa, Latinos and Televisual Redefinitions of the 'American' Pastime," *Journal of Sport & Social Issues* 26 (2002): 350.

60. Food and Drug Administration, "Crackdown on 'Andro' Products," *FDA Consumer Magazine* 38 (2004), http://www.fda.gov/fdac/features/2004/304_andro.html (accessed October 20, 2004)

61. Steve Marantz and Michael Knisley, "American Hero," *The Sporting News*, September 21, 1998, 20–1.

62. Mark Fitzgerald, "Furor Follows AP Disclosure on McGwire," *Editor & Publisher* 131 (1998), http://0-search.epnet.com.maurice.bgsu.edu:80/login.aspx?direct=true&db=aph&an=1037553 (accessed August 29, 2004).

63. John Hoberman, "Mark McGwire's Little Helper: The Androstenedione Debate,"

Think Muscle, http://www.thinkmuscle.com/articles/hoberman/mcgwire.htm (accessed April 17, 2006).

64. Cheryl Arnedt, "Poll: Clinton's Approval Ratings Improve," *ABC News*, last modified June 22, 2004, http://abcnews.go.com/sections/us/Polls/clinton_poll_040622.html (accessed August 7, 2005).

65. Daniel Okrent, "A Mac for All Seasons," *Time*, December 28, 1998–January 4, 1999, 142.

66. Jon L. Wertheim, Kevin Cook, and Mark Mravic, "Did Mac and Sammy Save Baseball?" *Sports Illustrated*, September 20, 1998, 38.

67. Christine Brennan, "No Matter the Result, Sosa's Power Will Be Forever Diminished," *USA Today*, June 5, 2003, 3C.

68. Jamie C. Harris, "Sosa Discovers Race as Glaring an Issue as the Cork in His Bat," *New York Amsterdam News*, June 19, 2005, 52.

69. Michael Eric Dyson, *Open Mike: Reflections on Philosophy, Race, Sex, Culture, and Religion* (New York: Basic *Civitas* Books, 2003), 213.

70. Kimberlé Crenshaw, "Color-Blind Dreams and Racial Nightmares: Reconfiguring Racism in the Post-Civil Rights Era," in *Birth of a Nation'hood: Gaze, Script, and Spectacle in the O.J. Simpson Case*, edited by Toni Morrison and Claudia Brodsky Lacour (New York: Pantheon, 1999), 117.

71. Brennan, 3C.

72. John Thorn, Phil Bimbaum, and Bill Deane, *Total Baseball: The Ultimate Baseball Encyclopedia*, 8th Edition (Wilmington, DE: Sport Media, 2004), 719; 23; 1086.

73. Michael Chabon, "Jose Canseco, Hero," *New York Times*, March 18, 2005, 21.

74. Tom Verducci, "Juice and Truth," *Sports Illustrated*, February 21, 2005, 41.

75. Mark Starr and Eve Conant, "A Major League Mess," *Newsweek*, March 28, 2005, 27.

76. Jack Curry, "2 Stars Leap to Hall of Fame, but Steroid Cloud Stops 3rd," *New York Times*, January 10, 2007, A1.

77. Bob Ley, "Baseball's Four Faces of Steroids," *Outside the Lines* (Bristol, CT: ESPN, August 7, 2005).

78. Verducci, "Making His Mark," 40.

79. Said, 136.

Chapter 2

1. Gerry Callahan, "Issue Too Big to Come Out," *Boston Herald*, May 24, 2002, 119.

2. Harriet L. Schwartz, "Out of Bounds," *Advocate*, March 18, 1997, 56.

3. Brendan Lemon, Albert Kim, and Kostya Kenned, "Not Out at the Plate," *Sports Illustrated*, June 3, 2002, 18.

4. Brendan Lemon, "Letter from the Editor," *Out*, May 2001, 15.

5. Chris Kline, "Tribe Ignores Past, Reaps Rewards," *Baseball America*, last modified September 4, 2003, http://www.baseballamerica.com/today/news/030904tadno.html (accessed August 8, 2004).

6. Billy Bean, *Going the Other Way: Lessons from a Life in and Out of Major League Baseball* (New York: Marlowe, 2003), xvi.

7. Bob Ley, "The World of the Gay Athlete," *Outside the Lines* (Bristol, CT: ESPN, December 16, 1998).

8. Bean, 217.

9. Ibid., 218.

10. Ibid., 217–8.

11. Dave Zirin, *What's My Name, Fool? Sports and Resistance in the United States* (Chicago: Haymarket, 2005), 213.

12. Jeff Pearlman, "At Full Blast," *Sports Illustrated*, December 27, 1999, 61.

13. S.L. Price, "Cat & Mouth Game," *Sports Illustrated*, March 13, 2000, 42.

14. Charles R. Lawrence III, "If He Hollers Let Him Go: Regulating Racist Speech on Campus," in *Words That Wound: Critical Race Theory, Assaultive Speech, and the First Amendment*, edited by Mari J. Matsuda, Charles Lawrence III, Richard Delgado, and Kimberlé Crenshaw (Boulder, CA: Westview, 1992), 451.

15. Wilbert A. Tatum, "Rock-a-Bye Rocker ...Out of This World," *New York Amsterdam News*, June 8, 2000, 12.

16. Price, 42.

17. Bean, 238.

18. Jay Mariotti, "Hearing an Ugly Side to Athletes," *The Sporting News*, May 14, 2001, 7.

19. Ibid., 7.

20. "Baseball and Gay Fans Come Together," *Outsports*, last modified August 3, 2004, http://www.outsports.com/baseball/2004/0803gaydays.htm (accessed July 20, 2005).

21. Patricia Hill Collins, *Fighting Words: Black Women and the Search for Justice* (Minneapolis: University of Minnesota Press, 1998), 83.

22. Rick Telander, "In Big Picture, Mariotti's Huge Part of Story," *Chicago Sun-Times*, June 26, 2007, 94.

23. Joe Cowley, "Selig Sends Guillén to School: Sox Manager Ordered to Attend Sensitivity Training, Pay Fine," *Chicago Sun-Times*, June 23, 2007, 126.

24. Ibid., 126.

25. Eric Anderson, *In the Game: Gay Athletes and the Cult of Masculinity* (Albany: State University of New York Press, 2005), 139.

26. Lawrence III, "If He Hollers Let Him Go," 461.

27. Ibid., 466.

28. Ibid., 466–7.

29. Jeff Pearlman, "Coming Out in the Big Leagues," *The Advocate*, January 15, 2008, 55.

30. Gene Wojciechowski, "Hardaway's Words of Hate Are Yesterday's News," *ESPN*, last modified February 17, 2007, http://sports.espn.go.com/espn/columns/story?columnist=wojciechwski_gene&id=2766874 (accessed May 12, 2008).

31. "Hardaway Axed by NBA for Anti-Gay Comments in Wake of Amaechi's Revelation That He's Gay," *Jet*, March 5, 2007, 49.

32. Lemon, "Letter from the Editor," 15.

33. David Nylund, "When in Rome: Heterosexism, Homophobia, and Sports Talk Radio," *Journal of Sport & Social Issues* 28, no. 2 (2004): 153.

34. Bean, 153.

35. Bob Ley, "The Gay Dilemma," *Outside the Lines* (Bristol, CT: ESPN, June 3, 2001).

36. "Baseball and Gay Fans Come Together."

37. Ley, "The Gay Dilemma."

38. Danae Clark, "Commodity Lesbianism," in *Popular Culture: Production and Consumption*, ed. C. Lee Harrington and Denise D. Bielby (Malden, MA: Blackwell Publishers, 2001), 88.

39. Bean, 234.

40. Dave Kindred, "Everything Evolves, Even the Word 'Babe,'" *The Sporting News*, June 3, 2002, 64.

41. Neal Travis, "In and Out with the Mets," *New York Post*, May 20, 2002, 011.

42. Ron Cook, "Sports Can't Get Out of the Closet," *Pittsburgh Post-Gazette*, May 24, 2002, C-1.

43. Rafael Hermoso, "Piazza Responds to Gossip Column," *New York Times*, May 22, 2002, D:5.

44. Kindred, "Everything Evolves," 64.

45. Tom D'Angelo, "Gay Issue Remains in Closet," *Palm Beach Post*, May 26, 2002, 7B.

46. Ibid., 7B.

47. Bruce Jenkins, "Baseball Isn't Ready to Open the Closet Door," *San Francisco Chronicle*, May 25, 2002, C2.

48. Harvey Araton, "Baseball Focuses on the Trivial," *New York Times*, May 23, 2002, 1.

49. Callahan, "Issue Too Big to Come Out."

50. John B. Thompson, *The Media and Modernity: A Social Theory of the Media* (Palo Alto, CA: Stanford University Press, 1995), 134.

51. Michel Foucault, *Discipline & Punish: The Birth of the Prison*, translated by Alan Sheridan (New York: Vintage, 1977), 202.

52. Kline.

53. Ibid.

54. Ibid.

55. "Indians Pitcher Asks Forgiveness for Role in Gay Porn Video," *CBS Sportsline*, last modified January 27, 2004, http://cbs.sports

line.com/mlb/story/7041300 (accessed: August 5, 2004).

56. Kline.

57. Collins, *Black Sexual Politics*, 186.

58. Ibid., 186.

59. Ibid., 186–6.

60. *John Geddes Lawrence and Tyron Garner, Petitioners vs. Texas*, U.S. 02-102 (2003).

61. Hillary Goodridge & Others vs. Department of Public Health & Other, SJC-08860 (2003).

62. Lawrence III, "The Id, the Ego," 237.

63. Chong-suk Han, "Gay Asian-American Male Seeks Home," *Gay & Lesbian Review Worldwide* 12, no. 5 (2005): 35.

64. Allen Luke, "Representing and Reconstructing Asian Masculinities: This Is Not a Movie Review," *Social Alternatives* 16, no. 3 (1997): 32.

65. Han, 35.

66. Robert Hanke, "Hegemonic Masculinity in *Thirtysomething*," *Critical Studies in Mass Communication* 7 (1990): 232.

67. Collins, *Black Sexual Politics*, 185–6.

68. Ibid., 185–6.

69. Nick Trujillo, "Hegemonic Masculinity on the Mound: Media Representations of Nolan Ryan and American Sports Culture," in *Reading Sport Critically: Critical Essays on Power and Representation*, edited by Susan Birrell and Mary G. McDonald (Boston: Northeastern University Press, 2000), 15.

70. Rick Weinberg, "95: Clemens Flings Shattered Bat at Piazza," 2004, *ESPN*, http://sports.espn.go.com/espn/espn25/story?page=moments/95 (accessed: July 13, 2004).

71. Ibid.

72. Collins, *Black Sexual Politics*, 189.

73. Tom Verducci, "Eight Men In," *Sports Illustrated*, July 28, 2003, 57.

74. Major League Baseball, "Mike Piazza: Player Information: Biography and Career Highlights," *MLB*, http://mlb.mlb.com/NASApp/mlb/team/player.jsp?player_id=120536 (accessed: October 10, 2005).

75. Trujillo, 16.

76. Jay Clarkson, "Contesting Masculinity's Makeover: *Queer Eye*, Consumer Masculinity, and 'Straight-Acting' Gays," *Journal of Communication Inquiry*, 29, no. 3 (2005): 240.

77. Hanke, 245.

78. MLB, "Mike Piazza."

79. Trujillo, 26.

80. Rick Reilly, "A Gentleman in a Pinstripe Suit," *Sports Illustrated*, July 12–19, 2004, 156.

81. Travis, 011.

82. Mike Donaldson, "What Is Hegemonic Masculinity?" *Theory and Society* 22, no. 5 (1993): 645.

83. Collins, *Black Sexual Politics*, 192.

84. Clarkson, 236.

85. Bradley Holms, "Queer Eye for the Red Sox," *Queer Eye for the Straight Guy* (United States: Scout Productions, 2005).

86. Gwen Knapp, "Is It Time to End the Hostility Toward Gays in the Pros?" *San Francisco Chronicle*, June 5, 2005, D1.

87. Holms, "Queer Eye."

88. Knapp, D1.

89. Ibid., D1.

90. L. Jon Wertheim, "Gays in Sport: A Poll," *Sports Illustrated*, April 18, 2005, 64

91. Ibid., 65.

92. Ibid., 65.

93. Eric H. Holder Jr., "Letter from the Attorney General to Congress on Litigation Involving the Defense of Marriage Act," Department of Justice, Office of Public Affairs, last modified February 23, 2011, http://www.justice.gov/opa/pr/2011/February/11-ag-223.html (accessed August 26, 2011)

94. "What Is the It Gets Better Project?" http://www.itgetsbetter.org/pages/about-it-gets-better-project/ (accessed August 26, 2011).

95. "San Francisco Giants Release 'It Gets Better' Video," *The Sporting News*, last modified June 1, 2010, http://aol.sportingnews.com/mlb/story/2011-06-01/san-francisco-giants-release-it-gets-better-video (accessed August 26, 2011).

96. Ibid.

97. Stephen Alexander, "Philadelphia Phillies to Preach in 'It Gets Better' Video," *Technorati*, last modified July 24, 2011, http://technorati.com/sports/baseball/article/philadelphia-phillies-to-preach-in-it/ (accessed August 26, 2011); Stephen Nohlgren, "Tampa Bay Rays to Join Antigay Bullying Movement 'It Gets Better,'" *St. Petersburg Times*, last modified August 10, 2011, http://www.tampabay.com/sports/baseball/rays/tampa-bay-rays-to-join-antigay-bullying-movement-it-gets-better/1185086 (accessed August 26, 2011).

98. "McDowell Back from Suspension," *ESPN*, last modified May 14, 2011, http://sports.espn.go.com/mlb/news/story?id=6541756 (accessed August 26, 2011).

99. Major League Baseball Disciplines Roger McDowell, *MLB*, last modified May 1, 2011, http://mlb.mlb.com/news/press_releases/press_release.jsp?ymd=20110501&content_id=18485548&vkey=pr_mlb&fext=.jsp&c_id=mlb (accessed August 26, 2011).

100. Callahan, "Issue Too Big to Come Out," 119.

101. Michael Wilbon and Tony Kornheiser, "Significance of Coming Out," *Pardon the Interruption* (Washington, DC: ESPN, October 26, 2005).

102. "California Ban on Same-Sex Marriage Struck Down," *CNN*, May 16, 2008, http://www.

cnn.com/2008/US/05/15/same.sex.marriage/ index.html?iref=newssearch; "New York to Recognize Gay Marriages," *CNN*, last modified May 29, 2008. http://www.cnn.com/2008/US/05/ 29/nygay.marriage/index.html?iref=newssearch (accessed August 26, 2011).

103. D'Angelo, 7B.

Chapter 3

1. Matt Crossman, "Three Tiers for the Stars," *The Sporting News*, July 28, 2003, 10.

2. *Jerry Maguire*, directed by Cameron Crowe (1996, Culver City, CA: Columbia TriStar, 2002), DVD.

3. Robert Sullivan, Venus Eskenazi, and Mike Williams, "Show Them the Money," *Time*, December 4, 2000, 63.

4. Mark Sappenfield, Todd Wilkinson, and Kris Axtman, "Enter the Era of the $49,000 at Bat," *Christian Science Monitor*, December 12, 2000, 1.

5. Tom Verducci, "The Lone Ranger," *Sports Illustrated*, September 9, 2002, 34.

6. Ibid., 34.

7. Collins, *Black Feminist Thought*, 45–6.

8. Ibid., 66.

9. Women of Color Policy Network, NYU Wager, "Policy Brief: Wage Disparities and Women of Color," http://wagner.nyu.edu/woc pn/publications/files/Pay_Equity_Policy_Brief. pdf (accessed November 20, 2011).

10. Ibid.

11. "*USA Today* Salaries Database," http://content.usatoday.com/sports/baseball/salaries/top25.aspx?year=2009 (accessed November 20, 2011). The highest paid players of color are: Alex Rodríguez, Vernon Wells, CC Sabathia, Johan Santana, Miguel Cabrera, Ryan Howard, Carlos Beltran, Carlos Lee, Alfonso Soriano, Carlos Zambrano, Torii Hunter, and Ichiro Suzuki.

12. Tim Kurkjian, "Worth Waiting For," *Sports Illustrated*, June 14, 1993, 68.

13. Bretón and Villegas, 18.

14. Ibid., 18.

15. Bretón, "Fields of Broken Dreams."

16. Michael Knisley, "Everybody Has the Dream," *The Sporting News*, February 19, 2001, 52.

17. Bretón "Fields of Broken Dreams."

18. Eric Nadel and Alex Rodríguez, "Q&A with Alex Rodríguez," *MLB*, last modified February 14, 2004, http://texas.rangers.mlb.com/NASApp/mlb/tex/news/tex_news.jsp?ymd=200 40214&content_id=637165<&vkey=news_tex &fext=.jsp (accessed March 21, 2005).

19. Kindred, "Class of '98," 14.

20. Tom Weir and Mike Todd, "Talking to Each Other," *USA Today*, April 14, 2004, 03C.

21. Ley, "Language Barriers."

22. Hernandez-Truyol, 910.

23. Marty Noble, "English Not Foreign to Pedro," *MLB*, http://www.mlb.com/NASApp/mlb/emailArticleServlet?aid=385316 (accessed March 12, 2005).

24. Wendel, 125.

25. Ibid., 125.

26. "What Are They Saying?" *USA Today*, April 14, 2004, 3C.

27. Hernandez-Truyol, 910–11.

28. Ibid., 893.

29. Wendel, 202.

30. Jesse Sanchez, "Alex the Man vs. A-Rod the Player," *MLB*, last modified April 13, 2004, http://mlb.mlb.com/NASApp/mlb/mlb/news/mlb_news.jsp?ymd=20040413&content_id =700961&vkey=news_mlb&fext=.jsp (accessed March 21, 2005).

31. Collins, *Black Feminist Thought*, 65.

32. Cesar Brioso, "Latinos Swing Into the Majors," *Hispanic*, April 2001, 48.

33. Allison Samuels and Mark Starr, "Ready for His Close-Up," *Newsweek*, April 9, 2001, 54.

34. "24-Hour Spanish Language Station Launching," *ESPN*, last modified January 7, 2004, http://espn.go.com/gen/news/2004/0107/ 1702456.html (accessed August 3, 2005).

35. "The 50 Most Beautiful People in the World," *People*, May 11, 1998, 157.

36. Gerry Callahan, "The Fairest of Them All," *Sports Illustrated*, July 8, 1996, 40.

37. Samuels and Starr, 54.

38. Summer Sanders, "Sexiest Athlete," *The Sports List* (FOX Sports, February 21, 2005).

39. Toby Miller, *Sportsex* (Philadelphia, Temple University Press, 2001), 40.

40. Laura Mulvey, "Visual Pleasure and Narrative Cinema," in *Film Theory and Criticism: Introductory Readings*, edited by Leo Braudy and Marshall Cohen (New York, Oxford University Press, 1999), 837.

41. Ibid., 838.

42. "Cheering on Women and Girls in Sport: Using Title IX to Fight Gender Role Oppression," *Harvard Law Review* 110, no. 7 (1997): 1631.

43. Ibid., 1631.

44. Miller, *Sportsex*, 39.

45. Thorn, Birnbaum, and Deane, 1531.

46. Jon Heyman, "The Best Player? A Clue: He Has Dazzled Seattle Fans," *The Sporting News*, January 10, 2000, 61.

47. Phil Barber, "Several Cuts Above," *The Sporting News*, July 10, 2000, 14.

48. Robert Burk, *Much More Than a Game: Players, Owners, & American Baseball Since 1921* (Chapel Hill: The University of North Carolina Press, 2001), 274.

49. Jim Caple, "Free Agency Simply Great

for Baseball," *ESPN*, last modified November 26, 2000, http://espn.go.com/mlb/columns/caple_jim/896034.html (accessed April 2, 2005).

50. Paul Forrester, "The Man Behind the Megamillion Dollar Players," *Christian Science Monitor*, April 3, 2001, 1.

51. "*USA Today* Salaries Database."

52. Ibid.

53. Ley, "Language Barriers."

54. Leslie Heywood and Shari L. Dworkin, *Built to Win: The Female Athlete as Cultural Icon* (Minneapolis: University of Minnesota Press, 2003), 103.

55. Sean Deveney, "Getting Leverage from a Buyout," *The Sporting News*, December 25, 2000, 54–5.

56. Forrester, 1.

57. Blain Newnham, "Avid Rangers Fans Should Have Taught A-Rod a Math Lesson," *Seattle Times*, December 14, 2000, D1.

58. Sappenfield *et al.*, 1.

59. "The 25 Most Intriguing People: Alex Rodríguez," *People*, December 25, 2000–January 1, 2001, 75.

60. Ross Atkin, "Is A-Rod Worth It? Some Say 'Yes,'" *Christian Science Monitor*, April 6, 2001, 12–13.

61. Robert Lipsyte and Peter Levine, *Idols of the Game: A Sporting History of the American Century* (Atlanta: Turner, 1995), 109.

62. "Julia Roberts," IMDb, http://www.imdb.com/name/nm0000210/ (accessed April 7, 2005).

63. Mark Feinsand, "One-on-One with Alex Rodríguez," *MLB*, last modified March 21, 2004, http://mlb.mlb.com/NASApp/mlb/mlb/news/mlb_news.jsp?ymd=20040324&content_id=66/622&vkey=news_mlb&fext=.jsp (accessed March 21, 2005).

64. Martha Hill Zimmer and Michael Zimmer, "Athletes as Entertainers: A Comparative Study of Earning Profiles," *Journal of Sport and Social Issues* 25, no. 2 (2001): 213.

65. Tom Verducci, "Stumbling Start," *Sports Illustrated*, April 9, 2001, 59.

66. Ibid., 59.

67. Ibid., 59.

68. Mary Ellen Egan, Victoria Murphy, and Nichole Ridgway, "The 400 Richest People in America," *Forbes*, October 9, 2000, 247.

69. Matthew Miller, Josephine Lee, and Steven Sun, "Forbes 400 Richest People in America," *Forbes*, October 6, 2003, 219.

70. James Richard Hill, "Will Rising Salaries Destroy Baseball?" in *Stee-Rike Four!: What's Wrong with the Business of Baseball?* Edited by Daniel R. Marburger (Westport, CT: Praeger, 1997), 56.

71. Joel Shuman, "Does A-Rod Deserve So Much Money? No," in *Baseball and Philosophy:*

Thinking Outside the Batter's Box, edited by Eric Bronson (Chicago: Open Court, 2004), 300.

72. Zirin, *What's My Name, Fool?* 101.

73. Tim Wise, "Membership Has Its Privileges: Thoughts on Acknowledging and Challenging Whiteness," in *White Privilege: Essential Readings on the Other Side of Racism*, edited by Paula S. Rothenberg (New York: Worth Publishers, 2002), 108.

74. McIntosh, 100.

75. Derrick Bell, "Wanted: A White Leader Able to Free Whites of Racism," in *The Derrick Bell Reader*, edited by Richard Delgado and Jean Stefancic (New York: New York University Press, 2005), 330.

76. George Lipsitz, "The White 2K Problem," *Cultural Values* 4 (2000): 519.

77. "*USA Today* Salaries Database."

78. Ibid.

79. David Leonard, "The Decline of the Black Athlete: An Online Exclusive: Extended Interview with Harry Edwards," *ColorLines* 3 (2000), http://search.proquest.com/docview/215537733?accountid=14925 (accessed September 3, 2011).

80. Chris Fowler, "Curt Flood," *SportsCentury* (Bristol, CT: ESPN, 2000).

81. Verducci, "Stumbling Start," 54.

82. Matthew Mankiewich, "Report: Sox Can Still Have A-Rod," *MLB*, December 4, 2003, http://texas.rangers.mlb.com/NASApp/mlb/mlb/news/mlb_news.jsp?ymd=20031204&content_id=612557&vkey=news_mlb&fext=.jsp&c_id=mlb (accessed March 21, 2005).

83. Ian Browne, "No Blessed Union Yet on Megadeal," *MLB*, last modified December 17, 2003, http://texas.rangers.mlb.com/NASApp/mlb/tex/news/tex_news.jsp?ymd=20031217&content_id=620263&vkey=news_tex&fext=.jsp&c_id=tex (accessed March 21, 2005).

84. "*USA Today* Salaries Database."

85. Ibid.

86. Mike Bauman, "Who Boos Louder at A-Rod?," *MLB*, last modified May 8, 2004, http://seattle.mariners.mlb.com/NASApp/mlb/sea/news/sea_news.jsp?ymd=20040508&content_id=738807&vkey=news_sea&fext=.jsp (March 21, 2005).

87. Albert Chen, "No Regrets," *Sports Illustrated*, May 31, 2004, 52.

88. Tom Verducci, "A-Rod Agonistes," *Sports Illustrated*, September 25, 2006, http://sports illustrated.cnn.com/2006/magazine/09/19/arod 0925/index.html (accessed September 3, 2011).

89. Caleb Breakey, "A-Rod Honored for Historic Month," *MLB*, last modified May 2, 2007, http://newyork.yankees.mlb.com/news/article.jsp?ymd=20070502&content_id=1942648&vkey=news_nyy&fext=.jsp&c_id=nyy (accessed September 3, 2011)

90. "Rodríguez Finalized $275m Deal with Yankees," *ESPN*, last modified December 13, 2007, http://sports.espn.go.com/mlb/news/story?id=3153171 (accessed September 3, 2011).

91. "*USA Today* Salaries Database."

92. Ibid.

93. Harvey Araton, "Pujols and Cardinals Call Off Talks," *New York Times*, February 17, 2011, B13.

94. Jon Heyman, "Cardinals, Pujols Fail to Reach Deal Before Wednesday Deadline," *Sports Illustrated*, last modified February 15, 2011, http://sportsillustrated.cnn.com/2011/writers/jon_heyman/02/15/cardinals-pujols-negotiations/index.html (accessed August 27, 2011)

95. "*USAToday* Salary Database."

96. Jonah Keri, "Is Albert Pujols Really Worth $250 Million?" *Grantland*, last modified December 8, 2011, http://www.grantland.com/blog/the-triangle/post/_/id/11778/is-albert-pujols-really-worth-250-million (accessed December 8, 2011).

97. Jayson Stark, "Angels Shock Baseball World," *ESPN*, last modified December 8, 2011, http://espn.go.com/mlb/hotstove11/story/_/id/7330869/los-angeles-angels-shock-world-ink-albert-pujols-cj-wilson (accessed December 8, 2011).

98. Collins, *Black Sexual Politics*, 155.

Chapter 4

1. Cheryl I. Harris, "Whiteness as Property," *Harvard Law Review* 106, no. 8 (1993): 1712–3.

2. Valerie Smith, "Reading the Intersection of Race and Gender in Passing Narratives," *Diacritics* 24 (1994): 44–5.

3. Lipsitz, "The White 2K Problem," 519.

4. Cynthia Gordy, "Setting the Record Straight," *Essence*, October 2006, 158.

5. Gail Ingham Berlage, "Effa Manley, a Major Force in Negro Baseball in the 1930s and 1940s," in *Out of the Shadows: African American Baseball from the Cuban Giants to Jackie Robinson*, edited by Bill Kirwin (Lincoln, NE: University of Nebraska Press, 2005), 129.

6. Jean Hastings Ardell, *Breaking Into Baseball: Women and the National Pastime* (Carbondale, IL: Southern Illinois University Press, 2005), 168.

7. The exact start date of professional baseball's segregation is not easy to pin down. The National Association banned integrated teams beginning in 1867. Chicago White Stockings player Cap Anson famously refused to play against the Toledo Blue Stockings in 1883 because of Moses Fleetwood Walker's presence. Walker and the remaining black players were pushed out of integrated teams by 1889. Baseball Commissioner Kenesaw Landis always asserted that black players were not banned from Major League Baseball. What is clear is that the separate-but-equal doctrine was being cemented throughout the nation and was finally codified by *Plessy v. Ferguson* in 1896.

8. "Eagle Owner Flays Rickey for Tactics in Player Deal," *Baltimore Afro-American*, November 3, 1945, 30.

9. Lawrence D. Hogan, *Shades of Glory: The Negro Leagues and the Story of African-American Baseball* (Washington, DC: National Geographic, 2006), 336.

10. Art Carter, "New Issue Looms on Satchell Paige," *Baltimore Afro-American*, June 15, 1940, 23.

11. Hogan, 354.

12. Ibid, 355.

13. Ibid., 355.

14. "Leon Day," *Baseball Hall of Fame*, http://www.baseballhalloffame.org/hofers/detail.jsp?playerId=492562 (accessed July 18, 2008).

15. "Monte Irvin," *Baseball Hall of Fame*, http://www.baseballhalloffame.org/hofers/detail.jsp?playerId=116403 (accessed July 18, 2008).

16. Lindsey Fraizer, "Pioneering Newcombe Eyes Top Honor," *MLB*, last modified February 16, 2007, http://mlb.mlb.com/news/article.jsp?ymd=20070214&content_id=1802262&vkey=news_mlb&fext=jsp&c_id=mlb (accessed May 8, 2008).

17. Leslie Heaphy, "Effa Manley: A Woman on a Mission," *Baseball Hall of Fame*, last modified February 15, 2007, http://www.baseballhalloffame.org/news/article.jsp?ymd=20070215&content_id=328&vkey=hof_news (accessed June 11, 2008).

18. The HOF also inducted Ray Brown, Willard Brown, Andy Cooper, Ulysses F. "Frank" Grant, Pete Hill, James Raleigh "Biz" Mackey, José Mendez, Alex Pompez, Cumberland Posey Jr., Louis Santop, George "Mule" Suttles, Ben Taylor, Cristobal Torriente, Sol White, Ernest "Jud" Wilson, and J.L. Wilkinson.

19. Delgado and Stefancic, xvii.

20. Derrick Bell, "*Brown v. Board of Education* and the Interest-Convergence Dilemma," in *The Derrick Bell Reader*, edited by Richard Delgado and Jean Stefancic (New York: New York University Press, 2005), 35.

21. Ardell, 56.

22. Sam Bernstein, "Ted Williams Pleads for Negro Leagues Inductions," *Baseball Hall of Fame*, last modified February 15, 2007, http://www.baseballhalloffame.org/news/article.jsp?ymd=20070215&content_id=282&vkey=hof_news (accessed June 11, 2008).

23. Bell, "Wanted," 532.

24. Crenshaw, "Color-Blind Dreams," 103.

25. Gordy, 158.

26. Ibid., 158.

27. James Overmyer, *Effa Manley and the Newark Eagles* (Metuchen, NJ: Scarecrow, 1993), 5–6.

28. Gordy, 158.

29. Art Carter, "From the Bench," *Baltimore Afro-American*, February 10, 1940, 21.

30. Art Carter, "From the Bench," *Baltimore Afro-American*, June 15, 1940, 21.

31. "Effa Manley Baseball Executive," *New Pittsburgh Courier*, June 3, 1981, 22.

32. Smith, "Reading the Intersection," 43.

33. Harris, "Whiteness as Property," 1713.

34. Quoted in Ibid., 1712.

35. Overmyer, 7.

36. Ibid., 6.

37. Joel Zoss and John Bowman, *Diamonds in the Rough: The Untold History of Baseball* (Lincoln, NE: University of Nebraska Press, 1989), 142.

38. Ibid., 148.

39. Luther Wright Jr., "Who's Black, Who's White, and Who Cares: Reconceptualizing the United States's Definition of Race and Racial Classification," *Vanderbilt Law Review* 48 (1995): 559.

40. Ibid., 515.

41. Ibid., 516.

42. Ibid., 517.

43. Ibid., 517.

44. Richard C. Paddock, "Of Color and Conviction: Stockton Recall Hinges on Definition of 'Black,'" *Los Angeles Times*, April 18, 1984, 12.

45. Overmyer, 6.

46. *Loving et ux v. Virginia* 388 U.S. 1 (1967).

47. Ibid.

48. Ibid., 8.

49. Klep was the first white player in the Negro Leagues who *acknowledged* his whiteness. According to the June 20, 1931, edition of the *Baltimore Afro-American*, Fred "Chick" Meade, who was white, "passed for colored to play with the Eastern League." 1.

50. Carter, "From the Bench," 21.

51. Wendell Smith, "Smitty's Sports-Spurts," *Pittsburgh Courier*, January 30, 1932, 16.

52. Stefan Fatsis, "Mystery of Baseball: Was William White Game's First Black? He Played a Big League Game in 1879 — Then Vanished; Mr. Morris Picks Up Trail," *Wall Street Journal*, Eastern Edition, 20 Jan. 2004, A.1.

53. Kerry Ann Rockquemore, "Forced to Pass and Other Sins Against Authenticity," *Women & Performance: A Journal of Feminist Theory* 15 (2005): 17.

54. Ellis Cashmore, "Tiger Woods and the New Racial Order," *Current Sociology* 56 (2008): 624.

55. Kenneth W. Mack and Jim Chen, "Barack Obama Before He Was a Rising Political Star," *Journal of Blacks in Higher Education* 45 (2004): 99.

56. Ibid., 29.

Chapter 5

1. Pat Conroy, "Hank Aaron's Pursuit of an Immortal and His Magic Number," in *Total Baseball: The Ultimate Baseball Encyclopedia*, 8th Edition, ed. John Thorn, Phil Bimbaum, and Bill Deane (Wilmington, DE: Sport Media, 2004), 309.

2. "Barry Bonds Moves Forward," *ESPN*, last modified May 30, 2012, http://espn.go.com/mlb/story/_/id/7981089/barry-bonds-moving-forward-felony-conviction (accessed June 1, 2012).

3. Ogden and Hilt, 216.

4. Richard Lapchick, *The 2006 Racial and Gender Report Card of the Associated Press Sports Editors* (Orlando, FL: The Institute for Diversity and Ethics in Sport, 2006), 5.

5. Thorn, Birnbaum, and Deane, 1045.

6. "Babe Ruth: Stats, Photos, Highlights," *MLB*, http://mlb.mlb.com/team/player.jsp?player_id=121578 (accessed August 27, 2011); Barry Bonds: Stats, Photos, Highlights, *MLB* http://mlb.mlb.com/team/player.jsp?player_id=111188 (accessed August 27, 2011).

7. Conroy, 390.

8. Thorn, Birnbaum, and Deane, 730.

9. Richard Goldstein, "Bobby Bonds, 57, a Star and the Father of Barry, Dies," *New York Times*, August 24, 2003, N35.

10. Ibid., N35.

11. Jeff Pearlman, *Love Me, Hate Me: Barry Bonds and the Making of an Antihero* (New York: HarperCollins, 2006) 32.

12. Ron Fimrite, "Remembering Bobby Bonds," *Sports Illustrated*, September 1, 2003, 59.

13. Ibid., 58.

14. Thorn, Birnbaum, and Deane, 714–16.

15. Ibid., 730.

16. Pearlman, Love Me, 26–33.

17. Richard Hoffer, "The Importance of Being Barry," *Sports Illustrated*, May 24, 1993, 12–22.

18. William Ladson, "The Complete Player," *The Sporting News*, July 12, 1999, 12.

19. Thorn, Birnbaum, and Deane, 719–20; 730; 1045.

20. Ken Rosenthal, "Bonds Excels Where It Counts: On the Field," *The Sporting News*, July 2, 2001, 14.

21. Barber, 14.

22. Jeff Pearlman, "Appreciating Bonds," *Sports Illustrated*, June 5, 2000, 48–9.

23. Todd Jones, "You Don't Have to Like Bonds to Appreciate Him," *The Sporting News*, November 4, 2002, 12.

24. Ibid., 51.

25. Rick Reilly, "He Loves Himself Barry Much," *Sports Illustrated*, August 27, 2001, 102.

26. Tony Kornheiser and Michael Wilbon, "Does Barry Deserve More Love?" *Pardon the Interruption* (Washington, DC: ESPN, September 13, 2004).

27. Rosenthal, 14.

28. "#6: McGwire and Sosa Chase Maris."

29. Steven Travers, *Barry Bonds: Baseball's Superman* (Champaign, IL: Sports Publishing, 2002), 120–1.

30. Rosenthal, 14.

31. Marcus Henry, "Barry Bonds Continues to Slam the Ball While Media Slams Him," *New York Amsterdam News*, August 14–20, 2003, 44.

32. Alysse Minkoff, "All of Rose's Thorns on Display," *ESPN*, last modified January 6, 2004, http://www.espn.go.com/page2/s/minkoff/040106.html (accessed March 21, 2005).

33. "Yankees Not Yet Willing to Forgive Gray," *ESPN*, last modified October 27, 1999 http://espn.go.com/mlb.news/1999/1026/135290.html (accessed April 2, 2005).

34. Collins, *Black Sexual Politics*, 186.

35. Dyson, 216.

36. Lipsitz, "The White 2K Problem," 521.

37. Michael Knisley, "A Worthy King," *The Sporting News*, October 8, 2001, 6.

38. Travers, 195.

39. Joe Sexton, "Baseball: It's Not Always Yo, Ho, Ho But Pirates Sail Along," *New York Times*, June 12, 1992, 15.

40. "Barry Bonds," *SportsCentury Greatest Athletes* (Santa Monica, CA: Genius Entertainment, 2007). DVD.

41. Ulish Carter, "Will Pirates Ever Win Again?" *New Pittsburgh Courier*, October 17–23, 2007, C5.

42. Howie Evans, "Bonds, Griffey, McGriff Pin Cushions for Sick Media Attacks," *New York Amsterdam News*, August 2–8, 2001, 44.

43. Suchon, 296.

44. Conroy, 310.

45. Quoted in Suchon, 296.

46. Lawrence III, "The Id, the Ego," 237.

47. Richard Dyer, "Entertainment and Utopia," in *The Cultural Studies Reader*, ed. Simon During (London: Routledge, 2003), 376–7.

48. Travers, 254.

49. Zirin, *What's My Name, Fool?* 244–5.

50. Douglass Kellner, *Media Spectacle* (London: Routledge, 2003), 73.

51. C.L. Cole and David L. Andrews, "America's New Son: Tiger Woods," in *Sport Stars: The Cultural Politics of Sporting Celebrity*, edited by David L. Andrews and Steven J. Jackson (New York: Routledge, 2001), 72.

52. Collins, *Black Sexual Politics*, 168.

53. Cashmore, *Making Sense of Sports*, 126.

54. Michael Bamberger, "What's Up with Tiger," *Sports Illustrated*, July 6, 1998, 18.

55. Michael Moore, *Stupid White Men...and Other Sorry Excuses for the State of the Nation!* (New York: HarperCollins, 2001), 66.

56. Conroy, 310.

57. Sarah Irwin, "Later Life, Inequality, and Sociological Theory," *Ageing and Society* 19.6 (1999): 699.

58. Tom Verducci, "The Producers," *Sports Illustrated*, June 4, 2001, 56.

59. Bob Klapisch, "Rocket: Perfectly Engineered to Pitch," *ESPN*, last modified May 25, 2003, http://sports.espn.go.com/mlb/columns/story?columnist=klapisch_bob&id=1558829 (accessed March 19, 2005).

60. Jeff Merron, "Hormonally Challenged," *ESPN*, last modified March 8, 2005, http://sports.espn.go.com/espn/page2/story?page=merron/050309&num=0 (accessed March 19, 2005).

61. Jayson Stark, "Goliath Not Yet Ready for Gotham," *ESPN*, last modified February 21, 2005, http://sports.espn.go.com/mlb/columns/story?columnist=stark_jayson&id=1993164 (accessed March 19, 2005).

62. Thorn, Birnbaum, and Deane, 1288.

63. Quoted in Suchon, 316.

64. Suchon, 20.

65. Tom Verducci, "Pushing 70," *Sports Illustrated*, October 8, 2001, 43.

66. Rosenthal, 14.

67. Travers, 195.

68. Bruce Jenkins, "Unprecedented, Unappreciated," *San Francisco Chronicle*, October 8, 2001, D2.

69. Glenn Dickey, "Deserving Bonds Has Got It All Over McGwire," *San Francisco Chronicle*, September 25, 2001, E2.

70. Thorn, Birnbaum, and Deane, 1045; 443.

71. Jeff Pearlman, "It's a Wrap," *Sports Illustrated*, October 15, 2001, 48.

72. Robert S. Brown, "Sport and the Healing of America After 9/11," in *Language, Symbols, and the Media: Communication in the Aftermath of the World Trade Center Attack*, edited by Robert E. Denton Jr. (New Brunswick, NJ: Transaction, 2004) 119.

73. Rebecca S. Kraus, "A Shelter in the Storm: Baseball Responds to September 11," *NINE: A Journal of Baseball and American Culture* 12, no.1 (2003): 92.

74. *Nine Innings from Ground Zero*, directed

by Ouisie Shapiro 2004 (United States: HBO, 2004). DVD.

75. Kraus, 96.

76. *Nine Innings from Ground Zero.*

77. Bell, *"Brown v. Board of Education,"* 39.

78. Jenkins, "Unprecedented," D2.

79. Tom Verducci, "Is Baseball in the Asterisk Era?" *Sports Illustrated*, March 15, 2004, 39.

80. Ibid., 39.

81. Karl Ravech and Mark McGwire, "Sunday Conversation," *SportsCenter* (Bristol, CT: ESPN, July 13, 2004).

82. Rick Morrissey, "Baseball May Need Big Share of Asterisk," *Chicago Tribune*, March 3, 2004, Final ed., Sports, 1.

83. "Players' Goal Was to Make Steroid Testing Permanent," *ESPN*, last modified March 12, 2003, http://espn.go.com/mlb/news/2003/0311/1521844.html (accessed March 12, 2005).

84. Skip Bayliss, "Prove It to Me," *ESPN*, last modified December 9, 2004, http://sports.espn.go.com/espn/page2/story?page=bayless/041210 (accessed January 27, 2005).

85. "Report: Bonds, Giambi, Sheffield Received Steroids," *ESPN*, last modified March 2, 2004. http://sports.espn.go.com/espn/wire?section=mlb&id=1748917 (accessed September 29, 2004).

86. George W. Bush, "State of the Union Address," January 20, 2004, http://www.whitehouse.gov/news/release/2004/01/10040120-7.html (accessed January 29, 2004).

87. "Implications by Track Star Infuriates Bonds," *ESPN*, last modified June 24, 2004, http://sports.espn.go.com/espn/print?id=1827368&type=story (accessed June 24, 2004).

88. Lance Williams and Mark Fainaru-Wada, "What Bonds Told the BALCO Grand Jury," *San Francisco Chronicle*, December 2, 2004, A1.

89. Bayliss.

90. Tim Keown, "You Gotta Disbelieve," *ESPN*, last modified December 7, 2004, http://sports.espn.go.com/espn/page2/story?page=keown/041207 (accessed January 27, 2005).

91. Steve Levy and Linda Cohn, "Jason Giambi," *SportsCenter* (Bristol, CT: ESPN, December 2, 2004.

92. McIntosh, 97.

93. Ibid., 100.

94. Tony Kornheiser and Michael Wilbon, "Will Test Clear Bonds's Name?" *Pardon the Interruption* (Washington, DC, ESPN, September 27, 2004).

95. John Saunders, Mitch Albom, Mike Lupica, and William C. Rhoden, "Jason Giambi," *The Sports Reporters* (New York: ESPN, December 5, 2004).

96. Keith Olbermann, "Asterisk Obsession," *Sports Illustrated*, September 7, 1998, 74.

97. Robert Whiting, *The Meaning of Ichiro:*

The New Wave from Japan and the Transformation of Our National Pastime (New York: Warner Books, 2004), 121.

98. Ralph Wiley, "Sour Grapes," *ESPN*, last modified March 4, 2004, http://sports.espn.go.com/espn/page2/story?page=wiley/040304 (accessed October 27, 2004).

99. Andrew Zimbalist, *May the Best Team Win* (Washington, DC: Brookings Institute Press, 2003), 99.

100. Howie Evans, "Barry Bonds Is Walking His Way to the Hall of Fame," *New York Amsterdam News* May 20–26, 2004, 48.

101. Michael Wilbon and Stephen A. Smith, "Should Rockies Pitch to Him?" *Pardon the Interruption* (Washington, DC, ESPN: September 2, 2004).

102. Tom Verducci, "SI's 2003 Baseball Awards," *Sports Illustrated*, September 29, 3002, 64.

103. Cole Wiley, "Let Us Be Wary of Celebrating Too Much," *ESPN*, last modified February 28, 2007. http://sports.espn.go.com/espn/blackhistory2007/columns/story?id=2782051 (accessed September 3, 2011).

104. Pat Forde, "Sports World Is Incubator for Larger Discussions to Come," *ESPN*, last modified May 24, 2007, http://sports.espn.go.com/espn/columns/story?columnist=forde_pat&id=2881430&sportCat=mlb. (accessed July 25, 2007).

105. Barry M. Bloom, "Many to Take Part in Honoring Robinson," *MLB*, last modified April 7, 2007, http://mlb.mlb.com/news/article.jsp?ymd=20070410&content_id=1890656&vkey=news_mlb&fext=.jsp&c_id=mlb (accessed September 3, 2011); Ben Walker, "Astros Roster Has No Black Players," *Yahoo*, last modified October 25, 2005, http://news.yahoo.com/s/ap/20051025/ap_on_sp_ba_ne/bbo_world_series_changing_diversity (accessed October 28, 2005).

106. Forde.

107. Dan Le Batard and Jayson Whitlock, "Bonds Not Indicted," *Pardon the Interruption* (Washington, DC: ESPN, July 20, 2006).

108. Collins, *Black Sexual Politics*, 80.

109. "Americans Conflicted About Bonds's Home Run Chase," *ESPN*, last modified May 6, 2007, http://sports.espn.go.com/mlb/news/story?id=2861930 (accessed May 6, 2007).

110. Ibid.

111. Ibid.

112. Jayson Stark, "Racial Issues Hover Over the Chase," *ESPN*, last modified May 6, 2007, http://sports.espn.go.com/mlb/columns/story?columnist=stark_jayson&id=2861938 (May 10, 2007).

113. Dave Zirin, Welcome to the Terrordome: The Pain, Politics, and Promise of Sports (Chicago: Haymarket, 2007), 162.

114. Kimberlé Crenshaw, "Bad Calls on the Racial Playing Field," *CommonDreams*, last modified October 11, 2003, http://www.com mondreams.org/views03/1011-08.htm (accessed September 3, 2011).

115. Dan Wojciechowski, "Bonds Record Holder Doesn't Enhance Baseball," *ESPN*, last modified August 7, 2007, http://sports.espn.go.com/espn/columns/story?columnist=wojcie chowski_gene&id=2963913&sportCat=mlb (accessed August 8, 2007).

116. Marantz and Knisley, 21.

117. Robert Miles, "Hollywood Ending," *ESPN the Magazine*, 4 June 2007, 48.

118. Bob Hertzel, "Vote Shows Bonds Had It All Despite Image," *The Sporting News* December 3, 1990, 40.

119. Warren Goldstein, "The Conundrum That Is Barry Bonds," *Chronicle of Higher Education* 53, no. 40 (2007), B10.

120. Todd Boyd, "You Can't Discuss Bonds Without Race," *ESPN*, last modified May 9, 2007, http://sports.espn.go.com/espn/page2/sto ry?page=boyd/070508 (accessed July 25, 2007).

121. Michael Wilbon and Tony Kornheiser, "Thoughts on Bud's Reaction," *Pardon the Interruption* (Washington, DC: ESPN, August 6, 2007).

122. Jim Reeves, "Bonds Cheated and Disgraced the Game and Hank Aaron," *Star-Telegram*, last modified August 8, 2007, http://www.star-telegram.com/sports/story/194941.html (accessed August 8, 2007).

123. Jim Rome, "Barry Bonds," *Jim Rome Is Burning* (Los Angeles: ESPN, August 7, 2007).

124. Wojciechowski, "Bonds's Record Holder."

125. John Saunders, Bob Ryan, Mike Lupica, and Dan Le Batard, "How Will History Remember Barry Bonds?" *The Sports Reporters* (New York, NY: ESPN August 12, 2007).

126. Zirin, *Welcome to the Terrordome*, 160.

127. Richard Lapchick, "Who's Covering Whom?: Sports Sections Lag in Diversity," *ESPN*, last modified June 22, 2006, http://sports.espn.go.com/espn/news/story?id=2496651 (accessed September 3, 2011); Richard Lapchick, "The 2006 Racial and Gender Report Card: Major League Baseball," (Orlando: The Institute for Diversity and Ethics in Sport, 2006), 1.

128. Lipsitz, "The White 2K Problem," 521.

129. Bob Ley, Ken Williams, and Howard Bryant, "Bonds's Image and Race," *Outside the Lines* (Washington, DC: ESPN, February 27, 2005).

130. Ley, Williams, and Bryant, "Bonds's Image and Race."

131. Henry, "Bonds Continues," 44.

132. Marvin Wamble, "No Brown on Bonds's Nose," *New Pittsburgh Courier*, March 16–20, 2005, C8.

133. Maulana Karenga, "Raceball, Baseball and Unforgivable Blackness: Hank, the King and Barry, the Man," *Los Angeles Sentinel*, June 1-June 7, 2006, A7.

134. Earl Ofari Hutchinson, "Don't Rush to Judgment on Bonds," *Chicago Defender*, November 21, 2007, 8.

135. "Grimsley's Attorney: Feds Asked Diamondbacks Pitcher to Wear Wire in Bonds Probe," *Associated Press*, June 9, 2006.

136. Le Batard and Whitlock, "Bonds Not Indicted."

137. John Saunders, Michael Kay, William C. Rhoden, and Mitch Albom. "A-Rod Hits 500." *The Sports Reporters* (New York: ESPN, August 5, 2007).

138. *Sports Reporters*, "A-Rod Hits 500."

139. Conroy, 390.

140. Michael Wilbon and Jay Mariotti, "Will Barry Every Play Again?" *Pardon the Interruption* (Washington, DC: ESPN, August 2, 2005).

141. Wiley, "Sour Grapes."

142. Travers, 216.

Chapter 6

1. Gene Wojciechowski, "Mitchell Report Has Flaws, But MLB, Players Need to Pay Attention," *ESPN*, last modified December 13, 2007, http://sports.espn.go.com/espn/columns/story?columnist=wojciechowski_gene&id=31 54051&sportCat=mlb. (accessed Dec. 14, 2007).

2. Jimmy Golen, "Court Ruling Small Consolation for Exposed Players," *Seattle Times*, last modified August 27, 2009, http://seattlet-imes.nwsource.com/html/sports/20097542 17_apbbobaseballdruglistreax.html (accessed September 5, 2011).

3. Tom Verducci, "Totally Juiced," *Sports Illustrated*, June 3, 2002, 34.

4. Ibid., 34.

5. Scott Reiss, Scott Van Pelt, and Buster Olney, "756," *SportsCenter* (Bristol, CT: ESPN, August 8, 2007).

6. George J. Mitchell, "Report to the Commissioner of Baseball of an Independent Investigation into the Illegal Use of Steroids and Other Performance Enhancing Substances by Players in Major League Baseball" (2007): SR-1.

7. Ibid., 168.

8. Ibid., 171.

9. Karl Ravech, John Kruk, and Steve Phillips, "Mitchell Report Special," *SportsCenter* (Bristol, CT: ESPN, December 13, 2007).

10. Jayson Stark, "Stories of Clemens, Bonds Similar, Yet Very Different," ESPN, last modified December 15, 2007, http://sports.espn.go.com/mlb/columns/story?columnist=stark_

jayson&id=3156189 (accessed September 30, 2007).

11. Howard Bryant, "Friction and Fractures Erode Faith in Mitchell's Investigation," *ESPN*, last modified December 11, 2007, http://sports.espn.go.com/mlb/news/story?id=3142651 (accessed December 11, 2007).

12. Jonathan Littleman, "Mitchell's Best Source Was a Towel Boy," *Yahoo! Sports*, last modified December 13, 2007, http://sports.yahoo.com/mlb/news;_ylt=AvYsAi12IKhPrITwSqtuqInZxLsF?slug=li-mitchellanalysis121307&prov=yhoo&type=lgns (accessed December 14, 2007).

13. Lester Munson, "Legal Questions Abound in Anticipation of Mitchell Report," *ESPN*, last modified December 6, 2007, http://sports.espn.go.com/mlb/columns/story?id=3142722 (accessed December 11, 2007).

14. "Source Saying Information on Clemens Will Be in Mitchell Report," December 13, 2007, ESPN.com, http://sports.espn.go.com/mlb/news/story?id=3153129 (accessed December 13, 2007).

15. Rachel Maddow and Dave Zirin, "And Justice for All?" *The Rachel Maddow Show* (New York, NY: MSNBC, February 27, 2009).

16. *Dr. Seuss' How the Grinch Stole Christmas*, directed by Chuck Jones (1966; Burbank, CA: Warner Home Video, 2000), DVD.

17. "Hall of Fame Voters Speak Out About Clemens," *ESPN*, last modified December 14, 2007, http://sports.espn.go.com/mlb/news/story?id=3155168 (accessed December 14, 2007).

18. Ibid.

19. Ibid.

20. Stark, "Stories of Clemens, Bonds Similar."

21. Lipsitz, "The White 2K Problem," 518.

22. Lipsitz, *The Possessive Investment in Whiteness*, vii.

23. C.L. Cole and Alex Mobley, "American Steroids: Using Race and Gender," *Journal of Sport & Social Issues* 29 no. 1 (2005): 6.

24. Zirin, *Welcome to the Terrordome*, 162.

25. Dan Wetzel, "Clemens Is No Different Than Bonds," *Yahoo! Sports*, last modified December 13, 2007, http://sports.yahoo.com/mlb/news?slug=dw-clemenssteroidsearly121307&prov=yhoo&type=lgns (accessed December 14, 2007).

26. Wiley, "Sour Grapes."

27. Wetzel.

28. Stark.

29. Bill Plaschke, "Don't Be Surprised if 'Rocket' Escapes Bonds Treatment," *Los Angeles Times*, October 2, 2006, D1.

30. Mike Bianchi, "Athlete's Paved the Way for Barack Obama's Run," *Orlando Sentinel*, November 5, 2008, D1.

31. Dave Zirin, "Did Tiger Woods Pave the Way for Barack Obama? Are You Kidding Me?" *Edge of Sports*, last modified November 13, 2008, http://www.edgeofsports.com/2008-11-13-388/index.html.

32. Bob Costas, Michael Wilbon, Cris Carter, and Jason Whitlock, "Race and the Media," *Costas Now* (New York: HBO, April 30, 2008).

33. "Deposition of: Andy Pettitte," Committee on Oversight and Governmental Reform, House of Representatives, Washington, DC, February 4, 2008.

34. "Interview of: Edward Charles Knoblauch," Committee on Oversight and Governmental Reform, House of Representatives, Washington, DC, February 1, 2008.

35. "The Mitchell Report: The Illegal Use of Steroids in Major League Baseball, Day 2," Committee on Oversight and Governmental Reform, House of Representatives, Second Session, Washington, DC, February 13, 2008.

36. Mike Greenberg and Mike Golic, *Mike & Mike in the Morning* (Bristol, CT: ESPN, February 13, 2008).

37. "Who Was More Credible, Clemens or McNamee?" *ESPN*, last modified February 13, 2008, http://sports.espn.go.com/mlb/news/story?id=3244809(accessed November 7, 2008).

38. Dave Shenin and Spencer S. Hsu, "Pitching Legend Roger Clemens Indicted on Charges of Lying to a Congressional Committee," *Washington Post*, last modified August 20, 2010, http://www.washingtonpost.com/wp-dyn/content/article/2010/08/19/AR2010081904125.html

39. Lester Munson, "Silence of Roger Clemens Lawyer," *ESPN*, last modified July 22, 2011, http://espn.go.com/espn/commentary/story/_/page/munson-110721/roger-clemens-trial-rusty-hardin-brilliant-rashard-mendenhall-twitter-champion (accessed August 28, 2011).

40. Joel Shuman, "Despite the Lies, Pettitte Hard to Hate," *New York Post*, February 20, 2008, 71.

41. Richard Justice, "It's Fitting to Forgive Andy After Apology," *Houston Chronicle*, February 19, 2008.

42. Greenberg and Golic, *Mike & Mike in the Morning*.

43. Tony Kornheiser and Michael Wilbon, "Andy Pettitte in HOF," *Pardon the Interruption* (Washington, DC: ESPN November 5, 2009).

44. "The Mitchell Report."

45. Lee Yobbi, "Coming Clean Has Its Rewards," *Santa Fe New Mexican*, last modified April 6, 2008 http://www.santafenewmexican.com/Sports/Coming-clean-has-its-rewards (accessed September 5, 2011).

46. Verducci, "A-Rod Agonistes."

47. John Saunders, Bob Ryan, Mike Lupica,

and Dan Le Batard, "Bonds Hits 755," *The Sports* Reporters (New York: ESPN, August 5, 2007).

48. Peter Gammons and Alex Rodríguez, "SC Exclusive: Alex Rodriquez Interview," *Sports-Center* (Bristol, CT: ESPN, February 9, 2009).

49. Bill Madden, "Alex a Total Bust. Forget Cooperstown, Rodriquez Has Earned a Spot in Hall of Shame," *New York Daily News*, February 8, 2009, 45.

50. Jayson Stark, "A-Rod Has Destroyed Game's History," *ESPN*, last modified February 8, 2009, http://sports.espn.go.com/mlb/columns/story?columnist=stark_jayson&id=3892788 (accessed November 2, 2009).

51. Steve Politi, "Forecast for A-Rod: Dark Cloud Overhead," *New Jersey Star-Ledger*, February 16, 2009, 33.

52. Buster Olney, "A-Rod Now Tarnished Forever," *ESPN*, last modified February 7, 2009, http://sports.espn.go.com/mlb/columns/story?columnist=olney_buster&id=3890934 (accessed November 2, 2009).

53. Hal Brodley, "Union Considers Grievance; Palmeiro Case Details Not Kept Confidential," *USA Today*, August 8, 2005, C3.

54. "Appeals Court Could Rehear Case," *ESPN*, last modified November 9, 2009, http://sports.espn.go.com/mlb/news/story?id=4639482 (accessed November 15, 2009).

55. "Players React to Court Ruling," *ESPN*, last modified August 26, 2009, http://sports.espn.go.com/mlb/news/story?id=4425039 (accessed November 15, 2009).

56. Michael S. Schmidt, "Court Rules U.S. Seized 2003 Tests Improperly," *New York Times*, August 27, 2009, B13.

57. Michael Butterworth, "Purifying the Body Politic: Steroids, Rafael Palmeiro, and the Rhetorical Cleansing of Major League Baseball," *Western Journal of Communication* 72, no. 2 (2008): 158.

58. Ibid., 157.

59. "Goodell to Seek Change in Labor Law," *ESPN*, last modified November 2, 2009 http://sports.espn.go.com/nfl/news/story?id=4617120 (accessed November 15, 2009).

60. "The NFL StarCaps Case: Are Sports' Anti-Doping Programs at League Crossroads?" *Subcommittee on Commerce, Trade and Consumer Protection*, Washington, DC, November 3, 2009.

61. Ibid.

62. Tom Verducci, "The Night the Lights Went Out in Mannywood," *Sports Illustrated*, May 18, 2009, 34.

63. Ibid., 34.

64. Ken Fidlin, "Manny Joins Cheat Club," *Toronto Sun*, May 8, 2009, Final Edition, Sports Section, S2.

65. Jeff Jacobs, "He Doesn't Get the Benefit of the Doubt," *Hartford Courant*, May 8, 2009, Final Edition, CT Sports, B1.

66. Fidlin, S2.

67. Beverly Ford, "So Manny Reasons to Wonder. Fans Shocked at Stars 50-Game Ban," *New York Daily News*, May 8, 2009, Sports Final Edition, 4.

68. Teri Thompson, Michael O'Keefe, and Nathanial Vinton, "Drug Spawns Manny's Ban. Use of Female Fertility Substance at Heart of Action," *New York Daily News*, May 8, 2009, Sports Final Edition, 84.

69. Mark Bechel and Jeff Pearlman, "Manny of the Year," *Sports Illustrated*, September 28, 1998, 100.

70. Steve Herrick, "The Wacky World of Manny Ramírez," *The Sporting News* March 8, 1998, 41.

71. Ben McGrath, "Waiting for Manny," *The New Yorker*, April 23, 2007, 38.

72. Bretón, 13.

73. Bob Padecky, "No Love Lost for Manny or Standing Ovation in Mannywood," *Santa Rosa Press Democrat*, October 16, 2009, C1.

74. Bill Chastain, "Manny Retires After Notification of Drug Issue," *MLB*, last modified April 9, 2011, http://mlb.mlb.com/news/article.jsp?ymd=20110408&content_id=17514236&vkey=news_mlb&fext=.jsp&c_id=mlb

75. Anthony Castrovince, "Manny's Exit from the Game Is Strangely Fitting," *MLB*, last modified April 8, 2011, http://mlb.mlb.com/news/article.jsp?ymd=20110408&content_id=17528732&vkey=news_mlb&fext=.jsp&c_id=mlb

76. Michael A. Schmidt, "Stars of Red Sox Title Years Are Linked to Doping," *New York Times*, July 31, 2009, A1.

77. "Ortiz's Reaction to Positive Result," *New York Times*, July 31, 2009: B13(L). *Academic One File*. Web. December 7, 2011.

78. Ronald Blum, "David Ortiz Thinks Legal Supplements and Vitamins Likely Caused Him to Land on a List of Alleged Drug Users Circulated by the Federal Government," *Today's Sunbeam*, last modified August 9, 2009, http://docs.newsbank.com/s/InfoWeb/aggdocs/NewsBank/129FAC4EC909DF90/0D0CB59C15C63E40?p_multi=TSSB (accessed September 5, 2011).

79. Joe Posnanski, "Baseball's Loveable Loser," *Sports Illustrated*, August 10, 2009, 14.

80. Tony Kornheiser and Dan Le Batard, "Papi Still Favors Suspensions," *Pardon the Interruption* (Washington, DC: ESPN, September 25, 2009).

81. Bob Raissman, "Roids Not Rage on ESPN to Justice to Bristol's Papi Coverage," *New York Daily News*, August 11, 2009, 62.

82. Ken Davidoff, "OK to Boo Papi, But Then Let It Go," *Newsday*, August 6, 2009, A61.

83. "McGwire Apologizes to La Russa, Selig,"

ESPN, last modified January 12, 2011, http://sports.espn.go.com/mlb/news/story?id=4816607.

84. Bob Costas and Mark McGwire, "Costas' Full McGwire Interview," *MLB*, last modified January 11, 2011, http://mlb.mlb.com/video/play.jsp?content_id=7148421&topic_id=7417714.

85. Gene Wojciechowski, "Line of Truth Starts Behind McGwire," *ESPN*, last modified January 11, 2011, http://sports.espn.go.com/espn/columns/story?columnist=wojciechowski_gene&page=wojciechowski/100112&sportCat=mlb.

86. "McGwire Evades Steroid Questions," *ESPN*, last modified January 18, 2011, http://sports.espn.go.com/mlb/news/story?id=4834393.

87. Howard Bryant, "McGwire Admittedly a Better Man," *ESPN*, last modified January 12, 2011, http://sports.espn.go.com/mlb/columns/story?columnist=bryant_howard&id=4817361.

88. Michael Wilbon and Tony Kornheiser, "Thoughts on Verdict," *Pardon the Interruption* (Washington, DC: ESPN, April 13, 2011).

89. Jayson Stark, "Barry Bonds Trial Reveals Ease of PEDs" *ESPN*, last modified April 13, 2011, http://sports.espn.go.com/mlb/columns/story?columnist=stark_jayson&id=6348022

90. Jemele Hill, "Do Steroid Era Players Value HOF?" *ESPN*, last modified April 15, 2011, http://sports.espn.go.com/espn/commentary/news/story?id=6362221

91. Jeff MacGregor, "The Bang (?) for Barry Bonds Bucks," *ESPN*, last modified April 18, 2011, http://sports.espn.go.com/espn/commentary/news/story?page=macgregor/110418.

92. George Dohrmann, "The U.S. vs. Barry Bonds," *Sports Illustrated*, March 28, 2011 pl.

93. Munson, "Silence of Roger Clemens Lawyer."

94. Costas et al., "Race and the Media."

95. Keith Olbermann, "Hall of Famers and Numbers Without Wings," *Baseball Nerd*, last modified November 28, 2009, http://keitholbermann.mlblogs.com/archives/2009/11/hall_of_famers_and_numbers_wit.html.

Chapter 7

1. Henry Aaron, "Jackie Robinson: Trailblazer," *Time*, last modified June 14, 1999, http://www.time.com/time/magazine/article/0,9171,991262,00.html (accessed August 28, 2011).

2. Robinson, 303.

3. Jules Tygiel, "The Great Experiment Fifty Years Later," in *The Cooperstown Symposium on Baseball and American Culture*, edited by Peter M. Rutkoff (Jefferson, NC: McFarland, 1997), 257.

4. Derrick A. Bell, "Who's Afraid of Critical Race Theory?" *University of Illinois Law Review* 893 (1995): 899.

5. Derrick Bell, "Racial Realism," *Connecticut Law Review* 24 no. 2 (Winter 1992): 364.

6. Arnold Rampersad, *Jackie Robinson: A Biography* (New York: Alfred A. Knopf, 1997), 126.

7. James W. Loewen, *Lies My Teacher Told Me: Everything Your American History Textbook Got Wrong*, revised edition (New York: Simon & Schuster, 2007), 168, 171.

8. Crenshaw, "Color-Blind Dreams," 103.

9. Bell, "*Brown v. Board of Education*," 523.

10. Ibid., 524–525.

11. Derrick Bell, "White Superiority in America: Its Legal Legacy, Its Economic Costs," *Villanova Law Review* 33 (1988): 767.

12. "Baseball Honors Jackie Robinson with Special Day," *Jet* 105, no. 18 (2004): 4–5.

13. Larry Stone, "Ken Griffey, Jr. on Jackie Robinson Day and the Decline of African Americans in Baseball," *Seattle Times*, last modified April 15, 2009, http://blog.seattletimes.nwsource.com/stone/2009/04/15/griffey_on_jackie_robinson_day.html (accessed August 28, 2011).

14. Anthony Castrovince, "Sabathia Cherishes Wearing No. 42," *MLB*, last modified April 15, 2007, http://mlb.mlb.com/news/article.jsp?ymd=20070415&content_id=1900140&vkey=news_mlb&fext=.jsp&c_id=mlb (accessed August 28, 2011.

15. Mark Newman, "'Sacred' No. 42 on Display in Baseball," *MLB*, last modified April 16, 2007, http://mlb.mlb.com/news/article.jsp?ymd=20070415&content_id=1901218&vkey=news_mlb&fext=.jsp&c_id=mlb (accessed August 28, 2011).

16. Castrovince, "Sabathia Cherishes Wearing No. 42."

17. "We're Killing the Meaning of Jackie Day," *NBC Sports*, last modified April 13, 2007, http://nbcsports.msnbc.com/id/17964581/ (accessed February 25, 2009).

18. Larry Stone, "It's Jackie Robinson Day: All Players Wear No. 42 Today, Thanks to Ken Griffey Jr.," *Seattle Times*, last modified April 15, 2011, http://seattletimes.nwsource.com/html/thehotstoneleague/2014783839_its_jackie_robinson_day_all_pl.html (accessed August 30, 2011)

19. Ibid.

20. Barry M. Bloom, "First Civil Rights Game Set for March 31," *MLB*, last modified December 4, 2006, http://mlb.mlb.com/news/article.jsp?ymd=20061204&content_id=1750068&vkey=news_mlb&fext=.jsp&c_id=mlb (accessed June 2, 2008).

21. Justice B. Hall, "Lee a Natural for Beacon of Change," *MLB*, last modified March 28, 2007, http://mlb.mlb.com/news/article.jsp?ymd=20070328&content_id=1863050&vkey=news_mlb&fext=.jsp&c_id=mlb (accessed August 20, 2011).

22. C. Richard King, Ellen J. Staurowsky, Lawrence Baca, Laurel R. Davis, and Cornel Pewewardy, "Of Polls and Race Prejudice: *Sports Illustrated*'s Errant 'Indian Wars,'" *Journal of Sport and Social Issues* 26, no. 4 (November 2002): 392.

23. Filip Bondy, "Selig's Civil Wrong," *New York Daily News*, last modified March 8, 2007, http://www.nydailynews.com/sports/2007/03/08/2007-03-08_seligs_uncivil_wrong-2.html (accessed August 28, 2011).

24. Lawrence III, "The Id, the Ego," 237.

25. Kimberly Roppolo, "Symbolic Racism, History, and Reality: The Real Problem with Indian Mascots," in *Genocide of the Mind: New Native American Writing*, edited by MariJo Moore (New York: Thunder's Mouth Press/Nation Books, 2003), 189.

26. Ibid.

27. Quoted on "If the Indians Win, Do Native Americans Get Civil Rights?" *Deadspin*, last modified March 31, 2007, http://deadspin.com/sports/mlb/if-the-indians-win-do-native-americans-get-civil-rights-248670.php (accessed August 27, 2011).

28. Bell, "Wanted," 539.

29. Spike Lee, Documentary Produced for Civil Rights Game, *MLB*, last modified March 31, 2007 http://mlb.mlb.com/mlb/events/civil_rights_game/y2007/index.jsp (accessed February 15, 2009).

30. Tygiel, 261.

31. *The Princess Bride*, directed by Rob Reiner (1987; Beverly Hills, CA: 20th Century–Fox, 2009). Blu-Ray.

32. Keith Olbermann and Ed Silverman, "#1 Remembering Robinson," *Countdown with Keith Olbermann*, MSNBC, April 13, 2007.

33. Randal C. Archibold, "Arizona Enacts Stringent Law on Immigration," *New York Times*, last modified April 23, 1010, http://www.nytimes.com/2010/04/24/us/politics/24immig.html (accessed September 1, 2011).

34. Janet Murguía, "MLB, Selig, Should Take Arizona Stand," *ESPN*, last modified May 21, 2010, http://sports.espn.go.com/espn/commentary/news/story?id=5207320 (accessed September 1, 2011).

35. Dave Zirin, "Strike Out Phoenix," *The Progressive* 74, no. 7 (2010): 42.

36. Michael Weiner, "Statement of MLBPA Executive Director Michael Weiner Regarding Arizona Immigration Law," *MLBPlayers*, last modified April 30, 2010, http://mlbplayers.mlb.com/pa/pdf/20100430_weiner_statement_on_arizona_immigration_law.pdf (accessed September 1, 2011).

37. Richard Lapchick, "The 2009 Racial and Gender Report Card: Major League Baseball," The Institute for Diversity and Ethics in Sport, April 15, 2009.

38. José E. Serrano. "Strike Two on Arizona Law, Commissioner Selig," *Congressional Documents and Publications*, June 17, 2010.

39. "Civil Rights Leaders Urge Players to Talk."

40. "All Star Game Ratings Down 8 Percent," *ESPN*, last modified July 13, 2011, http://espn.go.com/mlb/allstar11/story/_/id/6766927/mlb-all-star-game-ratings-hit-new-low-second-straight-year (accessed September 2, 2011).

41. Dave Zirin, "Why I'm Boycotting the All-Star Game," *Edge of Sports*, last modified July 11, 2011, http://www.edgeofsports.com/2011-07-11-635/index.html (accessed July 12, 2011).

42. Jeff MacGregor, "All-Stars, Mom, and ~~Protests~~ Apple Pie," *ESPN*, last modified July 12, 2011, http://espn.go.com/espn/commentary/story/_/page/macgregor-110711/the-mlb-all-star-game-apparently-marked-protests-arizona-proposed-illegal-immigration-legislation-shame (accessed September 2, 2011).

43. Mike Bauman, "Selig: Atlanta Is Perfect Place for CRG," *MLB*, last modified May 14, 2011, http://mlb.mlb.com/news/article.jsp?ymd=20110514&content_id=19086670&vkey=civilrights2011 (accessed September 2, 2011).

44. Cindy Boren, "Carlos Santana Uses Phillies-Braves Ceremony to Criticize Immigration Law," *Washington Post*, last modified May 15, 2011, http://www.washingtonpost.com/blogs/early-lead/post/carlos-santana-uses-phillies-braves-ceremony-to-criticize-immigration-law/2011/05/16/AFgS934G_blog.html (accessed September 2, 2011).

45. Dave Zirin, "Santana Is Booed for Using Baseball's Civil Rights Game to Speak Out for Civil Rights," *Edge of Sports*, last modified May 18, 2011, http://www.edgeofsports.com/2011-05-18-621/index.html (accessed May 19, 2011).

46. T.J. Holms, Morgan Freeman, and Carlos Santana, "Santana Sounds Off on Controversial Immigration Laws; Morgan Freeman: Immigration Is the New Civil Rights Struggle," *CNN*, last modified May 24, 2011, http://newsroom.blogs.cnn.com/2011/05/24/santana-sounds-off-on-controversial-immigration-moran-freeman-immigration-is-the-new-civil-rights-struggle/?iref=allsearch (accessed September 2, 2011).

47. Ibid.

48. Tim Wise, "With Friends Like These, Who Needs Glenn Beck? Racism and White Privilege on the Liberal-Left," Timwise.org, August 17, 2010, http://www.timwise.org/2010/08/with-friends-like-these-who-needs-glenn-beck-racism-and-white-privilege-on-the-liberal-left/ (accessed September 4, 2011).

49. "Jackie Robinson," National Baseball Hall of Fame and Museum, http://baseballhall.org/hof/robinson-jackie (accessed September 3, 2011).

50. Steven Wisensale, "The Black Knight: A

Political Portrait of Jackie Robinson," in *The Cooperstown Symposium on Baseball and American Culture*, ed. Peter M. Rutkoff (Jefferson, NC: McFarland, 1997), 190.

51. Doug Battema, "Jackie Robinson as Media's Mythological Black Hero," in *The Cooperstown Symposium on Baseball and American Culture*, edited by Peter M. Rutkoff (Jefferson, NC: McFarland, 1997), 211.

52. Robinson, 303.

Conclusion

1. *Bull Durham*, directed by Ron Shelton (1988; Santa Monica, CA: MGM Home Entertainment, 2002). DVD.

2. *Field of Dreams*, directed by Phil Alden Robinson (1989 Universal City, CA: Universal Pictures, 2004). DVD.

3. Bretón.

4. McIntosh, 123.

5. Lipsitz, "The White 2K Problem," 521.

6. Lori Preuitt, "Barry Bonds to Pay for Stow Kids' College," *NBC Bay Area*, May 26, 2011, http://www.nbcbayarea.com/news/local/Barry-Bonds-to-Pay-For-Stow-Kids-College-1225398 99.html.

7. William Zinsser, *On Writing Well: The Classic Guide to Writing Nonfiction*, 25th Anniversary Edition (New York: HarperCollins, 2001), 185.

Suggested Reading

While this book is informed by and cites a wide variety of sources, there are others well worth mentioning, particularly for readers who want more information on Critical Race Theory and the intersection of race and sport. This bibliographic essay provides a brief discussion of key texts.

For Critical Race Theory, there are several prospective starting points. One of the better options is William F. Tate IV's article "Critical Race Theory and Education: History, Theory, and Implications," which appears in the *Review of Research in Education* (vol. 22, pp. 195–247). Tate provides a brief history of the movement, the social theories which form the undercurrent of Critical Race Theory, as well as a discussion of some of the theory's key contributors. *Critical Race Theory: The Key Writings That Formed the Movement*, edited by Kimberlé Crenshaw, Neil Gotanda, Gary Peller, and Kendall Thomas (New York: New Press, 1995), does exactly what the anthology's title suggests: it provides access to some of the seminal essays that form the core of Critical Race Theory. Many of the concepts that recur throughout this book, including Derrick Bell's discussion of interest convergence, Kimberlé Crenshaw's concept of intersectionality and Charles R. Lawrence III's notion of unconscious racism are all contained in this anthology. Considered one of the founders of CRT, Derrick Bell has

a reader devoted to his writings. Edited by Richard Delgado and Jean Stefancic, *The Derrick Bell Reader* (New York: New York University Press, 2005) covers a great deal of ground. It should be noted that because Bell was such a prolific writer, the majority of the essays within the reader are truncated; however, citations are provided at the beginning of each work so readers can find the original, full-length source. Delgado and Stefancic also coauthored "Critical Race Theory: An Annotated Bibliography" (vol. 79, no. 2: 461–516) which appeared in the *Virginia Law Review* (vol. 79, no. 2: 461–516) and edited an anthology of more recent CRT writings entitled *Critical Race Theory: The Cutting Edge* (Philadelphia: Temple University Press, 2000). Of special note in this anthology is a section entitled "Beyond the Black-White Binary." Race relations in the United States have never been a simple bilateral issue and the essays contained in this section help move CRT toward a multilateral paradigm.

Using CRT to discuss sports did not originate with this book. Kevin Hylton's 2005 essay "'Race,' Sport and Leisure: Lessons from Critical Race Theory" (*Leisure* Studies vol. 24, no. 1: 81–98) highlights the core tenants of CRT and their relationship to sport studies, making the argument that race and racism should be at the center of sporting analysis. Hylton puts the arguments he laid out in the article into practice in his book *"Race" and Sport: Critical Race Theory* (New York: Routledge, 2009).

Anyone interested in the intersection of race and sport in the United States has a myriad of resources to choose from and because of that, this essay will focus solely on works that provide a general overview and were written for non-academic audiences. Harry Edwards' *The Revolt of the Black Athlete* (New York: Free Press, 1969) is as good a place as any to start. Edwards' involvement with the 1968 Olympic protest gave him a front-row seat to witness the centrality of race in sporting environments and the role politics plays in sporting structures. John Hoberman's work *Darwin's Athletes: How Sport Has Damaged Black America and Preserved the Myth of Race* (New York: Houghton Mifflin, 1997) discusses how the "fixation" on athletics from basketball to boxing to track, has reified racial stereotypes, damaged black communities, and led to anti-intellectual sentiments within those same communities. Many of Hoberman's critics would lay the blame not within black communities themselves but within society's power structure that gives black men the illusion of athletics as a way out. More recent though no less controversial analyses of race in sports come from William C. Rhoden's *Forty Million Dollar Slaves: The Rise, Fall, and Redemption of the Black Athlete* (New York: Three Rivers Press, 2006), Thabiti Lewis's *Ballers of the New School: Race and Sports in America* (Chicago: Third World Press, 2010) and Gerald Early's *A Level Playing Field: African American Athletes and the Republic of Sports* (Cambridge, MA: Harvard University Press, 2011). Though Early eschews the plantation metaphor, each of these

works makes the argument that despite the wealth and fame professional athletes enjoy, they are still constrained by racial systems in the United States.

Several anthologies delve into issues surrounding race and sport. Patrick B. Miller and David K. Wiggins's book *Sport and the Color Line: Black Athletes and Race Relations in Twentieth-Century America* (New York: Routledge, 2004) touches on subjects such as black women in track and field, Joe Louis, and scientific racism as it pertains to black athletic ability. *Reconstructing Fame: Sport, Race, and Evolving Reputations* (Jackson: University Press of Mississippi, 2008) edited by David C. Ogden and Joel Nathan Rosen features essays on Roberto Clemente, Paul Robeson, and Jim Thorpe. Finally, *Commodified and Criminalized: New Racism and African Americans in Contemporary Sport* (Lanham, MD: Rowman and Littlefield, 2011), edited by David J. Leonard and C. Richard King, includes discussions on Sheryl Swoopes, Freddy Adu, and Tiger Woods. All of these anthologies put race squarely in the center of their analyses and delve into the complicated history of race and sport in the United States.

Though it does not focus entirely on race, *Reading Sport: Critical Essays on Power and Representation* (Boston: Northeastern University Press, 2000), edited by Susan Birrell and Mary G. McDonald, includes essays on O.J. Simpson, Nancy Lopez, and Michael Jordan among others. In that same vein, *Sporting Stars: The Cultural Politics of Sporting Celebrity* (New York: Routledge, 2001), edited by David L. Andrews and Steven J. Jackson, includes essays on Venus Williams, Hideo Nomo, and Dennis Rodman.

Bibliography

Aaron, Henry. "Jackie Robinson: Trailblazer." *Time*, last modified June 14, 1999, http://www.time.com/time/magazine/article/0,9171,991262,00.html (accessed August 28, 2011).

Alexander, Stephen. "Philadelphia Phillies to Preach in 'It Gets Better' Video." *Technorati*, last modified July 24, 2011, http://technorati.com/sports/baseball/article/philadelphia-phillies-to-preach-in-it/ (accessed August 26, 2011).

"All Star Game Ratings Down 8 Percent." *ESPN*, last modified July 13, 2011, http://espn.go.com/mlb/allstar11/story/_/id/6766927/mlb-all-star-game-ratings-hit-new-low-second-straight-year (accessed September 2, 2011).

"Americans Conflicted About Bonds' Home Run Chase." *ESPN*, last modified May 6, 2007, http://sports.espn.go.com/mlb/news/story?id=2861930 (accessed May 6, 2007).

Anderson, Eric. *In the Game: Gay Athletes and the Cult of Masculinity*. Albany: State University of New York Press, 2005.

"Appeals Court Could Rehear Case." *ESPN*, last modified November 9, 2009, http://sports.espn.go.com/mlb/news/story?id=4639482 (accessed November 15, 2009).

Araton, Harvey. "Baseball Focuses on the Trivial." *New York Times*, May 23, 2002.

_____. "Pujols and Cardinals Call Off Talks." *New York Times* February 17, 2011.

_____. "Why Three Is Better Than One." *New York Times*, August 14, 1998.

Archibold, Randal C. "Arizona Enacts Stringent Law on Immigration." *New York Times*, last modified April 23, 1010, http://www.nytimes.com/2010/04/24/us/politics/24immig.html (accessed September 1, 2011).

Ardell, Jean Hastings. *Breaking into Baseball: Women and the National Pastime*. Carbondale: Southern Illinois University Press, 2005.

Arnedt, Cheryl. "Poll: Clinton's Approval Ratings Improve." *ABC News*, last modified June 22, 2004, http://abcnews.go.com/sections/us/Polls/clinton_poll_040622.html (accessed August 7, 2005).

Atkin, Ross. "Is A-Rod Worth It? Some Say 'Yes.'" *Christian Science Monitor*, April 6, 2001.

"Babe Ruth: Stats, Photos, Highlights." *MLB*, http://mlb.mlb.com/team/player.jsp?player_id=121578 (accessed August 27, 2011).

Bamberger, Michael. "What's Up with Tiger." *Sports Illustrated*, July 6, 1998.

Barber, Phil. "Several Cuts Above." *The Sporting News* July 10, 2000.

"Barry Bonds." *SportsCentury Greatest Athletes* 2007. Santa Monica, CA: Genius Entertainment, 2007. DVD.

"Barry Bonds: Stats, Photos, Highlights." *MLB*, http://mlb.mlb.com/team/player.jsp?player_id=111188 (accessed August 27, 2011).

"Barry Bonds Moves Forward." *ESPN*, last modified May 30, 2012, http://espn.go.com/mlb/story/_/id/7981089/barry-bonds-moving-forward-felony-conviction (accessed June 1, 2012).

"Baseball and Gay Fans Come Together." *Outsports*, last modified August 3, 2004, http://www.outsports.com/baseball/2004/0803gaydays.htm (accessed July 20, 2005).

"Baseball Honors Jackie Robinson with Special Day." *Jet* 105, no. 18 (2004).

Battema, Doug. "Jackie Robinson as Media's Mythological Black Hero." In *The Cooperstown Symposium on Baseball and American Culture*. Edited by Peter M. Rutkoff. 199–214. Jefferson, NC: McFarland, 1997.

Bauman, Mike. "Selig: Atlanta Is Perfect Place for CRG." *MLB*, last modified May 14, 2011, http://mlb.mlb.com/news/article.jsp?ymd=20110514&content_id=19086670&vkey=civilrights2011 (accessed September 2, 2011).

_____. "Who Boos Louder at A-Rod?" *MLB*, last modified May 8, 2004, http://seattle.mariners.mlb.com/NASApp/mlb/sea/news/sea_news.jsp?ymd=20040508&content_id=738807&vkey=news_sea&fext=.jsp (March 21, 2005).

Bayliss, Skip. "Prove It to Me." *ESPN*, last mod-

ified December 9, 2004, http://sports.espn.
go.com/espn/page2/story?page=bayliss/04
1210 (accessed January 27, 2005).

Bean, Billy. *Going the Other Way: Lessons from a
Life in and Out of Major League Baseball.* New
York: Marlowe, 2003.

Bechel, Mark, and Jeff Pearlman. "Manny of the
Year." *Sports Illustrated*, September 28, 1998.

Bell, Derrick. "*Brown v. Board of Education* and
the Interest-Convergence Dilemma." In *The
Derrick Bell Reader.* Edited by Richard Delgado and Jean Stefancic. 33–39. New York:
New York University Press, 2005.

_____. "Racial Realism." *Connecticut Law Re-
view* 24, no. 2 (Winter 1992) 363–379.

_____. "The Racism Is Permanent Thesis:
Courageous Revelations or Unconscious De-
nial of Racial Genocide." *Capital University
Law Review* 22, no. 1 (1993): 571–588.

_____. "Wanted: A White Leader Able to Free
Whites from Racism." *U.C. Davis Law Review*
33 (2000): 328–336.

_____. "White Superiority in America: Its Legal
Legacy, Its Economic Costs." *Villanova Law
Review* 33 (1988): 767–779.

Bell, Derrick A. "Who's Afraid of Critical Race
Theory?" *University of Illinois Law Review* 893
(1995): 893–910.

Berlage, Gail Ingham. "Effa Manley, a Major
Force in Negro Baseball in the 1930s and
1940s." In *Out of the Shadows: African Amer-
ican Baseball from the Cuban Giants to Jackie
Robinson.* Edited by Bill Kirwin. 128–146,
Lincoln: University of Nebraska Press, 2005.

Bernstein, Sam. "Ted Williams Pleads for Negro
Leagues Inductions." *National Baseball Hall
of Fame and Museum*, last modified February
15, 2007, http://www.baseballhalloffame.org/
news/article.jsp?ymd=20070215&content_
id=282&vkey=hof_news (accessed June 11,
2008).

Bianchi, Mike. "Athletes Paved the Way for Barack Obama's Run." *Orlando Sentinel*, November 5, 2008.

Birrell, Susan, and Mary G. McDonald. "Reading Sport, Articulating Power Lines: An Introduction." In *Reading Sport: Critical Essays
on Power and Representation.* Edited by Susan
Birrell and Mary G. McDonald. 3–12. Boston: Northeastern University Press, 2000.

Bloom, Barry M. "First Civil Rights Game Set
for March 31." *MLB*, last modified December
4, 2006,http://mlb.mlb.com/news/article.jsp
?ymd=20061204&content_id=1750068&
vkey=news_mlb&fext=.jsp&c_id=mlb (accessed June 2, 2008).

_____. "Many to Take Part in Honoring Robin-
son." *MLB*, last modified April 7, 2007, http:
//mlb.mlb.com/news/article.jsp?ymd=2007
0410&content_id=1890656&vkey=news_mlb

&fext=.jsp&c_id=mlb, (accessed September
3, 2011).

Blum, Ronald. "David Ortiz Thinks Legal Supplements and Vitamins Likely Caused Him
to Land on a List of Alleged Drug Users Circulated by the Federal Government." *Today's
Sunbeam*, last modified August 9, 2009, http:
//docs.newsbank.com/s/InfoWeb/aggdocs/
NewsBank/129FAC4EC909DF90/0D0CB
59C15C63E40?p_multi=TSSB (accessed September 5, 2011)

Bondy, Filip. "Selig's Civil Wrong." *New York
Daily News*, last modified March 8, 2007,
http://www.nydailynews.com/sports/2007
/03/08/2007-03-08_seligs_uncivil_wrong-
2.html (accessed August 28, 2011).

Boren, Cindy. "Carlos Santana Uses Phillies-
Braves Ceremony to Criticize Immigration
Law." *Washington Post*, last modified May 15,
2011, http://www.washingtonpost.com/blogs/
early-lead/post/carlos-santana-uses-phillies-
braves-ceremony-to-criticize-immigration-
law/2011/05/16/AFgS934G_blog.html (accessed September 2, 2011).

Boyd, Todd. "You Can't Discuss Bonds Without Race." *ESPN*, last modified May 9, 2007,
http://sports.espn.go.com/espn/page2/sto
ry?page=boyd/070508 (accessed July 25,
2007).

Boyer, Brooks. "2005 Chicago White Sox Advertising Campaign." *Chicago White Sox*,
http://chicago.whitesox.mlb.com/NASApp/
mlb/cws/fan_forum/campaigns/television/
index.jsp (accessed October 25, 2005).

Breakey, Caleb. "A-Rod Honored for Historic
Month." *MLB*, last modified May 2, 2007,
http://newyork.yankees.mlb.com/news/ar
ticle.jsp?ymd=20070502&content_id=194
2648&vkey=news_nyy&fext=.jsp&c_id=nyy
(accessed September 3, 2011).

Brennan, Christine. "No Matter the Result,
Sosa's Power Will Be Forever Diminished."
USA Today, June 5, 2003.

Bretón, Marcos. "Fields of Broken Dreams: Latinos and Baseball." *ColorLines* 3, no. 1 (2000)
http://search.proquest.com/docview/2155414
21?accountid=14925 (accessed September 3,
2011).

Bretón, Marcos, and José Luis Villegas. *Away
Games: The Life and Times of a Latin Baseball
Player.* New York: Simon & Schuster, 1999.

Brioso, Cesar. "Latinos Swing into the Majors."
Hispanic, April 2001.

Brodley, Hal. "Union Considers Grievance; Palmeiro Case Details Not Kept Confidential."
USA Today, August 8, 2005.

Brown, Robert S. "Sport and the Healing of
America After 9/11." In *Language, Symbols,
and the Media: Communication in the Aftermath of the World Trade Center Attack.* Edited

by Robert E. Denton, Jr. 117–127. New Brunswick, NJ: Transaction, 2004.

Browne, Ian. "No Blessed Union Yet on Megadeal." *MLB.COM*, December 17, 2003, http://texas.rangers.mlb.com/NASApp/mlb/tex/news/tex_news.jsp?ymd=20031217&content_id=620263&vkey=news_tex&fext=.jsp&c_id=tex (accessed March 21, 2005).

Bryant, Howard. "Friction and Fractures Erode Faith in Mitchell's Investigation." *ESPN*, last modified December 11, 2007, http://sports.espn.go.com/mlb/news/story?id=3142651 (accessed December 11, 2007).

_____. "McGwire Admittedly a Better Man." *ESPN*, last modified January 12, 2011, http://sports.espn.go.com/mlb/columns/story?columnist=bryant_howard&id=4817361 (accessed November 19, 2011).

Bull Durham. Directed by Ron Shelton. 1988. Santa Monica, CA: MGM Home Entertainment, 2002. DVD.

Burk, Robert. *Much More Than a Game: Players, Owners, & American Baseball Since 1921*. Chapel Hill: University of North Carolina Press, 2001.

Bush, George W. "State of the Union Address." January 20, 2004. http://www.whitehouse.gov/news/release/2004/01/10040120-7.html (accessed January 29, 2004).

Butterworth, Michael. "Purifying the Body Politic: Steroids, Rafael Palmeiro, and the Rhetorical Cleansing of Major League Baseball." *Western Journal of Communication* 72, no. 2 (2008): 145–168.

"California Ban on Same-Sex Marriage Struck Down." *CNN*, last modified May 16, 2008, http://www.cnn.com/2008/US/05/15/same.sex.marriage/index.html?iref=newssearch (accessed August 26, 2011).

Callahan, Gerry. "The Fairest of Them All." *Sports Illustrated*, July 8, 1996.

_____. "Issue Too Big to Come Out." *Boston Herald*, May 24, 2002.

Caple, Jim. "Free Agency Simply Great for Baseball." *ESPN*, last modified November 26, 2000, http://espn.go.com/mlb/columns/caple_jim/896034.html, (accessed April 2, 2005).

Carter, Art. "From the Bench," *Baltimore Afro-American*, February 10, 1940.

_____. "From the Bench," *Baltimore Afro-American*, June 15, 1940.

_____. "New Issue Looms on Satchell Paige," *Baltimore Afro-American*, June 15, 1940.

Carter, Ulish. "Will Pirates Ever Win Again?" *New Pittsburgh Courier*, October 17–23, 2007.

Cashmore, Ellis. *Making Sense of Sports*. Third Edition. London: Routledge, 2000.

_____. "Tiger Woods and the New Racial Order." *Current Sociology* 56 (2008): 621–634.

Castrovince, Anthony. "Manny's Exit from the Game Is Strangely Fitting." *MLB*, last modified April 8, 2011, http://mlb.mlb.com/news/article.jsp?ymd=20110408&content_id=17528732&vkey=news_mlb&fext=.jsp&c_id=mlb (accessed September 5, 2011).

_____. "Sabathia Cherishes Wearing No. 42." *MLB*, last modified April 15, 2007, http://mlb.mlb.com/news/article.jsp?ymd=20070415&content_id=1900140&vkey=news_mlb&fext=.jsp&c_id=mlb (accessed August 28, 2011.

Chabon, Michael . "Jose Canseco, Hero." *New York Times*, March 18, 2005.

Chastain, Bill. "Manny Retires After Notification of Drug Issue." *MLB*, last modified April 9, 2011, http://mlb.mlb.com/news/article.jsp?ymd=20110408&content_id=17514236&vkey=news_mlb&fext=.jsp&c_id=mlb.

"Cheering on Women and Girls in Sport: Using Title IX to Fight Gender Role Oppression." *Harvard Law Review* 110, no. 7 (1997): 1627–1644.

Chen, Albert. "No Regrets." *Sports Illustrated*, May 31, 2004.

Chen, David W. "Dominicans' Favorite Son: Sammy Sosa, Homerun Hitter." *New York Times*, September 5, 1998.

"Civil Rights Leaders Urge Players to Talk." *ESPN*, last modified July 12, 2010, http://sports.espn.go.com/mlb/allstar11/news/story?id=6759457 (accessed September 1, 2011).

Clark, Danae. "Commodity Lesbianism." In *Popular Culture: Production and Consumption*. Edited by C. Lee Harrington and Denise D. Bielby. 80–93. Malden, MA: Blackwell, 2001.

Clarkson, Jay. "Contesting Masculinity's Makeover: *Queer Eye*, Consumer Masculinity, and 'Straight-Acting' Gays." *Journal of Communication Inquiry* 29, no. 3 (2005): 235–255.

Cole, C.L., and Alex Mobley. "American Steroids: Using Race and Gender." *Journal of Sport & Social Issues* 29, no. 1 (2005): 3–8.

Cole C.L., and David L. Andrews. "America's New Son: Tiger Woods." In *Sport Stars: The Cultural Politics of Sporting Celebrity*. Edited by David L. Andrews and Steven J. Jackson. 70–86. New York: Routledge, 2001.

Collins, Patricia Hill. *Black Feminist Thought: Knowledge, Consciousness, and the Politics of Empowerment*, Revised Tenth Anniversary Edition. New York: Routledge, 2000.

_____. *Black Sexual Politics: African Americans, Gender, and the New Racism*. New York: Routledge, 2004.

_____. *Fighting Words: Black Women and the Search for Justice*. Minneapolis: University of Minnesota Press, 1998.

_____. *From Black Power to Hip Hop: Racism, Nationalism, and Feminism*. Philadelphia: Temple University Press, 2006.

Conroy, Pat. "Hank Aaron's Pursuit of an Immortal and His Magic Number." In *Total Baseball: The Ultimate Baseball Encyclopedia.* 8th Edition. Edited by John Thorn, Phil Birnbaum, and Bill Deane. 309–311. Wilmington, DE: Sport Media, 2004.

Cook, Ron. "Sports Can't Get Out of the Closet." *Pittsburgh Post-Gazette,* May 24, 2002.

Costas, Bob, and Mark McGwire. "Costas' Full McGwire Interview." *MLB,* last modified January 11, 2011, http://mlb.mlb.com/video/play.jsp?content_id=7148421&topic_id=7417714 (accessed November 19, 2011).

Costas, Bob, Michael Wilbon, Cris Carter, and Jason Whitlock. "Race and the Media." *Costas Now.* New York: HBO, April 30, 2008.

Cowley, Joe. "Selig Sends Guillen to School: Sox Manager Ordered to Attend Sensitivity Training, Pay Fine." *Chicago Sun-Times,* June 23, 2007.

Crenshaw, Kimberlé. "Bad Calls on the Racial Playing Field." *CommonDreams.Org,* October 11, 2003, http://www.commondreams.org/views03/1011-08.htm (accessed September 3, 2011).

_____. "Color-Blind Dreams and Racial Nightmares: Reconfiguring Racism in the Post-Civil Rights Era." In *Birth of a Nation'hood: Gaze, Script, and Spectacle in the O.J. Simpson Case.* Edited by Toni Morrison and Claudia Brodsky Lacour. 97–168. New York: Pantheon, 1999.

_____. "Demarginalizing the Intersection of Race and Sex: A Black Feminist Critique of Antidiscrimination Doctrine, Feminist Theory, and Antiracist Politics." In *Feminist Legal Theories.* Edited by Karen K. Maschke. 23–51. New York: Garland, 1997.

Crossman, Matt. "Three Tiers for the Stars." *The Sporting News,* July 28, 2003.

Curry, Jack. "2 Stars Leap to Hall of Fame, But Steroid Cloud Stops 3rd." *New York Times,* January 10, 2007.

D'Angelo, Tom. "Gay Issue Remains in Closet." *Palm Beach Post,* May 26, 2002.

Davidoff, Ken. "OK to Boo Papi, But Then Let It Go." *Newsday,* August 6, 2009.

Dedman, Bill. "It's a Race for the Record, but Is It Also About Race?" *New York Times,* September 20, 1998.

Delgado, Richard, and Jean Stefancic. "Introduction." In *Critical Race Theory: The Cutting Edge.* Edited by Richard Delgado and Jean Stefancic. xv–xix. Philadelphia: Temple University Press, 2000.

"Deposition of: Andy Pettitte." *Committee on Oversight and Governmental Reform, House of Representatives.* Washington, DC, February 4, 2008.

Deveney, Sean. "Getting Leverage from a Buyout." *The Sporting News,* December 25, 2000.

Dickey, Glenn. "Deserving Bonds Has Got It All Over McGwire." *San Francisco Chronicle,* September 25, 2001.

Dohrmann, George. "The U.S. vs. Barry Bonds." *Sports Illustrated,* March 28, 2011.

Donaldson, Mike. "What Is Hegemonic Masculinity?" *Theory and Society* 22, no. 5 (1993): 643–657.

Dr. Seuss' How the Grinch Stole Christmas. Directed by Chuck Jones 1966. Burbank, CA, Warner Home Video, 2000. DVD.

Dyer, Richard. "Entertainment and Utopia." In *The Cultural Studies Reader.* Edited by Simon During. 371–381. London: Routledge, 2003.

Dyson, Michael Eric. *Open Mike: Reflections on Philosophy, Race, Sex, Culture, and Religion.* New York: Basic Civitas Books, 2003.

"Eagle Owner Flays Rickey for Tactics in Player Deal." *Baltimore Afro-American,* November 3, 1945.

"Effa Manley Baseball Executive." *New Pittsburgh Courier,* June 3, 1981.

Egan, Mary Ellen, Victoria Murphy, and Nichole Ridgway. "The 400 Richest People in America." *Forbes,* October 9, 2000.

Evans, Howie. "Barry Bonds Is Walking His Way to the Hall of Fame." *New York Amsterdam News,* May 20–26, 2004.

_____. "Bonds, Griffey, McGriff Pin Cushions for Sick Media Attacks." *New York Amsterdam News,* August 2–8, 2001.

Fatsis, Stefan. "Mystery of Baseball: Was William White Game's First Black? He Played a Big League Game in 1879 — Then Vanished, Mr. Morris Picks Up Trail." *Wall Street Journal,* Eastern Edition, January 20, 2004.

Feinsand, Mark. "One-on-One with Alex Rodríguez." *MLB,* last modified March 21, 2004, http://mlb.mlb.com/NASApp/mlb/mlb/news/mlb_news.jsp?ymd=20040324&content_id=667622&vkey=news_mlb&fext=.jsp (accessed March 21, 2005).

Fidlin, Ken. "Manny Joins Cheat Club." *Toronto Sun,* May 8, 2009.

Field of Dreams. Directed by Phil Alden Robinson. 1989. Universal City, CA. Universal Pictures, 2004. DVD.

"The 50 Most Beautiful People in the World." *People,* May 11, 1998.

Fimrite, Ron. "Remembering Bobby Bonds." *Sports Illustrated,* September 1, 2003.

"The First Inning: Our Game: 1840s–1900." *Baseball.* Directed by Ken Burns. 1994. PBS Distribution, 2010. DVD.

Fitzgerald, Mark. "All's Quiet When Sosa Smacks 62nd." *Editor & Publisher,* September 19, 1998.

_____. "Furor Follows AP Disclosure on Mc-Gwire." *Editor & Publisher* 131 (1998), http://0-search.epnet.com.maurice.bgsu.edu:80/login.aspx?direct=true&db=aph&an=1037 553 (accessed August 29, 2004).

Food and Drug Administration. "Crackdown on 'Andro' Products." *FDA Consumer Magazine* 38 (2004), http://www.fda.gov/fdac/features/2004/304_andro.html (accessed October 20, 2004).

Ford, Beverly. "So Manny Reasons to Wonder. Fans Shocked at Star's 50-Game Ban." *New York Daily News*, May 8, 2009.

Forde, Pat. "Sports World Is Incubator for Larger Discussions to Come." *ESPN*, last modified May 24, 2007, http://sports.espn.go.com/espn/columns/story?columnist=forde_pat&id=2881430&sportCat=mlb. (accessed July 25, 2007).

Forrester, Paul. "The Man Behind the Megamillion Dollar Players." *Christian Science Monitor*, April 3, 2001.

Foucault, Michel. *Discipline & Punish: The Birth of the Prison.* Trans. Alan Sheridan. New York: Vintage, 1977.

Fowler, Chris. "Curt Flood." *SportsCentury.* Bristol, CT: ESPN, 2000.

Frazier, Lindsey. "Pioneering Newcombe Eyes Top Honor." *MLB*, last modified February 16, 2007, http://mlb.mlb.com/news/article.jsp?ymd=20070214&content_id=1802262&vkey=news_mlb&fext=jsp&c_id=mlb (accessed May 8, 2008).

Gammons, Peter, and Alex Rodríguez. "SC Exclusive: Alex Rodriquez Interview." *SportsCenter.* Bristol, CT: ESPN, February 9, 2009.

Goldstein, Richard. "Bobby Bonds, 57, a Star and the Father of Barry, Dies." *New York Times*, August 24, 2003.

Goldstein, Warren. "The Conundrum That Is Barry Bonds." *Chronicle of Higher Education* 53, no. 40 (2007).

Golen, Jimmy. "Court Ruling Small Consolation For Exposed Players." *Seattle Times*, last modified August 27, 2009, http://seattletimes.nwsource.com/html/2009754217_apbbobaseballdruglistreax.html (accessed September 5, 2011).

Gomez, Pedro. "Latin Players Could Use More Support." *The Sporting News*, June 2, 2002.

"Goodell to Seek Change in Labor Law." *ESPN*, last modified November 2, 2009, http://sports.espn.go.com/nfl/news/story?id=461712 0 (accessed November 15, 2009).

Gordy, Cynthia. "Setting the Record Straight." *Essence*, October 2006.

Greenberg, Mike, and Mike Golic. *Mike and Mike in the Morning.* Bristol, CT: ESPN, February 13, 2008.

"Grimsley's Attorney: Feds Asked Diamondbacks Pitcher to Wear Wire in Bonds Probe." *Associated Press*, June 9, 2006.

Hall, Justice B. "Lee a Natural for Beacon of Change." *MLB*, last modified March 28, 2007, http://mlb.mlb.com/news/article.jsp?ymd=20070328&content_id=1863050&vkey=news_mlb&fext=.jsp&c_id=mlb (accessed August 20, 2011).

"Hall of Fame Voters Speak Out About Clemens." *ESPN*, last modified December 14, 2007, http://sports.espn.go.com/mlb/news/story?id=3155168 (accessed December 14, 2007).

Han, Chong-suk. "Gay Asian-American Male Seeks Home." *Gay & Lesbian Review Worldwide* 12, no. 5 (2005): 35–6.

Hanke, Robert. "Hegemonic Masculinity in *Thirtysomething*." *Critical Studies in Mass Communication* 7 (1990): 231–238.

"Hardaway Axed by NBA for Anti-Gay Comments in Wake of Amaechi's Revelation That He's Gay." *Jet*, March 5, 2007.

Harris, Cheryl I. "Whiteness as Property." *Harvard Law Review* 106, no. 8 (1993): 1707–1791.

Harris, Jamie C. "Sosa Discovers Race as Glaring an Issue as the Cork in His Bat." *New York Amsterdam News*, June 19, 2005.

Heaphy, Leslie. "Effa Manley: A Woman on a Mission." *Baseball Hall of Fame*, last modified February 15, 2007, http://www.baseballhalloffame.org/news/article.jsp?ymd=20070215&content_id=328&vkey=hof_news (accessed June 11, 2008).

Henry, Marcus. "Barry Bonds Continues to Slam the Ball While Media Slams Him." *New York Amsterdam News*, August 14–20, 2003.

Henry III, William A. "Beyond the Melting Pot." *Time*, April 28, 1990.

Hermoso, Rafael. "Piazza Responds to Gossip Column." *New York Times*, May 22, 2002.

Hernandez-Truyol, Berta Esperanza. "Borders (En)Gendered: Normativities, Latinas, and a LatCrit Paradigm." *New York University Law Review* 72 (1997): 882–927.

Herrick, Steve. "The Wacky World of Manny Ramírez." *The Sporting News*, March 8, 1998.

Hertzel, Bob. "Vote Shows Bonds Had It All Despite Image." *The Sporting News*, December 3, 1990.

Heyman, Jon. "The Best Player? A Clue: He Has Dazzled Seattle Fans." *The Sporting News*, January 10, 2000.

_____. "Cardinals, Pujols Fail to Reach Deal Before Wednesday Deadline." *Sports Illustrated*, last modified February 15, 2011, http://sportsillustrated.cnn.com/2011/writers/jon_heyman/02/15/cardinals-pujols-negotiations/index.html (accessed August 27, 2011).

Heywood, Leslie, and Shari L. Dworkin. *Built to Win: The Female Athlete as Cultural Icon.*

Minneapolis: University of Minnesota Press, 2003.

Hill, James Richard. "Will Rising Salaries Destroy Baseball?" In *Stee-Rike Four!: What's Wrong with the Business of Baseball?* Edited by Daniel R. Marburger. 55–60. Westport, CT: Praeger, 1997.

Hill, Jemele. "Do Steroid Era Players Value HOF?" *ESPN*, last modified April 15, 2011, http://sports.espn.go.com/espn/commentary/news/story?id=6362221 (accessed September 5, 2011).

Hillary Goodridge & Others vs. Department of Public Health & Other, SJC-08860 (2003).

Hoberman, John. *Darwin's Athletes: How Sport Has Damaged Black America and Preserved the Myth of Race*. Boston: Houghton Mifflin, 1997.

_____. "Mark McGwire's Little Helper: The Androstenedione Debate." *Think Muscle* (2006), http://www.thinkmuscle.com/articles/hoberman/mcgwire.htm (accessed April 17, 2006).

Hoffer, Richard. "The Importance of Being Barry." *Sports Illustrated*, May 24, 1993.

Hogan, Lawrence D. *Shades of Glory: The Negro Leagues and the Story of African-American Baseball*. Washington, DC: National Geographic, 2006.

Holder, Jr., Eric H. "Letter from the Attorney General to Congress on Litigation Involving the Defense of Marriage Act." Department of Justice, Office of Public Affairs, February 23, 2011, http://www.justice.gov/opa/pr/2011/February/11-ag-223.html (accessed August 26, 2011).

Holms, Bradley. "Queer Eye for the Red Sox." *Queer Eye for the Straight Guy*. United States: Scout Productions, 2005. DVD.

Holms, T.J., Morgan Freeman, and Carlos Santana. "Santana Sounds Off on Controversial Immigration Laws; Morgan Freeman: Immigration Is the New Civil Rights Struggle." *CNN*, last modified May 24, 2011, http://newsroom.blogs.cnn.com/2011/05/24/santana-sounds-off-on-controversial-immigration-moran-freeman-immigration-is-the-new-civil-rights-struggle/?iref=allsearch (accessed September 2, 2011).

hooks, bell. *Killing Rage: Ending Racism*. New York: Henry Holt, 1995.

Hutchinson, Earl Ofari. "Don't Rush to Judgment on Bonds." *Chicago Defender*, November 21, 2007

Hylton, Kevin. "'Race,' Sport and Leisure: Lessons from Critical Race Theory." *Leisure Studies* 24.1 (2005): 81–98.

"If The Indians Win, Do Native Americans Get Civil Rights? *Deadspin.com*, March 31, 2007, http://deadspin.com/sports/mlb/if-the-india-ns-win-do-native-americans-get-civil-rights-248670.php (accessed August 27, 2011).

"Implications by Track Star Infuriates Bonds." *ESPN*, last modified June 24, 2004, http://sports.espn.go.com/espn/print?id=1827368&type=story (accessed June 24, 2004).

"Indians Pitcher Asks Forgiveness for Role in Gay Porn Video." *CBS Sportsline*, last modified January 27, 2004, http://cbs.sportsline.com/mlb/story/7041300 (accessed: August 5, 2004).

"Interview of: Edward Charles Knoblauch." Committee on Oversight and Governmental Reform, House of Representatives. Washington, DC, February 1, 2008.

Irwin, Sarah. "Later Life, Inequality, and Sociological Theory." *Ageing and Society* 19.6 (1999): 691–715.

"Jackie Robinson." *National Baseball Hall of Fame and Museum*, http://baseballhall.org/hof/robinson-jackie (accessed September 3, 2011).

Jacobs, Jeff. "He Doesn't Get the Benefit of the Doubt." *Hartford Courant*, May 8, 2009.

Jarvie, G., and I. Reid. "Race Relations, Sociology of Sport and the New Politics of Race and Racism." *Leisure Studies* 16.4 (1997): 211–19.

Jenkins, Bruce. "Baseball Isn't Ready to Open the Closet Door." *San Francisco Chronicle*, May 25, 2002.

_____. "Unprecedented, Unappreciated." *San Francisco Chronicle*, October 8, 2001.

Jerry Maguire. Directed by Cameron Crowe. 1996, Culver City, CA: Columbia TriStar, 2002. DVD.

John Geddes Lawrence and Tyron Garner, Petitioners vs. Texas, U.S. 02-102 (2003).

Jones, Todd. "You Don't Have to Like Bonds to Appreciate Him." *The Sporting News*, November 4, 2002.

Juffer, Jane. "Who's The Man? Sammy Sosa, Latinos and Televisual Redefinitions of the 'American' Pastime." *Journal of Sport & Social Issues* 26, no. 4 (2002): 337–359.

"Julia Roberts." *IMDb*, http://www.imdb.com/name/nm0000210/ (accessed April 7, 2005).

Justice, Richard. "It's Fitting to Forgive Andy After Apology." *Houston Chronicle*, February 19, 2008.

Karenga, Maulana. "Raceball, Baseball and Unforgivable Blackness: Hank, The King and Barry, The Man." *Los Angeles Sentinel*, June 1–7, 2006.

Kellner, Douglass. *Media Spectacle*. London: Routledge, 2003.

Keown, Tim. "You Gotta Disbelieve." *ESPN*, last modified December 7, 2004, http://sports.espn.go.com/espn/page2/story?page=keown/041207 (accessed January 27, 2005).

Keri, Jonah. "Is Albert Pujols Worth $250 Million?" *Grantland,* last modified December 8, 2011, http://www.grantland.com/blog/the-triangle/post/_/id/11778/is-albert-pujols-really-worth-250-million (accessed December 8, 2011).

Kindred, Dave. "The Class of '98." *The Sporting News,* December 21, 1998.

_____. "Everything Evolves, Even the Word 'Babe.'" *The Sporting News,* June 3, 2002.

King, C. Richard, Ellen J. Staurowsky, Lawrence Baca, Laurel R. Davis, and Cornel Pewewardy, "Of Polls and Race Prejudice: *Sports Illustrated*'s Errant 'Indian Wars.'" *Journal of Sport and Social Issues* 26, no. 4 (November 2002): 381–402.

Klapisch, Bob. "Rocket: Perfectly Engineered to Pitch." *ESPN,* last modified May 25, 2003, http://sports.espn.go.com/mlb/columns/story?columnist=klapisch_bob&id=1558829 (accessed March 19, 2005).

Kline, Chris. "Tribe Ignores Past, Reaps Rewards." *Baseball America,* last modified September 4, 2003, http://www.baseballamerica.com/today/news/030904tadno.html (accessed August 8, 2004).

Knapp, Gwen. "Is It Time to End the Hostility Toward Gays in the Pros?" *San Francisco Chronicle,* June 5, 2005.

Knisley, Michael. "A Worthy King." *The Sporting News,* October 8, 2001.

_____. "Everybody Has the Dream." *The Sporting News,* February 19, 2001.

Knisley, Michael, and Steve Marantz. "A Finish with a Flourish." *The Sporting News,* October 5, 1998.

Koppett, Leonard. *Koppett's Concise History of Major League Baseball.* New York: Carroll & Gaf, 2004.

Kornheiser, Tony, and Dan Le Batard. "Papi Still Favors Suspensions." *Pardon the Interruption.* Washington, DC: ESPN, September 25, 2009.

Kornheiser, Tony and Michael Wilbon. "Andy Pettitte in HOF." *Pardon the Interruption.* Washington, DC: ESPN, November 5, 2009.

_____. "Does Barry Deserve More Love?" *Pardon the Interruption.* Washington, DC: ESPN, September 13, 2004.

_____. "Will Test Clear Bonds' Name?" *Pardon the interruption.* Washington, DC, ESPN, September 27, 2004.

Kraus, Rebecca S. "A Shelter in the Storm: Baseball Responds to September 11." *NINE: A Journal of Baseball and American Culture* 12, no.1 (2003): 88–101.

Kurkijan, Tim. "Worth Waiting For." *Sports Illustrated,* June 14, 1993.

Ladson, William. "The Complete Player." *The Sporting News,* July 12, 1999.

Lapchick, Richard. "1998 Racial and Gender Report Card." Boston: The Center for the Study of Sport in Society, 1998.

_____. "2004 Racial and Gender Report Card." Orlando, FL: The Institute for Diversity and Ethics in Sport, 2005.

_____. "The 2006 Racial and Gender Report Card of the Associated Press Sports Editors." Orlando, FL: The Institute for Diversity and Ethics in Sport, 2006.

_____. "The 2006 Racial and Gender Report Card: Major League Baseball." Orlando: The Institute for Diversity and Ethics in Sport, 2006.

_____. "The 2008 Racial and Gender Report Card of the Associated Press Editors." Orlando, FL: The Institute for Diversity and Ethics in Sport, 2008.

_____. "The 2009 Racial and Gender Report Card: Major League Baseball." Orlando, FL: The Institute for Diversity and Ethics in Sport, April 15, 2009.

_____. "Who's Covering Whom?: Sports Sections Lag in Diversity." *ESPN,* last modified June 22, 2006, http://sports.espn.go.com/espn/news/story?id=2496651 (accessed September 3, 2011).

Lawrence III, Charles R. "The Id, The Ego, and Equal Protection: Reckoning with Unconscious Racism." In *Critical Race Theory: The Key Writings That Formed the Movement.* Edited by Kimberlé Crenshaw, Neil Gotanda, Gary Peller, and Kendall Thomas. 235–256. New York: The New Press, 1995.

_____. "If He Hollers Let Him Go: Regulating Racist Speech on Campus." In *Words That Wound: Critical Race Theory, Assaultive Speech, and the First Amendment.* Edited by Mari J. Matsuda, Charles Lawrence III, Richard Delgado, and Kimberlé Crenshaw. 53–88. Boulder, CA: Westview, 1992.

Le Batard, Dan, and Jason Whitlock. "Bonds Not Indicted." *Pardon the Interruption.* Washington, DC: ESPN, July 20, 2006.

Lee, Spike. Documentary Produced for Civil Rights Game, *MLB,* last modified March 31, 2007, http://mlb.mlb.com/mlb/events/civil_rights_game/y2007/index.jsp (accessed February 15, 2009).

Lemon, Brendan. "Letter from the Editor." *Out,* May 2001.

Lemon, Brendan, Albert Kim, and Kostya Kenned. "Not Out at the Plate." *Sports Illustrated,* June 3, 2002.

"Leon Day." *National Baseball Hall of Fame and Museum,* http://www.baseballhalloffame.org/hofers/detail.jsp?playerId=492562 (accessed July 18, 2008).

Leonard, David. "The Decline of the Black Athlete: An Online Exclusive: Extended Interview with Harry Edwards." *ColorLines* 3

(2000), http://search.proquest.com/docview/215537733?accountid=14925 (accessed September 3, 2011).

Levy, Steve, and Linda Cohn. "Jason Giambi." *SportsCenter*. Bristol, CT: ESPN, December 2, 2004.

Ley, Bob. "Baseball's Four Faces of Steroids." *Outside the Lines*. Bristol, CT: ESPN, August 7, 2005.

_____. "The Gay Dilemma." *Outside the Lines*. Bristol, CT: ESPN, June 3, 2001.

_____. "Language Barriers." *Outside the Lines Nightly*. Bristol, CT: ESPN, June 12, 2003.

_____. "The World of the Gay Athlete." *Outside the Lines*. Bristol, CT: ESPN, December 16, 1998.

Ley, Bob, Ken Williams, and Howard Bryant. "Bonds's Image and Race." *Outside the Lines*. Washington, DC: ESPN, February 27, 2005.

Lipsitz, George. *The Possessive Investment in Whiteness: How White People Profit from Identity Politics*. Philadelphia: Temple University Press, 2006.

_____. "The White 2K Problem." *Cultural Values* 4, no. 4 (2000): 518–524.

Lipsyte, Robert, and Peter Levine. *Idols of the Game: A Sporting History of the American Century*. Atlanta: Turner, 1995.

Littleman, Jonathan. "Mitchell's Best Source Was a Towel Boy." *Yahoo! Sports*, last modified December 13, 2007, http://sports.yahoo.com/mlb/news;_ylt=AvYsAi12IKhPrITwSqtuqInZxLsF?slug=li-mitchellanalysis121307&prov=yhoo&type=lgns (accessed December 14, 2007).

Loewen, James W. *Lies My Teacher Told Me: Everything Your American History Textbook Got Wrong*. Revised edition. New York: Simon & Schuster, 2007.

Looney, Douglas S. "Sosa: Big Home Runs, Bigger Smiles." *Christian Science Monitor*, July 2, 1999.

Loving et ux. v. Virginia 388 U.S. 1 (1967).

Luke, Allen. "Representing and Reconstructing Asian Masculinities: This is Not a Movie Review." *Social Alternatives* 16, no. 3 (1997): 32–4.

McCarver, Tim. *The Perfect Season: Why 1998 Was Baseball's Greatest Year*. New York: Villard, 1999.

McDonald, Mary G., and Susan Birrell. "Reading Sport Critically: A Methodology for Interrogating Power." *Sociology of Sport Journal* 16, no. 4 (1999): 283–300.

"McDowell Back from Suspension," *ESPN*, last modified May 14, 2011, http://sports.espn.go.com/mlb/news/story?id=6541756 (accessed August 26, 2011).

McGrath, Ben. "Waiting for Manny." *The New Yorker*, April 23, 2007.

MacGregor, Jeff. "All-Stars, Mom, and ~~Protests~~ Apple Pie." *ESPN*, last modified July 12, 2011, http://espn.go.com/espn/commentary/story/_/page/macgregor-110711/the-mlb-all-star-game-apparently-marked-protests-arizona-proposed-illegal-immigration-legislation-shame (accessed September 2, 2011).

_____. "The Bang (?) for Barry Bonds Bucks." *ESPN*, last modified April 18, 2011, http://sports.espn.go.com/espn/commentary/news/story?page=macgregor/110418 (accessed September 5, 2011).

"McGwire Apologizes to La Russa, Selig." *ESPN*, last modified January 12, 2011, http://sports.espn.go.com/mlb/news/story?id=4816607 (accessed November 19, 2011).

"McGwire Evades Steroid Questions." *ESPN*, last modified January 18, 2011, http://sports.espn.go.com/mlb/news/story?id=4834393 (accessed November 19, 2011).

McIntosh, Peggy. "White Privilege: Unpacking the Invisible Knapsack." In *White Privilege: Essential Readings on the Other Side of Racism*. Third Edition. Edited by Paula Rothenberg, 123–127. New York: Worth, 2002.

Mack, Kenneth W., and Jim Chen. "Barack Obama Before He Was a Rising Political Star." *The Journal of Blacks in Higher Education* 45 (2004): 99.

McNary, Kyle. *Black Baseball: A History of African Americans & the National Game*. New York: Sterling, 2003.

Madden, Bill. "Alex a Total Bust. Forget Cooperstown, Rodríguez Has Earned a Spot in Hall of Shame." *New York Daily News*, February 8, 2009.

Maddow, Rachel, and Dave Zirin, "And Justice for All?" *The Rachel Maddow Show*. New York: MSNBC, February 27, 2009.

"Major League Baseball Disciplines Roger McDowell," *MLB*, last modified May 1, 2011, http://mlb.mlb.com/news/press_releases/press_release.jsp?ymd=20110501&content_id=18485548&vkey=pr_mlb&fext=.jsp&c_id=mlb (accessed August 26, 2011).

Major League Baseball. "Mike Piazza: Player Information: Biography and Career Highlights." *MLB.COM* http://mlb.mlb.com/NASApp/mlb/team/player.jsp?player_id=120536 (accessed: October 10, 2005).

Mankiewich, Matthew. "Report: Sox Can Still Have A-Rod." *MLB*, last modified December 4, 2003, http://texas.rangers.mlb.com/NASApp/mlb/mlb/news/mlb_news.jsp?ymd=20031204&content_id=612557&vkey=news_mlb&fext=.jsp&c_id=mlb (accessed March 21, 2005).

Marantz, Steve, and Michael Knisley. "American Hero." *The Sporting News*, September 21, 1998.

Mariotti, Jay. "Hearing an Ugly Side to Athletes." *The Sporting News*, May 14, 2001.

Merron, Jeff. "Hormonally Challenged." *ESPN*, last modified March 8, 2005, http://sports. espn.go.com/espn/page2/story?page=merron/ 050309&num=0 (accessed March 19, 2005).

Miles, Robert. "Hollywood Ending." *ESPN the Magazine*, June 4, 2007.

Miller, Matthew, Josephine Lee, and Steven Sun. "Forbes 400 Richest People in America." *Forbes* October 6, 2003.

Miller, Toby. *Sportsex*. Philadelphia: Temple University Press, 2001.

Minkoff, Alysse. "All of Rose's Thorns on Display." *ESPN*, last modified January 6, 2004, http://www.espn.go.com/page2/s/minkoff/ 040106.html (accessed March 21, 2005).

Mitchell, George J. "Report to the Commissioner of Baseball of an Independent Investigation into the Illegal Use of Steroids and Other Performance Enhancing Substances by Players in Major League Baseball." 2007.

"The Mitchell Report: The Illegal Use of Steroids in Major League Baseball, Day 2." *Committee on Oversight and Governmental Reform. House of Representatives*, Second Session, Washington, DC, February 13, 2008.

Monaghan, Peter. "'Critical Race Theory': Some Startling Analyses." *Chronicle of Higher Education*, June 23, 1993.

"Monte Irvin, *National Baseball Hall of Fame and Museum*, http://www.baseballhalloffame. org/hofers/detail.jsp?playerId=116403 (accessed July 18, 2008).

Moore, Michael. *Stupid White Men...and Other Sorry Excuses for the State of the Nation!* New York: HarperCollins, 2001.

Morrissey, Rick. "Baseball May Need Big Share of Asterisk." *Chicago Tribune*, March 3, 2004.

Mulvey, Laura. "Visual Pleasure and Narrative Cinema." *Film Theory and Criticism: Introductory Readings*. Fifth Edition. Edited by Leo Braudy and Marshall Cohen, 833–844. New York: Oxford University Press, 1999.

Munson, Lester. "Legal Questions Abound in Anticipation of Mitchell Report." *ESPN*, last modified December 6, 2007, http://sports. espn.go.com/mlb/columns/story?id=3142722 (accessed December 11, 2007).

_____. "Silence of Roger Clemens Lawyer." *ESPN*, last modified July 22, 2011, http:// espn.go.com/espn/commentary/story/_/page/ munson-110721/roger-clemens-trial-rusty-hardin-brilliant-rashard-mendenhall-twitter-champion (accessed August 28, 2011).

Murguía, Janet. "MLB, Selig Should Take Arizona Stand." *ESPN*, last modified May 21, 2010, http://sports.espn.go.com/espn/com mentary/news/story?id=5207320 (accessed September 1, 2011).

Nadel, Eric, and Alex Rodríguez. "Q&A with Alex Rodríguez." *MLB*, last modified February 14, 2004, http://texas.rangers.mlb.com/ NASApp/mlb/tex/news/tex_news.jsp?ymd=2 0040214&content_id=637165<&vkey=news _tex&fext=.jsp (accessed March 21, 2005).

"New York to Recognize Gay Marriages." *CNN*, last modified May 29, 2008. http://www.cnn. com/2008/US/05/29/nygay.marriage/index. html?iref=newssearch (accessed August 26, 2011).

Newman, Mark. "'Sacred' No. 42 on Display in Baseball." *MLB*, last modified April 16, 2007, http://mlb.mlb.com/news/article.jsp?ymd= 20070415&content_id=1901218&vkey=news_ mlb&fext=.jsp&c_id=mlb (accessed August 28, 2011).

Newnham, Blain. "Avid Rangers Fans Should Have Taught A-Rod a Math Lesson." *Seattle Times*, December 14, 2000.

"The NFL StarCaps Case: Are Sports' Anti-Doping Programs at League Crossroads?" *Subcommittee on Commerce, Trade and Consumer Protection*. Washington, DC, November 3, 2009.

Nine Innings from Ground Zero. Directed by Ouisie Shapiro. 2004. United States: HBO, 2004. DVD.

Noble, Marty. "English Not Foreign to Pedro." *MLB*, http://www.mlb.com/NASApp/mlb/ emailArticleServlet?aid=385316 (accessed March 12, 2005).

Nohlgren, Stephen. "Tampa Bay Rays to Join Antigay Bullying Movement 'It Gets Better.'" *St. Petersburg Times*, last modified August 10, 2011, http://www.tampabay.com/sports/base ball/rays/tampa-bay-rays-to-join-antigay-bullying-movement-it-gets-better/1185086 (accessed August 26, 2011).

"#6: McGwire and Sosa Chase Maris." *The Headliners*. Bristol, CT: ESPN, 2004.

Nylund, David. "When in Rome: Heterosexism, Homophobia, and Sports Talk Radio," *Journal of Sport & Social Issues* 28, no. 2 (2004): 136–168.

Ogden, David C., and Michael L. Hilt. "Collective Identity and Basketball: An Explanation for the Decreasing Number of African-Americans on America's Baseball Diamonds." *Journal of Leisure Research* 35, no. 2 (2003): 213–227.

Okrent, Daniel. "A Mac For All Seasons." *Time*, December 28, 1998-January 4, 1999.

Olbermann, Keith. "Asterisk Obsession." *Sports Illustrated*, September 7, 1998.

_____. "Hall of Famers and Numbers Without Wings." *Baseball Nerd Times*, last modified November 28, 2009, http://keitholbermann. mlblogs.com/archives/2009/11/hall_of_famers _and_numbers_wit.html (accessed September 5, 2011).

Olbermann, Keith, and Ed Silverman. "#1 Remembering Robinson." *Countdown with Keith Olbermann*. MSNBC, April 13, 2007.

Olney, Buster. "A-Rod Now Tarnished Forever." *ESPN*, last modified February 7, 2009, http://sports.espn.go.com/mlb/columns/story?columnist=olney_buster&id=3890934 (accessed November 2, 2009).

"Ortiz's Reaction to Positive Result." *New York Times*, last modified July 31, 2009, http://find.galegroup.com.proxy.lib.wayne.edu/gtx/start.do?prodId=SPN.SP00&userGroupName=lom_waynesu. (accessed 23 November 23, 2009).

Overmyer, James. *Effa Manley and the Newark Eagles*. Metuchen, NJ: Scarecrow, 1993.

Paddock, Richard C. "Of Color and Conviction: Stockton Recall Hinges on Definition of 'Black.'" *Los Angeles Times*, April 18, 1984.

Padecky, Bob. "No Love Lost for Manny or Standing Ovation in Mannywood." *Santa Rosa Press Democrat*, October 16, 2009.

Pearlman, Jeff. "Appreciating Bonds." *Sports Illustrated*, June 5, 2000.

_____. "At Full Blast." *Sports Illustrated*, December 27, 1999.

_____. "Coming Out in the Big Leagues." *The Advocate*, January 15, 2008.

_____. "It's a Wrap." *Sports Illustrated*, October 15, 2001.

_____. *Love Me, Hate Me: Barry Bonds and the Making of an Antihero*. New York: HarperCollins, 2006.

Pincus, Fred L. "Discrimination Comes in Many Forms: Individual, Institutional, and Structural." In *Readings for Diversity and Social Justice*. Edited by Maurianne Adams, Warren J. Blumenfeld, Rosie Castañeda, Heather W. Hackman, Madeline L. Peters, Ximena Zúñiga. 31–34. New York: Routledge, 2000.

Plaschke, Bill. "Don't Be Surprised if 'Rocket' Escapes Bonds Treatment." *Los Angeles Times*, October 2, 2006.

"Players' Goal Was to Make Steroid Testing Permanent," *ESPN*, last modified March 12, 2003, http://espn.go.com/mlb/news/2003/0311/1521844.html (accessed March 12, 2005).

"Players React to Court Ruling." *ESPN*, last modified August 26, 2009, http://sports.espn.go.com/mlb/news/story?id=4425039 (accessed November 15, 2009).

Politi, Steve. "Forecast for A-Rod: Dark Cloud Overhead." *New Jersey Star-Ledger*, February 16, 2009.

Posnanski, Joe. "Baseball's Loveable Loser." *Sports Illustrated*, August 10, 2009.

Preuitt, Lori. "Barry Bonds to Pay for Stow Kids' College," *NBC Bay Area*, *Times*, last modified May 26, 2011, http://www.nbcbayarea.com/news/local/Barry-Bonds-to-Pay-For-Stow-Kids-College-122539899.html (accessed November 19, 2011).

Price, S.L. "Cat & Mouth Game." *Sports Illustrated*, March 13, 2000.

The Princess Bride. Directed by Rob Reiner. 1987. Beverly Hills, CA: 20th Century–Fox, 2009. Blu-Ray.

Raissman, Bob. "Roids Not Rage on ESPN to Justice to Bristol's Papi Coverage." *New York Daily News*, August 11, 2009.

Rampersad, Arnold. *Jackie Robinson: A Biography*. New York: Alfred A. Knopf, 1997.

Ravech, Karl, John Kruk, and Steve Phillips. "Mitchell Report Special." *SportsCenter*. Bristol, CT: ESPN, December 13, 2007.

Ravech, Karl, and Mark McGwire. "Sunday Conversation." *SportsCenter*. Bristol, CT: ESPN, July 13, 2004.

Reeves, Jim. "Bonds Cheated and Disgraced the Game and Hank Aaron." *Star-Telegram*, August 8, 2007, http://www.star-telegram.com/sports/story/194941.html (accessed August 8, 2007).

Reilly, Rick. "A Gentleman in a Pinstripe Suit." *Sports Illustrated*, July 12–19, 2004.

_____. "He Loves Himself Barry Much." *Sports Illustrated*, August 27, 2001.

_____. "The Magical and Mysterious Oz." *Sports Illustrated*, April 24, 2005.

_____. "Pride of the Yankees." *Sports Illustrated*, September 28, 1998.

Reiss, Scott, Scott Van Pelt, and Buster Olney. "756." *SportsCenter*. Bristol, CT: ESPN, August 8, 2007.

"Report: Bonds, Giambi, Sheffield Received Steroids." *ESPN*, last modified March 2, 2004, http://sports.espn.go.com/espn/wire?section=mlb&id=1748917 (accessed September 29, 2004).

Robinson, Jackie. "Letter to Michael Hamilburg." In *First Class Citizenship: The Civil Rights Letters of Jackie Robinson*. Edited by Michael G. Long. 302–3. New York: Times, 2007.

Rock, Pete, Ed O.G., and Masta Ace. "Wishing." *My Own Worst Enemy*. Fatbeats, 2004.

Rockquemore, Kerry Ann. "Forced to Pass and Other Sins Against Authenticity." *Women & Performance: A Journal of Feminist Theory* 15, no. 1 (2005): 17–32.

"Rodríguez Finalized $275m Deal with Yankees." *ESPN*, last modified December 13, 2007, http://sports.espn.go.com/mlb/news/story?id=3153171 (accessed September 3, 2011).

Rome, Jim. "Barry Bonds." *Jim Rome Is Burning*. Los Angeles, CA: ESPN August 7, 2007.

Roppolo, Kimberly. "Symbolic Racism, History, and Reality: The Real Problem with Indian Mascots." In *Genocide of the Mind: New Native*

American Writing. Edited by MariJo Moore. 187–198. New York: Thunder's Mouth Press/ Nation Books, 2003.

Rosenthal, Ken. "Bonds Excels Where It Counts: On the Field." *The Sporting News,* July 2, 2001.

Rushin, Steve. "Sam the Ham." *Sports Illustrated,* September 14, 1998.

Said, Edward. "The President and the Baseball Player." *Cultural Critique* 43 (1999): 136–138.

Samuels, Allison, and Mark Starr. "Ready for His Close-Up." *Newsweek,* April 9, 2001.

"San Francisco Giants Release 'It Gets Better' Video," *The Sporting News,* last modified June 1, 2010, http://aol.sportingnews.com/mlb/story/2011-06-01/san-francisco-giants-release-it-gets-better-video (accessed August 26, 2011).

Sanchez, Jesse. "Alex the Man vs. A-Rod the Player." *MLB,* last modified April 13, 2004, http://mlb.mlb.com/NASApp/mlb/mlb/news/mlb_news.jsp?ymd=20040413&content_id=700961&vkey=news_mlb&fext=.jsp (accessed March 21, 2005).

Sanders, Summer. "Sexiest Athlete." *The Sports List,* FOX Sports, February 21, 2005.

Sappenfield, Mark, Todd Wilkinson, and Kris Axtman. "Enter the Era of the $49,000 at Bat." *Christian Science Monitor,* December 12, 2000.

Saunders, John, Bob Ryan, Mike Lupica, and Dan Le Batard. "Bonds Hits 755." *The Sports Reporters.* New York: ESPN, August 5, 2007.

_____. "How Will History Remember Barry Bonds?" *The Sports Reporters.* New York: ESPN August 12, 2007.

Saunders, John, Michael Kay, William C. Rhoden, and Mitch Albom. "A-Rod Hits 500." *The Sports Reporters.* New York: ESPN, August 5, 2007.

Saunders, John, Mitch Albom, Mike Lupica, and William C. Rhoden. "Jason Giambi." *The Sports Reporters.* New York: ESPN, December 5, 2004.

Schmidt, Michael S. "Court Rules U.S. Seized 2003 Tests Improperly." *New York Times,* August 27, 2009.

_____. "Stars of Red Sox Title Years Are Linked to Doping." *New York Times* July 31, 2009.

Schwartz, Harriet L. "Out of Bounds." *Advocate,* March 18, 1997.

Serrano, José E. "Strike Two on Arizona Law, Commissioner Selig." *Congressional Documents and Publications,* June 17, 2010.

Sexton, Joe. "Baseball: It's Not Always Yo, Ho, Ho But Pirates Sail Along." *New York Times,* June 12, 1992.

Shenin, Dave, and Spencer S. Hsu. "Pitching Legend Roger Clemens Indicted on Charges of Lying to a Congressional Committee." *Washington Post,* last modified August 20,

2010, http://www.washingtonpost.com/wp-dyn/content/article/2010/08/19/AR201008190 4125.html (accessed September 5, 2011).

Shuman, Joel. "Despite the Lies, Pettitte Hard to Hate." *New York Post,* February 20, 2008.

_____. "Does A-Rod Deserve So Much Money? No." In *Baseball and Philosophy: Thinking Outside the Batter's Box.* Edited by Eric Bronson. 297–299. Chicago: Open Court, 2004.

Smith, Gary. "Home Run Fever." *Sports Illustrated,* August 3, 1998.

_____. "The Race Is On." *Sports Illustrated,* September 21, 1998.

Smith, Valerie. "Reading the Intersection of Race and Gender in Passing Narratives." *Diacritics* 24 (1994): 43–57.

Smith, Wendell. "Smitty's Sports-Spurts." *Pittsburgh Courier,* January 30, 1932.

"Source Saying Information on Clemens Will Be in Mitchell Report." *ESPN,* last modified December 13, 2007, http://sports.espn.go.com/mlb/news/story?id=3153129 (accessed December 13, 2007).

Stark, Jayson. "A-Rod Has Destroyed Game's History." *ESPN,* last modified February 8, 2009, http://sports.espn.go.com/mlb/columns/story?columnist=stark_jayson&id=389 2788 (accessed November 2, 2009).

_____. "Angels Shock Baseball World," *ESPN,* last modified December 8, 2011, http://espn.go.com/mlb/hotstove11/story/_/id/7330869/los-angeles-angels-shock-world-ink-albert-pujols-cj-wilson (accessed December 8, 2011).

_____. "Barry Bonds Trial Reveals Ease of PEDs." *ESPN,* last modified April 13, 2011, http://sports.espn.go.com/mlb/columns/story?columnist=stark_jayson&id=6348022 (accessed September 5, 2011).

_____. "Goliath Not Yet Ready for Gotham." *ESPN,* last modified February 21, 2005, http://sports.espn.go.com/mlb/columns/story?columnist=stark_jayson&id=1993164 (accessed March 19, 2005).

_____. "Racial Issues Hover Over the Chase," *ESPN,* last modified May 6, 2007, http://sports.espn.go.com/mlb/columns/story?columnist=stark_jayson&id=2861938 (May 10, 2007).

_____. "Stories of Clemens, Bonds Similar, Yet Very Different." *ESPN,* last modified December 15, 2007, http://sports.espn.go.com/mlb/columns/story?columnist=stark_jayson&id=3156189 (accessed September 30, 2007).

Starr, Mark, and Eve Conant. "A Major League Mess." *Newsweek,* March 28, 2005.

Stein, Joel, Dan Cray, Maureen Harrington, Staci D. Kramer, and Romeh Ratnesar. "The Fun Is Back." *Time,* July 27, 1998.

Stein, Joel, and Julie Grace. "Grand Slam." *Time,* September 28, 1998.

Stone, Larry. "It's Jackie Robinson Day: All Players Wear No. 42 Today, Thanks to Ken Griffey Jr." *Seattle Times*, last modified April 15, 2011, http://seattletimes.nwsource.com/html/thehotstoneleague/2014783839_its_jackie_robinson_day_all_pl.html (accessed August 30, 2011).

_____. "Ken Griffey Jr. on Jackie Robinson Day and the Decline of African Americans in Baseball." *Seattle Times*, last modified April 15, 2009, http://blog.seattletimes.nwsource.com/stone/2009/04/15/griffey_on_jackie_robinson_day.html (accessed August 28, 2011).

Suchon, Josh. *This Gracious Season: Barry Bonds & The Greatest Year in Baseball*. Los Angeles: Winter Publications, 2002.

Sullivan, Robert, Venus Eskenazi, and Mike Williams. "Show Them the Money." *Time*, December 4, 2000.

Tatum, Wilbert A. "Rock-a-Bye Rocker...Out of This World." *New York Amsterdam News*, June 8, 2000.

Telander, Rick. "In Big Picture, Mariotti's Huge Part of Story." *Chicago Sun-Times*, June 26, 2007.

Thompson, John B. *The Media and Modernity: A Social Theory of the Media*. Palo Alto, CA: Stanford University Press, 1995.

Thompson, Teri, Michael O'Keefe, and Nathanial Vinton. "Drug Spawns Manny's Ban. Use of Female Fertility Substance at Heart of Action." *New York Daily News*, May 8, 2009.

Thorn, John. "Why Baseball." In *Total Baseball: The Ultimate Baseball Encyclopedia* edited by John Thorn, Phil Birnbam, and Bill Dean. 3–5. Wilmington, DE: Sport Media, 2004.

Thorn, John, Phil Birnbaum, and Bill Deane. *Total Baseball: The Ultimate Baseball Encyclopedia*. 8th Edition Wilmington, DE: Sport Media, 2004.

Travers, Steven. *Barry Bonds: Baseball's Superman*. Champaign, IL: Sports Publishing, 2002.

Travis, Neal. "In and Out with the Mets." *New York Post*, May 20, 2002.

Trucios-Haynes, Enid. "Why Race Matters: Lat-Crit Theory and Latina/o Racial Identity." *Berkeley La Raza Law Journal* 11/12 (2000): 1–42.

Trujillo, Nick. "Hegemonic Masculinity on the Mound: Media Representations of Nolan Ryan and American Sports Culture." In *Reading Sport Critically: Critical Essays on Power and Representation*. Edited by Susan Birrell and Mary G. McDonald. 14–39. Boston: Northeastern University Press, 2000.

"The 25 Most Intriguing People: Alex Rodríguez." *People*, December 25, 2000–January 1, 2001.

"24-Hour Spanish Language Station Launching." *ESPN*, last modified January 7, 2004, http://espn.go.com/gen/news/2004/0107/1702456.html (accessed August 3, 2005).

Tygiel, Jules. "The Great Experiment Fifty Years Later." In *The Cooperstown Symposium on Baseball and American Culture*. Edited by Peter M. Rutkoff. 257–270. Jefferson, NC: McFarland, 1997.

"*USA Today* Salaries Database." http://content.usatoday.com/sports/baseball/salaries/top25.aspx?year=2009 (accessed November 20, 2011).

Verducci, Tom. "A-Rod Agonistes." *Sports Illustrated*, last modified September 25, 2006, http://sportsillustrated.cnn.com/2006/magazine/09/19/arod0925/index.html (accessed September 3, 2011).

_____. "Eight Men In." *Sports Illustrated*, July 28, 2003.

_____. "Is Baseball in the Asterisk Era?" *Sports Illustrated*, March 15, 2004.

_____. "Juice and Truth." *Sports Illustrated*, February 21, 2005.

_____. "The Lone Ranger." *Sports Illustrated*, September 9, 2002.

_____. "Making His Mark." *Sports Illustrated*, September 14, 1998.

_____. "The Night the Lights Went Out in Mannywood." *Sports Illustrated*, May 18, 2009.

_____. "The Producers." *Sports Illustrated*, June 4, 2001.

_____. "Pushing 70." *Sports Illustrated*, October 8, 2001.

_____. "SI's 2003 Baseball Awards." *Sports Illustrated*, September 29, 3002.

_____. "Sosa: So, So Fun." *Sports Illustrated*, September 7, 1998.

_____. "Stumbling Start." *Sports Illustrated*, April 9, 2001.

_____. "Totally Juiced," *Sports Illustrated*, June 3, 2002.

Walker, Ben. "Astros Roster Has No Black Players." *YAHOO*, last modified October 25, 2005, http://news.yahoo.com/s/ap/2005102 5/ap_on_sp_ba_nc/bbo_world_series_changing_diversity (accessed October 28, 2005).

Wamble, Marvin. "No Brown on Bonds's Nose." *New Pittsburgh Courier*, March 16–20, 2005.

Weinberg, Rick. "95: Clemens Flings Shattered Bat at Piazza." *ESPN*, http://sports.espn.go.com/espn/eopn25/story?page=moments/95 (accessed: July 13, 2004).

Weiner, Michael. "Statement of MLBPA Executive Director Michael Weiner Regarding Arizona Immigration Law." *MLB Players*, last modified April 30, 2010, http://mlbplayers.mlb.com/pa/pdf/20100430_weiner_statement_on_arizona_immigration_law.pdf (accessed September 1, 2011).

Weir, Tom, and Mike Todd. "Talking to Each Other." *USA Today*, April 14, 2004.

Wendel, Tim. *The New Face of Baseball: The*

One-Hundred Year Rise and Triumph of Latinos in America's Favorite Sport. New York: HarperCollins, 2003.

"We're Killing the Meaning of Jackie Day." *NBC Sports*, last modified April 13, 2007, http://nbcsports.msnbc.com/id/17964581/ (accessed February 25, 2009).

Wertheim, L. Jon. "Gays in Sport: A Poll." *Sports Illustrated*, April 18, 2005.

Wertheim, L. Jon, Kevin Cook, and Mark Mravic. "Did Mac and Sammy Save Baseball?" *Sports Illustrated*, September 20, 1998.

Wetzel, Dan. "Clemens Is No Different Than Bonds." December 13, 2007, *Yahoo! Sports*, http://sports.yahoo.com/mlb/news?slug=dw-clemenssteroidsearly121307&prov=yhoo&type=lgns (accessed December 14, 2007).

"What Are They Saying?" *USA Today*, April 14, 2004.

"What is the It Gets Better Project?" http://www.itgetsbetter.org/pages/about-it-gets-better-project/ (accessed August 26, 2011).

Whiting, Robert. *The Meaning of Ichiro: The New Wave from Japan and the Transformation of Our National Pastime.* New York: Warner, 2004.

"Who Was More Credible, Clemens or McNamee?" *ESPN*, last modified February 13, 2008, http://sports.espn.go.com/mlb/news/story?id=3244809 (accessed November 7, 2008).

Wilbon, Michael, and Jay Mariotti. "Will Barry Ever Play Again?" *Pardon the Interruption.* Washington, DC: ESPN, August 2, 2005.

Wilbon, Michael, and Stephen A. Smith. "Should Rockies Pitch To Him?" *Pardon the Interruption.* Washington, DC: ESPN, September 2, 2004.

Wilbon, Michael, and Tony Kornheiser. "Significance of Coming Out." *Pardon the Interruption*, Washington, DC: ESPN, October 26, 2005.

_____. "Thoughts on Bud's Reaction." *Pardon the Interruption.* Washington, DC: ESPN, August 6, 2007.

_____. "Thoughts on Verdict." *Pardon the Interruption.* Washington, DC: ESPN, April 13, 2011.

Wildman Stephanie M., and Adrienne D. Davis. "Language and Silence: Making Systems of Privilege Visible." In *Critical Race Theory: The Cutting Edge.* Edited by Richard Delgado and Jean Stefancic. 657–663. Philadelphia: Temple University Press, 2000.

Wiley, Cole. "Let Us Be Wary of Celebrating Too Much." *ESPN*, last modified February 28, 2007, http://sports.espn.go.com/espn/blackhistory2007/columns/story?id=2782051 (accessed September 3, 2011).

Wiley, Ralph. "Sour Grapes," *ESPN*, last modified March 4, 2004, http://sports.espn.go.com/espn/page2/story?page=wiley/040304 (accessed October 27, 2004).

Williams, Lance, and Mark Fainaru-Wada. "What Bonds Told the BALCO Grand Jury." *San Francisco Chronicle*, December 2, 2004.

Wise, Tim. "Membership Has Its Privileges: Thoughts on Acknowledging and Challenging Whiteness." In *White Privilege: Essential Readings on the Other Side of Racism*, edited by Paula S. Rothenberg. 133–136. New York: Worth Publishers, 2002.

_____. "With Friends Like These, Who Needs Glenn Beck? Racism and White Privilege on the Liberal-Left." *Timwise*, last modified August 17, 2010, http://www.timwise.org/2010/08/with-friends-like-these-who-needs-glenn-beck-racism-and-white-privilege-on-the-liberal-left/ (accessed September 4, 2011).

Wisensale, Steven. "The Black Knight: A Political Portrait of Jackie Robinson." In *The Cooperstown Symposium on Baseball and American Culture.* Edited by Peter M. Rutkoff. 189–198. Jefferson, NC: McFarland, 1997.

Wojciechowski, Gene. "Bonds' Record Holder Doesn't Enhance Baseball." *ESPN*, last modified August 8, 2007, http://sports.espn.go.com/espn/columns/story?columnist=wojciechowski_gene&id=2963913&sportCat=mlb (accessed August 8, 2007).

_____. "Hardaway's Words of Hate Are Yesterday's News." *ESPN*, last modified February 17, 2007, http://sports.espn.go.com/espn/columns/story?columnist=wojciechowski_gene&id=2766874 (accessed May 12, 2008).

_____. "Line of Truth Starts Behind McGwire." *ESPN*, last modified January 11, 2011, http://sports.espn.go.com/espn/columns/story?columnist=wojciechowski_gene&page=wojciechowski/100112&sportCat=mlb (accessed November 19, 2011).

_____. "Mitchell Report Has Flaws, but MLB, Players Need to Pay Attention." *ESPN*, last modified December 13, 2007, http://sports.espn.go.com/espn/columns/story?columnist=wojciechowski_gene&id=3154051&sportCat=mlb. (accessed December 14, 2007).

Women of Color Policy Network, NYU Wager. "Policy Brief: Wage Disparities and Women of Color," http://wagner.nyu.edu/wocpn/publications/files/Pay_Equity_Policy_Brief.pdf (accessed November 20, 2011).

Wright Jr., Luther. "Who's Black, Who's White, and Who Cares: Reconceptualizing the United States's Definition of Race and Racial Classification." *Vanderbilt Law Review* 48 (1995): 513–569.

"Yankees Not Yet Willing to Forgive Gray." *ESPN*, last modified October 27, 1999, http://espn.go.com/mlb.news/1999/1026/135290.html (accessed April 2, 2005).

Yobbi, Lee. "Coming Clean Has Its Rewards." *Santa Fe New Mexican*, last modified April 6, 2008, http://www.santafenewmexican.com/Sports/Coming-clean-has-its-rewards (accessed September 5, 2011).

Zimbalist, Andrew. *May The Best Team Win.* Washington, DC: Brookings Institute Press, 2003.

Zimmer, Martha Hill, and Michael Zimmer. "Athletes as Entertainers: A Comparative Study of Earning Profiles." *Journal of Sport and Social Issues* 25, no. 2 (2001): 202–215.

Zinsser, William. *On Writing Well: The Classic Guide to Writing Nonfiction.* 25th Anniversary Edition. New York: HarperCollins, 2001.

Zirin, Dave. "Did Tiger Woods Pave the Way for Barack Obama? Are You Kidding Me?" *Edge of Sports*, November 13, 2008, http://www.edgeofsports.com/2008-11-13-388/index.html (accessed January 14, 2009).

_____"Santana is Booed for Using Baseball's Civil Rights Game to Speak Out for Civil Rights." *Edge of Sports*, last modified May 18, 2011, http://www.edgeofsports.com/2011-05-18-621/index.html, (accessed May 19, 2011).

_____. "Strike Out Phoenix." *The Progressive* 74, no. 7 (2010): 42.

_____. *Welcome to the Terrordome: The Pain, Politics, and Promise of Sports.* Chicago: Haymarket, 2007.

_____. *What's My Name, Fool? Sports and Resistance in the United States.* Chicago: Haymarket, 2005.

_____. "Why I'm Boycotting the All-Star Game." *Edge of Sports*, July 11, 2011, http://www.edgeofsports.com/2011-07-11-635/index.html (accessed July 12, 2011).

Zoss, Joel, and John Bowman. *Diamonds in the Rough: The Untold History of Baseball.* Lincoln: University of Nebraska Press, 1989.

Index